A Bill of Rights

WORCESTER COLLEGE OF TECHNOLOGY

D0271242

AUSTRALIA
LBC Information Services

CANADA and USA
The Carswell Company
Toronto

NEW ZEALAND
Brooker's
Auckland

SINGAPORE and MALAYSIA
Thomson Information (S.E. Asia)
Singapore

A Bill of Rights?

Michael Zander

Professor of Law, London School of Economics

Fourth Edition

With a Foreword by Lord Scarman

London
Sweet & Maxwell
1997

First Edition   1975
Reprinted   1977
Reprinted   1977
Second Edition   1979
Barry Rose (Publishers) Limited

Third Edition   1985
Fourth Edition   1997
Sweet & Maxwell Ltd

Published by Sweet and Maxwell Ltd of
100 Avenue Road, London NW3 3PF.
Laserset by LBJ Enterprises Ltd
Aldermaston and Chilcompton.
Printed in England by Clays Ltd, St Ives plc.

No natural forests were destroyed to make this product;
only natural timber was used and re-planted.

A catalogue record for this book is
available from the British Library

ISBN 0-421-58430-0

All rights reserved. U.K. statutory material in this publication is
acknowledged as Crown copyright.
No part of this publication may be reproduced or transmitted, in any
form or by any means, or stored in any retrieval system of any nature,
without prior written permission, except for permitted fair dealing under
the Copyright, Designs and Patents Act 1988, or in accordance with the
terms of a licence issued by the Copyright Licensing Agency in respect of
photocopying and/or reprographic reproduction. Application for
permission for other use of copyright material including permission to
reproduce extracts in other published works shall be made to the
publishers.
Full acknowledgment of author, publisher and source must be given.

©
M. Zander
1997

A Bill of Rights?

Foreword to the Fourth Edition

Now, indeed, the time has come for a fourth edition of this excellent study of the pros and cons of incorporating the European Convention of Human Rights into the statute law of the United Kingdom. Laws for the protection of the rights of individuals are of little value to the citizen if he cannot enforce them directly in the courts of his own country. The practical value to the citizen of incorporating in an Act of Parliament the human rights which by signing and ratifying the convention Britain has recognised are his rights is that they would be directly enforceable by him without the delays, the expense and the burden of going, with his lawyers, to argue his case in Strasbourg. And there is further advantage not only to the litigant but to the nation: our courts would be able to assist directly in the development of the law protecting human rights.

August 1996   Scarman

Introduction

It is widely known that the United Kingdom is one of the few countries in the world which has neither a written constitution nor its own Bill of Rights. It is not quite so widely known that the United Kingdom has available to it a Bill of Rights in the form of the European Convention on Human Rights. To get a remedy under the Convention one has to go to Strasbourg which is quite far away, quite expensive and very slow. This work is mainly about the question whether the European Convention on Human Rights should become accessible to the citizens of this country through proceedings brought in the ordinary courts of this country — or, in other words, whether the United Kingdom should have the European Convention as its Bill of Rights. A subsidiary question addressed is whether, rather than taking the European Convention off-the-peg, it would be better to craft a home-grown Bill of Rights. Most of the book deals with the fundamental questions of what is a Bill of Rights and what are its strengths and weaknesses.

The first edition of this work appeared in 1975, very shortly after Sir Leslie Scarman (as he then was) had made the subject a talking-point in his 1974 Hamlyn Lectures. Sir Leslie wrote the Foreword. It is a source of great delight to me that Lord Scarman, now aged 85 and enjoying a well-earned retirement, should have agreed to again write a Foreword. No one has done more than he to advance this cause.

My position has consistently been, and remains, that, on balance, after weighing all the pros and cons, it is desirable and indeed important to have an accessible Bill of Rights. This position is based on the firm belief that although a Bill of Rights is not the only, nor always the best way of dealing with grievances, it can reach grievances that no other remedy can reach. A working Bill of Rights is therefore a resource that no fully developed democracy should be without.

But there are problems and this work seeks to look squarely at them. It raises for consideration each of the many arguments that have been advanced against the concept of a Bill of Rights. I hope that it will be felt that the arguments of the doubters and sceptics have been treated fairly — for they merit the most anxious consideration. This is not an issue on which it is easy to be absolutely for or absolutely against. It is more nuanced — an issue on which reasonable people can disagree and on which there is much to be said on both sides of the question. When one comes down on one side or the other of the argument, it will, for most people be "on balance".

In the twenty or so years since this debate first started, there can be no question that those who believe in the value of an accessible Bill of Rights have gained a great deal of significant support – especially amongst senior judges and on the political Left, including now the support of the Labour Party. The fact that one of the main political parties has adopted the cause and that it is supported amongst the higher reaches of the judiciary means that what was previously only a subject of talk could now become a subject of practical politics. If so, I believe that this will prove to be one of the most important constitutional developments of this era.

The book starts in Chapter 1 with a detailed history of the debate, establishing its progress, who took part, what they said and with what contemporary result or reaction. Chapter 2 outlines the arguments for a Bill of Rights. Chapter 3, by far the longest in the book, treats the many issues raised by those who oppose the idea. Chapter 4 deals with practical questions that arise as soon as one decides to go ahead with such a project.

I believe that the burden of making the case lies on those who propose such change. It is my hope that at the end of the book the reader may be persuaded that the potential gains in having an accessible Bill of Rights outweigh the potential risks.

Michael Zander
London

September 1996

CONTENTS

1. THE HISTORY OF THE BILL OF RIGHTS DEBATE 1968–1996

1968–1974

Until 1974 the question of a Bill of Rights for Britain was a subject that attracted little interest. But in December 1974, Lord Justice Scarman (as he then was) delivered the first of his Hamlyn Lectures[1] in which he proposed that there should be an entrenched Bill of Rights. What was significant was not simply that a promi nent judge was making a call for a Bill of Rights, but that his suggestion was treated as an event of major importance. *The Guardian* made the story the front page lead;[2] other newspapers took up the cry; profiles of Sir Leslie and discussion of the proposal appeared in many of the leading papers. In a matter of days the issue became fashionable and a topic of some political moment.

Although it was Sir Leslie Scarman who made the subject a serious issue for debate, the question of a Bill of Rights, or some equivalent, had in fact been raised previously on a number of occasions.

The credit for opening up the subject in a considered way goes to Mr Anthony Lester,[3] widely regarded as Britain's foremost civil liberties lawyer and one of the most influential personalities in this debate. In a pamphlet written in 1968, *Democracy and Individual Rights*[4], Mr Lester drew attention to the threats to the individual citizen from a variety of sources — "Parliament, the Civil Service, Local Government, or those clusters of private, oligarchal power which compete with Government in significance and scale".[5]

Parliament, he said, had on occasion reacted to popular preju dice or mass hysteria against a minority. At the start of the century, the sudden influx of mainly Jewish refugees from the pogroms of Eastern Europe had driven a timid government to pass the Aliens

---

[1] Leslie Scarman, *English Law — The New Dimension* (1974), see especially pp.18–21. Lord Justice Scarman became a Lord of Appeal in Ordinary in 1978.
[2] December 5, 1974.
[3] Now Lord Lester of Herne Hill Q.C.
[4] Fabian Tract No. 390.
[5] *Ibid.* at p.2.

Act 1905. Xenophobia and war hysteria had led to the Aliens Act 1914, which passed all its parliamentary stages in a single August day. Both statutes were passed as emergency acts; both were still in force in 1968.

In 1962, "after a blatantly racist campaign against the immigration of coloured Commonwealth citizens", Parliament had passed the first Commonwealth Immigrants Act, conferring sweeping powers over tens of thousands of migrant workers and their families without opportunity of a proper hearing or appeal. In 1965, the Labour Government had bowed to further pressure and put an inflexible limit on immigration from the Commonwealth. In 1968, the Government had whipped the Commonwealth Immigrants Bill through all its parliamentary stages in one week. The Act deprived a group of United Kingdom citizens of their previously unfettered right to enter the country. In these instances,

> " . . . the hallowed safeguards of our Parliamentary system were swiftly swept aside. Constitutional conventions, the sense of fair play of our legislators, the consciences of individual Members of Parliament, the Opposition, the independent judiciary, the Press, and public opinion were of no avail."[6]

More typical of denial of individual freedom by Parliament, according to Mr Lester, was the careless delegation to the executive of absolute and arbitrary powers. An example was the delegation of sweeping powers to the immigration officer in the Aliens Acts. Another was the system of security tests for an accused government employee — he could not be represented, was not entitled to know the evidence against him, could not bring witnesses to contradict what he might guess is the evidence against him, and the evidence was not on oath. Another was the control over the issuing of passports. Mr Lester instanced the withdrawal of the passport of Sir Frederick Crawford as part of the British Government's campaign against U.D.I. in Rhodesia. The Commonwealth Secretary even declined to give the House of Commons any reasons for this action.

Other examples were the lack of adequate machinery to investigate complaints against the police, the inadequate machinery to investigate criminal cases, and the then refusal by the social security authorities to publish the "A" code governing supplementary benefits.

In the field of local government, democratic and legal controls were, if anything, even weaker and the abuse of bureaucratic power

[6] *Ibid.* at p.4.

was more likely. Allocation of council housing, local decisions about such matters as education, censorship or control of meetings were all apt to be decided on the basis of unpublished criteria, without any hearing or appeal by the individuals affected. Mr Lester called for a code of administrative procedure to govern the civil service, and for a Bill of Rights. But he doubted whether it would be wise to entrust a Bill of Rights to the judges. It would be wrong to give the judges the power to overrule Parliament. "It might take years to get the English Bench to interpret a Bill of Rights as a living document rather than an Income Tax Act".[7] (As will be seen, Mr Lester subsequently changed his mind over this.) There was also the risk that "some might use such a Bill to undermine radical social or economic legislation".[8]

According to Mr Lester, the solution was to enact a Bill of Rights which initially would not be enforceable by the courts. Instead there could be a Constitutional Council with the power (like the Ombudsman) only to make recommendations to Parliament about the compatability of legislation or executive action with the provisions of the Bill of Rights. Such a compromise might be necessary in order to obtain immediate political support for the Bill. But "the ultimate objective ought to be a Bill which is enforceable by the individual before a proper court".

> "That objective will not be reached until the judiciary can be trusted by Parliament to perform the major task of applying the Bill of Rights in a progressive and liberal spirit; it is a challenge to the Bench and the legal profession to win that trust."[9]

Mr Lester's final recommendation for immediate action was cautious — establish a Bill of Rights by enacting into English law the European Convention on Human Rights but make it merely an educative force, at least for the time being.

Over the next few years, the subject was sporadically ventilated in Parliament. On April 23, 1969, Lord Lambton (Conservative) sought leave to introduce a Ten-Minute Rule Bill "to preserve the rights of the individual". His main motivation, he said,[10] was to restore citizens rights which had been eroded. He instanced the Race Relations Act which curtailed freedom of speech, the educational policies of the Labour Government which denied parental choice and the Town and Country Planning Acts which, he said,

---

[7] *Ibid.* at p.15.
[8] *Ibid.*
[9] *Ibid.*
[10] *Hansard*, H.C. Vol. 782, col. 474 (April 23, 1969).

3

limited the rights of farmers. Factory and health inspectors had rights of entry to private places. Passports had been withheld for political opinions.

His Bill was modelled on the Canadian Act for the Protection of Human Rights and Fundamental Freedoms 1960. This ensured that all future legislation was checked by the Canadian Minister of Justice to ensure that it did not conflict with the Act. A similar check should be made here by the Attorney-General, said Lambton. Such an act would ensure individual rights.

The motion was opposed by Labour MP, Mr Alex Lyon, (subsequently Minister of State at the Home Office) though diffidently, as he said, "because any radical conscience, aware of the need to preserve the liberty of the individual, must always seek some new institution to enable that to be done". A Bill of Rights would put a fetter on Parliament's capacity to change the law.

If the fetter were progressive and liberal, that might be desirable. But if it was conservative (whether through a constitutional court, a supreme court, a committee, or the Attorney-General) and regressive, "then the inflexibility of our machinery for changing the law when obvious social injustice appeared, would make it a gravely retrograde measure for human liberty".[11] The debate lasted a total of 14 minutes. No-one else spoke, and Lord Lambton's proposed Bill was rejected by 161 votes to 137.

Mr Lester at that time was Labour (later he was to become one of the first members of the Social Democratic Party founded by Mr Roy Jenkins, Mrs Shirley Williams, Dr David Owen and Mr William Rodgers). Lord Lambton was Conservative. The next major contribution, again in 1969, came from three Liberals — Mr John Macdonald Q.C., with his pamphlet *A Bill of Rights*,[12] Lord Wade, who initiated a debate in the House of Lords and Mr Emlyn Hooson Q.C., who introduced a Ten-Minute Rule Bill in the House of Commons.

Mr Macdonald's pamphlet, based on the work of a group of Liberal lawyers, went further than Mr Lester's — advocating a Bill of Rights enforceable in the ordinary courts. The need for such protection, he thought, derived from a variety of causes. He instanced: (1) the growth of bureaucracy and the individual's difficulties in presenting his case; (2) new threats to privacy from telephone-tapping, industrial espionage and the computer; (3) the increasing concentration of power in Whitehall, in industry and in the mass media; and (4) growing intolerance, exemplified by Mr Enoch Powell M.P., against minorities.

[11] *Hansard*, H.C. Vol. 782, cols. 477–478 (April 23, 1969).
[12] Liberal Party pamphlet.

His tract included a draft Bill with clauses giving rights in 24 specific areas — for instance, banning discrimination (on grounds of race, religion, sex, national or social origin); guaranteeing security of the person against injury without consent; freedom of speech and opinion; freedom of religion, of association and assembly; freedom from unlawful arrest or detention; liberty to marry freely; to educate children ("in such manner as the parent shall think fit"), etc. Mr Macdonald did not think it was necessary for the Bill of Rights to be entrenched in the sense that it would require any special parliamentary majority to pass or amend. It was enough, he thought, to provide that the Bill could only be validly amended by legislation which specifically stated an intention to do so.

On June 18, 1969, Lord Wade started a four-hour debate in the House of Lords based on the Macdonald pamphlet. His motion was:

> " . . . to call attention to the need for protection of human rights and fundamental freedoms, to the increasing power of the State in relation to the individual, and to the threat to personal privacy resulting from technological advance; and to possible measures, including the enactment of a Bill of Rights."[13]

He referred to earlier proposals: Lord Reading's Preservation of the Rights of the Subject Bill 1947, Lord Samuel's Liberties of the Subject Bill 1950, and Lord Mancroft's Rights of Privacy Bill 1961. Although the subject, therefore, was not new, it was, he thought, becoming increasingly important.

Lord Wade referred especially to the growing concentration of governmental powers, to the speed with which important bills were sometimes rushed through Parliament and to invasions of privacy. On enforceability, he adopted the proposal of Mr John Macdonald, that the rights proclaimed be capable of being determined by the ordinary courts.

Lord Gardiner, the Lord Chancellor, responding to the motion, said he was "an old civil rights man".[14] But in spite of his desire to be constructive, he found himself unable to agree that a Bill of Rights was the best way to advance. The problem with Bills of Rights, he thought, was that either they contained things that were already law, in which case they were not needed, or they were in such general terms that it was impossible to say what effect they would have. He thought it would be better to move on specific

[13] *Hansard*, H.L. Vol. 302, col. 1026 (June 18, 1969).
[14] *Ibid*, col. 1039.

5

issues such as improvements in legal aid, intrusions into privacy, extensions to the jurisdiction of the Ombudsman or better remedies in the field of administrative law.

Less than a month after Lord Wade's debate, Mr Emlyn Hooson Q.C., raised the same matter in the Commons. On July 22, 1969, he was granted leave to introduce the John Macdonald draft Bill of Rights under the Ten-Minute Rule Bill procedure.[15] Apart from his own speech in favour, there was no debate. The Bill was read a first time and ordered to be printed. It never had a second reading.

The other main event in this field in 1969 was the publication in April of a pamphlet, *New Charter*,[16] by the then Mr Quintin Hogg, M.P., Opposition Front Bench spokesman on Home Office Affairs. Though published by the Conservative Political Centre, the views were stated to be those of the author alone and not the Party.

Reluctantly, Mr Hogg had come to the conclusion that there was need for constitutional reform. Parliament had become ". . . virtually an elective dictatorship. The party system makes the supremacy of a government like the present, automatic and almost unquestioned".[17] Debates in successive Parliaments under different governments had dwindled to a ritual. There were signs of revolt in Scotland and Wales. There was need for a constitutional conference to consider agreed solutions.

He thought reform might include regional legislatures with Ministers, on the model of parliaments. There could be a chain of subordinate legislatures "with rights protected by the judiciary, but themselves popularly elected".[18] The Westminster Parliament would retain a reserve of sovereignty. The central Ministers of Education, Transport and Finance would retain power to control policy for the entire country. The Chancellor of the Exchequer would keep the power to raise taxes. But, as with Northern Ireland, a slice of the taxes would be handed back to the regions.[19]

On individual rights Mr Hogg thought that there was need for some form of Human Rights Bill. He had formerly agreed with the traditional view that what was crucial was not rights but remedies. On this view, general declarations of rights, like Magna Carta, the American Declaration of Independence, or the United Nations Universal Declaration on Human Rights were marks of a primitive legal system — "necessary to its development, but something to get over and done with in the formative stages".

---

[15] *Hansard*, H.C. Vol. 787, col. 1519 (July 22, 1969).
[16] Conservative Political Centre, No. 430, 1969.
[17] *Ibid.* at p.7.
[18] *Ibid.* at p.10.
[19] *Ibid.* at p.11.

6

He had changed his mind. The old remedies had proved themselves inadequate. He did not think that the problem was adequately defined as that of controlling the executive or criticising the caprices of individual Ministers. Ministers were only using the powers of Parliament delegated to them by a parliamentary majority usually after inadequate discussion.

> "It is the arbitrary rule of the modern Parliament itself which needs consideration. Every other country . . . has insisted on safeguards of this kind, and in theory we are committed to it. Admittedly the Universal Declaration of Human Rights to which we put our name was not intended to be enforceable. But the European Convention — which embodies many of the same rights — is enforceable, and we are party to it."[20]

Cannot, he asked, our own judiciary be entrusted with some of the powers which, at least in theory, we have entrusted to a European Court?

Less than two years later, however, Mr Hogg, now restored to the House of Lords as Lord Hailsham, had changed his mind. On November 26, 1970, Lord Arran moved the second reading of his Bill of Rights — based on the Canadian Bill of Rights enacted in 1960.[21] He hoped his Bill would be referred to a Select Committee. But Lord Hailsham, the then Lord Chancellor, said, "not only that this bill will not do" but also set out his "basic difficulties about accepting a Bill of Rights of any kind".[22]

One was that general declarations of rights reflected an unsophisticated state of the law. They were less a system of constitutional law in which rights could be enforced, than landmarks in the struggle which brought such a system into being. Thus, the right to life was better expressed in the Fatal Accidents Act 1846, than in any general statement. The right to associate became the Trade Unions Act of 1871. "Thou shalt love thy neighbour" became, amongst other things, the employer's duty to fence dangerous machinery or the farmer's duty to keep his cattle off the highway. "Thou shalt not commit adultery" became a decree nisi for divorce, with appropriate orders for custody, maintenance and costs.

The fact that we had subscribed to the Universal Declaration and to the European Convention illustrated rather than conflicted with this view. International law was precisely at the stage at which general declarations were required to give guidance as to what was acceptable conduct in international affairs.

[20] *Ibid.* at p.12.
[21] *Hansard*, H.L. Vol. 313, col. 243 (November 26, 1970).
[22] *Ibid*, cols. 255–256.

Lord Hailsham told their Lordships, however, that he was not adamantly opposed to any form of new written constitution — though he doubted whether it was possible to enact any such constitution in such a way as to prevent a later Parliament from undoing it. He would not positively say that he was against all Bills of Rights — but he was against this one.

Lord Gardiner, following Lord Hailsham, reminded the House that in the June 1969 debate on Lord Wade's proposal, he had said why he was not a Bill of Rights man. He had promised, however, to keep an open mind on the subject, and he thought this attempt very much better. Although he would not vote for it, he equally would not vote against it, because it was proposed to send the Bill to a Select Committee. The Select Committee could add to it, subtract from it, call evidence, and get expert help.[23]

After a debate of nearly four hours, however, Lord Arran withdrew his Motion and the Bill.

A few months later, on April 2, 1971, Mr Sam Silkin Q.C., future Labour Attorney-General, moved the second reading of a Protection of Human Rights Bill. The purpose of this would have been to establish a United Kingdom Commission of Human Rights to base its work on the European Convention on Human Rights. The task of the Commission would be "to investigate, report and recommend". It was to have no power to enforce. It would be able to receive complaints from anyone claiming to be the victim of a violation of human rights contrary to the European Convention. If it found the complaint admissible and if it concluded that injustice had been done, it would be able to report to Parliament. It would then be for the Government to decide whether or not to act on the report. There would be no right of appeal from the Commission to the courts, but the right of petition to the European Commission would be preserved.

Introducing his Bill, Mr Silkin said that it would give the humblest citizen the right of complaint to a new body over any violation, whether by private or public bodies, "of those rights and freedoms which society believes should be protected but which remain for the time being outside the protection of the law".[24]

Mr Silkin's motion was seconded by Mr Peter Archer Q.C., then Chairman of the Society of Labour Lawyers and later Solicitor-General.[25] The dangers to be guarded against, he thought, included those created by government. "The techniques at the disposal of governments these days can make them extremely dangerous". But

---

[23] *Hansard*, H.L. Vol. 313, cols. 269–275 (November 26, 1970).
[24] *Hansard*, H.C. Vol. 814, col. 1854 (April 2, 1971).
[25] *Ibid*, cols. 1860–1863.

there were other relationships too. Very serious distress could be caused by an employer, by a landlord, or by a neighbour. Sometimes to safeguard individuals it was necessary to give more power to governmental officials, such as industrial tribunals, to rent officers or to judges. While he was speaking, the House was counted out for lack of 40 members present.

In 1974, Mr Silkin returned to the problem in an unpublished paper written for internal Labour Party use. In this he proposed a Citizens' Rights Commission, to "investigate complaints of injustice or abuse of power emanating from any source — even from a statute itself — so that action might be taken upon them". The Commission would be a single, comprehensive body with power to investigate, report and publicise. It would in some circumstances have the power to conciliate and even "to initiate and pursue proceedings in the courts". It would take over the functions of the Race Relations Board, of the (then proposed) sex discrimination board, etc. Investigation of complaints would be likely to lead to the recognition of certain customary principles of justice. But it would be for Parliament to enact any such principles into law.

The chief event of 1974 was the delivery in December by Sir Leslie Scarman of his Hamlyn Lectures, *English Law — The New Dimension*. The main burden of the lectures was the crisis facing English law from a number of directions. One was the pressure of the international human rights movement. Both the General Assembly's Universal Declaration of Human Rights and the more recent European Convention on Human Rights reflected "a rising tide of opinion which, in one way or another, will have to be accommodated in the English legal system".

> "This may be thought difficult stuff for the common law. Charters, constitutions, broadly generalised declarations of right, just do not fit. We have no written constitution."[26]

There were many who thought that the incorporation of human rights legislation into English law was unnecessary.

> "The point is a fair one: and deserves to be taken seriously. When times are normal and fear is not stalking the land, English law sturdily protects the freedom of the individual and respects human personality. But when times are abnormally alive with fear and prejudice, the common law is at a disadvantage: it cannot resist the will, however frightened and prejudiced it may be, of Parliament".[27]

[26] Leslie Scarman, *English Law — The New Dimension* (1974), p.14.
[27] *Ibid*. at p.15.

9

One example was the war-time decision in *Liversidge v. Anderson*.[28] A more recent instance was the inability of the courts to correct the retrospective effect of the Immigration Act 1971. It was the helplessness of the law in face of the legislative sovereignty of Parliament which made it difficult for the legal system to accommodate the concept of fundamental and inviolable human rights.

> "Means, therefore, have to be found whereby (1) there is incorporated into English law a declaration of such rights; and (2) these rights are protected against all encroachments, including the power of the state, even when that power is exerted by a representative legislative institution, such as Parliament. . ."[29]

The idea of any law superior to that of Parliament was foreign to modern British ears, but in the past English law had recognised the concept of a fundamental law.

Sir Leslie doubted whether "the deeply disturbing practices of interrogation to which resort was had in Northern Ireland would have occurred, had British law possessed, at the time, a fully developed code of fundamental human rights".[30]

> "The legal system must now ensure that the law of the land will itself meet the exacting standards of human rights declared by international instruments, to which the United Kingdom is a party, as inviolable. This calls for entrenched or fundamental laws protected by a Bill of Rights — constitutional law which it is the duty of the courts to protect even against the power of Parliament. In other words, there must be a constitutional restraint placed upon the legislative power which is designed to protect the individual citizen from instant legislation conceived in fear or prejudice and enacted in breach of human rights."[31]

A second main pressure point identified by Sir Leslie Scarman was the trend toward political devolution. Inevitably, devolution would bring with it a role for the courts "and it will be a role similar in character to that which, under the guidance of the European Court of Justice, has to be assumed by the courts when faced with a question as to the validity of Community legislation".

Moreover citizens' rights would have to be safeguarded not only against administrative or executive tyranny but "against the ambitions, the excess of zeal, and sometimes the prejudice or panic, of the central regional legislatures".

---

[28] [1942] A.C. 206, H.L.
[29] Leslie Scarman, *English Law — The New Dimension* (1974), p.15.
[30] *Ibid.* at p.18.
[31] *Ibid.* at pp.19–20.

"Where else in the plethora of these new law-making bodies will one find an independent arbiter capable of declaring and enforcing the rights of the citizen than in the courts . . . It is perhaps too often forgotten that one of the merits of the rule of law is that it is a curb on power — irrespective of the person or institution who wields it."[32]

1975–1978

Shortly after these lectures, there were two significant contributions to the debate from leading Conservatives. Sir Keith (later Lord) Joseph, first in a talk to Conservative lawyers on March 17, 1975 and subsequently in a pamphlet entitled *Freedom Under Law*,[33] developed his view that a Bill of Rights was needed to protect the rule of law. He instanced as examples of the breakdown of law and order the Clay Cross incident, the campaign in favour of the Shrewsbury pickets, the threat to freedom of the press in the form of Mr Michael Foot's trade union legislation and a tax policy the effect of which would be to destroy a substantial proportion of independent business. The rule of law was focused on individuals — their person, property, rights, freedom and good name. "The rule of law begins with the individual, because individuals are real, whereas society is an abstraction."[34]

There was no way of retaining Parliament's control over the executive unless the flow of legislation was reduced. "Cut down legislation and save the law." Respect for the law was deep-rooted in Britain but this was changing now with highly political and controversial legislation abrogating traditional rights. Governments that received a minority of the poll, used the majesty of the law to dress up their prejudices and panic expedients.

"If some people or groups, be they trade unions or ratepayers, can enjoy widespread sympathy when they defy politically unpopular laws, the next step is for people to defy any laws they find inconvenient. Until recently, people of all classes regarded the law as basically just . . . Today the law is becoming a party-political football . . . If we are to save the law from Parliament and Parliament from itself, we need a new safeguard."[35]

Sir Keith saw the answer in a Bill of Rights. One function of such a basic document would be to outline the division of powers,

[32] *Ibid.* at pp.67–68.
[33] Conservative Political Centre.
[34] *Ibid*, at p.6.
[35] *Ibid.* at p.13.

11

as far as possible restoring to the courts their function of protection of individuals and corporate bodies.

Secondly, a Bill of Rights would provide a self-imposed restraint on Parliament. It might lay down various kinds of parliamentary majorities needed for different kinds of legislation.

A constitutional court would be needed to vet legislation, delegated or not, for compliance with the Bill of Rights. But Sir Keith did not spell out his proposals beyond these general prescriptions. The analysis of the problem occupied virtually the whole of his short pamphlet. The remedies he proposed were described in 18 lines of print.

The other entry in the lists was Lord Hailsham, now once again of the opinion that something needed to be done. In May 1975, in four long articles in *The Times*,[36] he urged the need for a written constitution for the United Kingdom. Legislation of major importance was passed with totally inadequate debate. Parliament was reduced to little more than a rubber stamp. But "by far the most serious criticism of Parliament at the moment is the enormous power of the executive within it".[37] The executive commanded the entire resources of the civil service. The Prime Minister could choose the moment to call an election.

At the same time, there was increasing disaffection and growing numbers of protest movements. There had been blockades outside the ports by fishermen against Norwegian fish, and inside the ports by farmers against French eggs and Irish cattle. There had been a work to contract by consultants and a protest by hospital staff against private patients. Scottish and Welsh nationalism aimed at the authority of Westminster. What united all this activity from the National Front at one extreme, to the International Marxists at the other, was the belief that whichever party was in power the central government did not correspond to the needs or wishes of the people.

> "We are living in a paradoxical situation in which Government has rarely seemed so oppressive, or at the same time so easy to defy with impunity."[38]

Lord Hailsham rehearsed some of the disadvantages of having a Bill of Rights. An attempt to entrench the Bill would either be ineffective or an unacceptable fetter on Parliament. The result would be to bring the judges into the political arena. A Bill of Rights would add significantly to the expenses and uncertainties of litigation. In India, for instance, actions brought for constitutional

[36] *The Times*, May 2, 16, 19 and 20, 1975.
[37] *The Times*, May 16, 1975.

12

remedies ran into many thousands a year and created some bitter disputes between the judiciary and Parliament.

Until recently, Lord Hailsham had concluded that the best way forward was by way of the European Convention. But for three reasons he had changed his mind. One was the demand for devolution to Scotland and Wales which would require some measure of judicial control. It would necessarily involve definition of the rights of individuals and minorities, against both central and local authority.

The second reason was that the present Labour Government was persistently proposing legislation that "would almost certainly be caught by any Bill of Rights legislation, however formulated".[39] The most obvious example, he thought, was trade union legislation — though he did not specify in what regard it offended. Legislation of both Governments regarding immigration might also have fallen foul of a Bill of Rights.

The third reason, which he thought even more conclusive than the other two, was that the country was heading for some form of crisis too deep-seated to be capable of piecemeal adjustment.

The reform he envisaged[40] would consist of a written constitution for the whole of the United Kingdom. The legislative power of Parliament would be divided and restricted on terms not very different from that accorded to Ulster in the Government of Ireland Act 1920, but entrenched by the provision of a legal and judicial machinery adequate to enforce devolution.

The rights of the individual and of minority groups would have to be protected by entrenched provisions both against local and central authority. And the right of Parliament to amend the constitution or override the provincial legislatures on matters within their devolved authority would have to be limited and defined. The whole edifice would have to be crowned and the law enforced by a Constitutional Court with separate divisions for the different portions of the realm and ultimate appeal to whatever replaced the Appellate Committee of the present House of Lords.

The next development was a brief debate in the House of Commons on a motion put by Mr James Kilfedder (Ulster Unionist) on July 7, 1975. He moved that the Government recommend the setting up of a Royal Commission to investigate and report on the subject of a Bill of Rights extending to the whole of the United Kingdom.[41] The motion was supported by, amongst

---

[39] *Ibid.*

[40] *The Times,* May 9, 1975. See further Lord Hailsham's later book, *The Dilemma of Democracy* (1978), pp.170–174.

[41] *Hansard,* H.C. Vol. 894, col. 32 (July 7, 1975).

others, Mr Edward du Cann and opposed by Mr Enoch Powell. Dr Shirley Summerskill, Minister of State at the Home Office, said that the Government was not "committed against a Bill of Rights" but there were many difficulties. One was the problem of entrenchment; another was whether a Bill of Rights should be broadly or narrowly written; a third was the possibility of conflict between the Bill of Rights and existing law. The Government hoped that the debate would continue. Mr Kilfedder withdrew his motion without a division. During the debate no Labour Member spoke, apart from Dr Summerskill. Mr du Cann stated that the Leader of the Opposition had set up a special committee under the chairmanship of Sir Michael Havers, former Solicitor-General, to study the problem of a Bill of Rights.[42]

In the following week, a Bill of Rights Bill was introduced by a Liberal M.P., Mr A. J. Beith, with the support of Liberal colleagues including Mr Jeremy Thorpe, Mr Emlyn Hooson, Q.C. and Mr David Steel. The Bill was introduced in a short speech by Mr Beith under the Ten-minute Rule Bill procedure, but there was no further debate.[43] The Bill was simply read a first time and ordered to be printed.

In the meanwhile, the Labour Party had also become active in the summer and autumn of 1975. A paper prepared by the Human Rights Sub-Committee of the Home Policy Committee of the National Executive urged the adoption of the European Convention on Human Rights into United Kingdom law. The Human Rights Sub-Committee was chaired by Mrs Shirley Williams, and included Lord Gardiner, former Lord Chancellor, and the Law Officers Mr Sam Silkin and Mr Peter Archer.[44] The Sub-Committee's proposal was considered by the Home Policy Committee under the chairmanship of Mr Anthony Wedgwood Benn (later Mr Tony Benn).[45] The Home Policy Committee and the National Executive itself decided not to allow the Sub-Committee's paper to be issued as official Labour Party policy, but it was decided that the paper could be published as a discussion document.[46] It was launched on February 15, 1976 at a press conference addressed by Mrs Shirley Williams and the Solicitor-General, Mr Peter Archer.

The Sub-Committee's paper, "Charter of Human Rights", was brief — a mere 11 pages. It argued that better protection of human

[42] *Ibid*. col. 72.
[43] *Hansard*, H.C. Vol. 895, cols. 1270–1273 (July 15, 1975).
[44] It also included Mr Anthony Lester and the writer.
[45] Mr Benn has consistently been opposed to any form of Bill of Rights.
[46] Until Mr John Smith's speech in March 1993, see p.32–34 below, that was the nearest the Labour Party came to support for a Bill of Rights.

rights was needed even though Britain had as good a record in this field as any other country. ("The protection of human rights is not a form of international competition. The fact that we may be better provided than this or that foreign country is of less concern than whether we are doing as much as we should and whether any new forms of protection would assist us.") The purpose of a Charter of Human Rights (avoidance of the term Bill of Rights was intentional), would be to "provide a new method for the citizen who believed himself to be the victim of injustice to seek a remedy". Such a Charter was desirable because the system was "less sensitive and responsive than it should be to the grievances of individuals or groups in the community". It was time for the scales to be tipped back in favour of the ordinary person. The way to do this would be to incorporate the European Convention as a United Kingdom statute. This would not infringe the sovereignty of Parliament since Parliament would still be able to pass any statute to cancel or modify any of its provisions. A Charter of Human Rights would be an indication of concern for the individual. There was a widespread feeling that the individual was more and more the object of forces he could not control in the increasingly complex conditions of modern society. A Labour Government, with its tendency to prefer centralised and planning solutions to those of the free market, was especially open to the charge that it regarded the individual as subservient to the greater good of the community. Yet civil liberties were a traditional concern of the Labour Party, and were wholly compatible with socialism. Incorporation of the European Convention of Human Rights into United Kingdom law could "provide the Labour Government with a major initiative which would demonstrate its commitment to individual liberties without endangering its programme".

Only three days before publication of the Labour Party's discussion document, Mr Roy Jenkins, the Home Secretary, indicated that he too was moving in the direction of considering the incorporation of the European Convention.[47] In a speech to the Birmingham Law Society on February 12, 1975, he discussed the advantages and disadvantages of such a step. He was careful not to state any concluded view on the question, but suggested that the question of guarantees of human rights was one of mounting concern. It had caught the attention of an increasing number of lawyers and politicians, and particularly over the previous few months, there had been a growing public interest in the subject. The Government had undertaken a study of the problem and the two main political parties were proceeding with their own studies. He hoped that the discussion would continue.

[47] Mr Anthony Lester was employed at the Home Office as his Special Adviser.

The Times, commenting editorially on Mr Jenkins' speech,[48] said he had advertised the Government's serious interest in the question. But it was for the reformers to make the case for so major an innovation. Lord Hailsham, though he had since changed his mind, had earlier pointed out that Bills of Rights might be less efficacious than they sounded.[49] The rights they purported to guarantee were defined with considerable generality. The declaration that one had a right to life was fine and good, but the place to look for its legal effect was the Fatal Accidents Act of 1846 and other prosaic enactments. Also, Bills of Rights were most needed in times of national emergency, but they normally provided for derogation from them at such times "just when they are most needed". Furthermore, there was a problem of passing more power to the judges who were, and should remain, unaccountable if their independence was to be preserved.

The Sunday Times appeared to take a more favourable view. In an editorial on February 15, 1975 it said that incorporation of the European Convention into United Kingdom law was now a campaign of serious people. It would not destroy parliamentary sovereignty "but would introduce a new factor into Parliament's consideration of what politically or morally it could do". Advocacy of a Bill of Rights entailed support for something new and therefore uncertain, but it also proclaimed "a conviction that individual liberties are not now well protected". But the *Daily Telegraph*[50] warned that in these dramatic times "we cannot rely for the defence of liberty on a barricade of parchment". Since the Labour Party's Discussion Document stated that incorporation of the European Convention would not prevent a Labour Government from acting, there was nothing here to comfort those who looked to a Bill of Rights to give some protection from the constant extension of State power. On the other hand, some Tories wished to see clauses entrenched so as to make it harder for Parliament constantly to enlarge the sphere of the executive. But legislation of this kind would call for a far greater measure of agreement about the fundamentals of a good society than existed at that time. This last point troubled *The Economist*[51] as well. Both Mr Jenkins and the Labour Party's document preferred to take the European Convention "off the peg" rather than drafting a tailor-made Bill of Rights. But this was a "generation old, Hitler aftermath definition of civil liberties". A Bill of Rights, to have

[48] *The Times*, February 13, 1976.
[49] But see Lord Hailsham's reply, *The Times*, February 17, 1976.
[50] *Daily Telegraph*, February 16, 1976.
[51] *The Economist*, February 21, 1976.

16

some chance of survival, needed to emerge from bi-partisan agreement but, if drafting of an appropriate modern document meant that such agreement could not emerge, the rights of individuals would be sacrificed to the rights of the political parties.

Further fuel was added to the fire in the succeeding weeks and months. On March 5, 1976 the Standing Advisory Commission on Human Rights for Northern Ireland published a discussion paper on the Bill of Rights problem in which it enumerated the arguments for and against the proposal and posed some questions that required to be answered. The Advisory Commission, under the chairmanship of the late Lord Feather, invited written submissions and comments by the end of the following month "in order to avoid delay in the completion of work on a subject of such importance"[52].

In March 1976 Lord Wade moved a debate in the House of Lords on a fresh Bill designed to incorporate the European Convention into United Kingdom law.[53] The first clause of his Bill would have given the force of law to the Convention lock, stock and barrel, and the second clause provided that in case of conflict between the Convention or its Protocols and any pre-existing statute the Convention was to prevail. In case of subsequent legislation, however, the Convention should prevail "unless subsequent enactment shall explicitly state otherwise".[54] Lord Hailsham, now again critical, objected that for various reasons the Bill in such a form would not quite do. For one thing he did not think "that a Private Members' Bill altering the British Constitution is really on".[55] He feared that Bills of Rights might be a form of bogus protection. ("Show me a nation with a Bill of Rights and I will show you a nation which has fewer actual human rights than England or Britain, because the escape clauses are used, often quite ruthlessly by the Executive of the time."[56]) He believed that there was a need for a written constitution with entrenched clauses. It was not possible to deal with the issue piecemeal. It was necessary to tackle the sovereignty of Parliament by having devolved Assemblies. The device of a Bill of Rights was a delusive protection. He wanted to see something more comprehensive and effective. But he hoped that the Bill would be given a second reading. He had put down a motion referring the issue to a Select Committee, but whether he moved the motion would depend on the reply to the debate of the Minister of State, Lord Harris.

[52] Standing Advisory Commission on Human Rights, *Bill of Rights*, March 5, 1976, para. 17.
[53] *Hansard*, H.L. Vol. 369, col. 775 (March 25, 1976).
[54] *Ibid.*
[55] *Ibid.* col. 777.
[56] *Ibid.* cols. 784–785.

Before Lord Harris spoke there were speeches from a number of other peers. Lord Gardiner who in 1969, during the debate on Lord Wade's earlier Bill, had been against a Bill of Rights, said he had changed his mind. He had previously thought that a Bill of Rights "was something outside our legal traditions"[57]. But for various reasons he had concluded that this was not so. First, there was the need to improve the power of Parliament and of the people as against that of the executive. Secondly, it would be sad if we did not play a full part in a strong and growing international movement of human rights. Thirdly, it would be required in the context of devolution. Fourthly, taking proceedings in Strasbourg was too slow. Fifthly, it would enable the judges to develop the law and practice more quickly than if it were left to the executive and the legislature. Taking the European Convention was better than trying to draft a fresh Bill of Rights. He did not think that the judges would have real difficulties in interpreting the document. Lord Brockway and Lord Banks also spoke in favour of the proposal.

But Lord Denning M.R. and Lord Lloyd of Hampstead disagreed. The Master of the Rolls, usually one to support the citizen against the Big Battalions, said that a Bill of Rights, with entrenched clauses, would be "contrary to all our history and tradition"[58]. If judges were given power to overthrow sections of Acts of Parliament, they would become political, their appointments would be based on political grounds and the "reputation of our Judiciary would suffer accordingly".[59] Many of the principles of the European Convention had been developed by English judges. "In so far as those articles simply enunciate principles which have been culled from the law of England, we do not need them".[60] But the Convention went further. It used high-sounding phrases, such as were common in the legislation of European countries "quite contrary to our system".[61] Such phrases might be brought into play by individuals who might "tend to disrupt and embarrass our society".[62] Lord Denning was not usually regarded as a champion of the status quo, but in this context he was clearly alarmed by the unsettling implications of a Bill of Rights. He thought that it might be "taken advantage of by disgruntled people who will bring proceedings before the courts challenging the orderly system of our country".[63] They might be turned down, but there would be a great

[57] *Hansard*, H.L. Vol. 369, col. 788 (March 25, 1976).
[58] *Ibid*. col. 797.
[59] *Ibid*.
[60] *Ibid*. col. 798.
[61] *Ibid*.
[62] *Ibid*.
[63] *Ibid*. col. 800.

deal of litigation: "people praying in aid of these fundamental rights, as they say, and giving much embarrassment and disturbance to society".[64] (Lord Denning subsequently changed his mind. Mr Anthony Lester giving the F.A. Mann Lecture in November 1983 stated that Lord Denning had authorised him to say that he was now in favour of incorporation of the Convention into United Kingdom law.[65])

Lord Lloyd, a distinguished academic lawyer and a Labour supporter, said he was opposed to handing over major policy issues for resolution by the judges. Surely Parliament, with all its faults, was better qualified to make political judgments.[66] He did not accept that human rights were seriously threatened under our system. If problems arose they could be dealt with by individual pieces of legislation. The enactment of a Bill of Rights would be "to throw the whole of our law into a state of total uncertainty for almost an indefinite period".[67] Almost any Act could be impugned in legal proceedings. Only the lawyers would benefit.

Lord Harris, the Minister of State at the Home Office, said that Lord Wade's Bill came in the middle of a growing public debate on the issue. The Government was still some way from being able to form an informed and balanced judgment. In the Government's view the need was for wide public discussion. Its own officials were still studying the problem and were likely to report shortly. It would be best to await the fruits of those labours.[68] In the event, however, the House gave the Bill an unopposed second reading and Lord Hailsham did not press his motion.

Less than three weeks' later, on April 14, 1976, the Attorney-General, Mr Sam Silkin, said at Queen's University, Belfast, that the time might have come for Britain to consider taking the historic step of incorporating the European Convention into our law. Giving the Macdermott Lecture, Mr Silkin did not come out categorically for such a step but his remarks clearly indicated that this was his own preferred solution. It was the strongest statement yet by any Government Minister in favour of incorporating the European Convention.

The momentum of events continued, with two further developments in June 1976. In the middle of the month the Home Office

[64] *Ibid.*
[65] Anthony Lester,"Fundamental Rights: The United Kingdom Isolated?" (1984) Pub.L. 46 at 63, n.83.
[66] *Hansard*, H.L. Vol. 369, col. 794.
[67] *Ibid.* col 795.
[68] *Ibid.* cols. 807–813.

published its Discussion Document[69] to which Lord Harris had referred in the debate on Lord Wade's Bill in March. The document was said to arise out of the public discussion that had been generated by Lord Scarman's Hamlyn Lectures, Lord Hailsham's articles in *The Times*, the studies initiated by both the Labour and the Conservative Parties and the work of the Northern Ireland Standing Advisory Commission on Human Rights. It described the existing arrangements for the remedying of grievances and then launched into a detailed resumé of the issues raised by a proposal for a Bill of Rights. There were problems of the rights to be covered in such a document, of whether it should have higher status than ordinary law, and whether it should be enforceable against private parties as well as public authorities. The basic question was whether we should move in the direction of legislation giving special protection to fundamental rights. It set out three main options — to leave things as they were: to incorporate the European Convention into United Kingdom law; or to draft a new Bill of Rights. Although the document offered no opinion between the three alternatives, it focused principal attention on the second — confirming the general view that if a Bill of Rights were to be adopted, the European Convention was the most likely choice. The 26-page paper was a lucid and useful account of the issues raised for consideration — including some detailed treatment of the possible impact on United Kingdom law and practice of application of some particular provisions of the Convention and the First Protocol.

But the chief interest in the document lay not so much in its content, but in the composition of the Working Party that drew it up, and in the constitutional innovation of publishing a paper drawn up by senior civil servants. Departments represented on the Working Party were the Cabinet Office, the Civil Service Department, the Foreign and Commonwealth Office, the Northern Ireland Office, the Law Officer's Department, the Lord Advocate's Department and the Treasury Solicitor's Department. It was clear from this list that the governmental machine was taking the question of a Bill of Rights with great seriousness.

This was confirmed a few days later at an unusual conference organised over the weekend of June 18–20, 1976 by the British Institute of Human Rights[70] at Highgate House, a country house in

---

[69] Home Office Discussion Paper, *Legislation on Human Rights: with particular reference to the European Convention*, June 1976. The value of publication was however somewhat diminished by the fact that the Discussion Document was not available from HMSO.

[70] Mr Anthony Lester and the writer were actively involved in the organisation of the conference.

Northamptonshire. Some 40 participants had been invited to consider whether Britain should have a Bill of Rights and, if so, what should be its incidents. The British contingent included Ministers (the Lord Chancellor, Lord Elwyn-Jones, and the Attorney-General, Mr Sam Silkin); judges (Lord Gardiner, Lord Justice Scarman, the Chief Justice of Northern Ireland, Sir Robert Lowry and Mr Justice Templeman); representatives of the Conservative Opposition (Mr Ian Percival Q.C., Shadow Solicitor-General, and Mr Leon Brittan M.P.); the chairman of the Liberal Lawyers, Mr John Macdonald, Q.C.; and senior civil servants (including the Permanent Under-Secretary of State and the Deputy Under-Secretary of State at the Home Office, the Deputy Clerk of the Crown in the Lord Chancellor's Office, the Deputy Legal Secretary to the Law Officers, the Treasury Solicitor, and the Legal Adviser to the Foreign and Commonwealth Office). Participants from the United States included former Justice of the Supreme Court, the Hon. Tom Clark; former Watergate Special Prosecutor, Professor Archibald Cox; the Secretary of State for Transportation, Mr William Coleman; and the Hon. J. Skelly Wright of the United States Federal Court of Appeal. The President of the European Commission of Human Rights and two fellow Commissioners also came, as did the Secretary to the Austrian Cabinet and a member of the French Conseil d'Etat.

The conference was opened by the Home Secretary, Mr Roy Jenkins, who said that he had reached the conclusion that the European Convention should be incorporated into our domestic law.[71] But because of the official positions of most of those who attended, it was agreed that no publicity should be given to the views of individuals. The press statement after the meeting said that although a wide range of opinion was expressed on whether it would be desirable to enact a Bill of Rights in Great Britain, the majority certainly felt that such a step would be feasible if it were thought desirable. Some felt that the enactment of a Bill of Rights would do good, whilst others questioned whether it would add anything to existing safeguards for human rights. Another doubt expressed was whether a Bill of Rights might slow down the administrative process. The main advantage of a Bill of Rights "was seen to be as a set of standards or guidelines for legislators, civil servants and all public officials by which their conduct could

---

[71] A few weeks later, in September 1976, Mr Jenkins wrote ". . . for my part . . . I am inclined to share the view expressed by the Attorney-General in his Macdermott lecture on the Rights of Man and the Rule of Law, and am disposed to favour adopting the Convention into our law in order to provide more effective remedies for violations of the Convention". (1976) 73 Law Soc.Gaz. 774.

21

be judged by impartial judges on a case by case basis". The general view was that "if we were to have a Bill of Rights, the incorporation of the existing European Convention . . . was the most that could be regarded as politically realistic, at least initially".

At the conclusion of the meeting there were many present (including the writer) who felt that the Bill of Rights lobby had made significant progress in persuading some of the sceptics about the idea — including some in very high places.

Until this point there had been no sign of the official view of the Conservative Opposition. Sir Michael Havers (Shadow Attorney-General and chairman of the committee set up by the Leader of the Opposition to consider the problem) declared himself in favour of incorporation of the European Convention in an article in the *Daily Mail* on August 4, 1976. His committee, however, never published a report. But in November 1976 a subcommittee of the Society of Conservative Lawyers, including seven Q.C.s, published a report, *Another Bill of Rights?*, which proposed "that the European Convention of Human Rights should be given statutory force as over-riding domestic law where the two codes conflict". Curiously, the report also argued that there was no need for a Bill of Rights. Apparently, in the view of the authors, the European Convention did not qualify as a Bill of Rights. The reasoning which led the sub-committee to this conclusion was not explained but it seems that by a Bill of Rights it meant a new document that would protect, *inter alia*, values of especial concern to Conservatives. ("Unfortunately, we see no prospect whatever of sufficient all-party support for a Bill of Rights that could provide any effective safeguard of the rights that Conservatives, and many Liberals, believe to be crucial to a free society.") On the other hand, any Bill of Rights could only operate as an effective safeguard if it commanded the respect and confidence of those whom it sought to protect and to this end it must carry sufficient all-party support to make it extremely unlikely that any of its provisions would become bones of contention at general elections of the foreseeable future. Since such all-party support was not likely to be forthcoming, a Bill of Rights was not the right approach. The report did not discuss any of the problems connected with incorporation of the European Convention. Most of the report was concerned with proposed improvements in the system of administrative law. In fact, the entire discussion of the European Convention in a document of some 22 pages, consisted of a mere three lines — but the recommendation to incorporate the Convention was, nevertheless, unqualified and categorical.

Moreover, it shortly became apparent that the Conservative Front Bench had decided to support the campaign to secure the incorporation of the European Convention, at least in the context of the devolution legislation. On January 14, 1977 Mr Leon Brittan, then Opposition Front Bench spokesman on devolution (and later, in 1984, to become Home Secretary in Mrs Thatcher's second Government) told an audience in North Berkshire that amendments would be moved to the Scotland and Wales Bill to make the European Convention effective in Scotland and Wales. "I believe", he was quoted as saying, "that if these amendments are passed and the provisions relating to the Bill of Rights are seen to work in Scotland and Wales, the case for a United Kingdom Bill of Rights would be immeasurably strengthened."[72]

Mr Brittan's promise did not come to fruition on the first devolution Bill. The Opposition amendments tabled in regard to the European Convention were not reached before the Bill was eventually withdrawn. But the matter was put to the test when the Scotland Bill was in the committee stage. On February 1, 1978, Mr Brittan for the Opposition moved two new clauses and a related schedule designed "to provide Scotland with a Bill of Rights".[73] The rights and freedoms to be provided were those in the European Convention on Human Rights, with slight alterations to make them appropriate to a devolved legislature. The amendment was opposed by the Government. Mr John Smith, future Leader of the Labour Party, but then Minister of State in the Privy Council Office, said it would not be wise to take a decision on this important question in the context of the Scotland Bill. The Government had issued its Discussion Paper. The matter required further consideration. The amendment was put to the vote (with the whips on) and was defeated by 251 votes to 227 — a Government majority of 24.[74] This was the first occasion on which the House of Commons voted on the substantive question of the incorporation of the European Convention. It was also the first — and only — occasion to date on which incorporation of the European Convention has ever officially been proposed by the Conservative Party.

A few months earlier, on November 23, 1977, the Northern Ireland Standing Advisory Commission on Human Rights had published a lengthy report on the issue.[75] The Report was an important contribution to the literature on this subject. It provided a full analysis of the relevant issues. It stated that there was

---

[72] *The Times*, January 15, 1978.
[73] *Hansard*, H.C. Vol. 943, col. 491 (February 1, 1978).
[74] *Ibid*. col. 580.
[75] Northern Ireland Standing Advisory Commission on Human Rights, *The Protection of Human Rights by law in Northern Ireland*, Cmnd. 7009 (1977).

widespread support in Northern Ireland for a Bill of Rights, though for a variety of very different reasons. A substantial majority of the witnesses had favoured a United Kingdom rather than a Northern Ireland measure — especially in the context of direct rule. It appeared that a Bill of Rights limited to Northern Ireland would not be widely welcomed. There was a widespread feeling that those who lived in the United Kingdom should, so far as possible, share similar fundamental rights and freedoms. The overwhelming weight of evidence given to the Committee had favoured the use of the European Convention on Human Rights as the basis for any Bill of Rights, whether for Northern Ireland alone or for the whole United Kingdom. The Committee concluded that there was a need for better protection of human rights in Northern Ireland and one of the principal steps that should be taken to this end would be to make the European Convention part of domestic law for the United Kingdom as a whole. Failing this, there should be a clear and enforceable charter of human rights for Northern Ireland alone.

A few weeks after the debate and vote in the House of Commons the subject was taken up again very generally by the House of Lords which after a debate set up a Select Committee on a Bill of Rights.[76] The debate was initiated, yet again, by Lord Wade. The Liberal Peer moved his Bill, which was intended to incorporate the European Convention into the domestic law of Britain. This time Lord Hailsham did move his amendment to refer the Bill to a Select Committee. If he had thought that the Bill would find its way onto the statute book that session he would have been content to give it a second reading, put down his amendments, and send it to the Commons. But he was sure that the Government did not intend to allow the Bill to prosper. A good Select Committee could produce a valuable report which would add a definite and constructive contribution to the debate and possibly elucidate some of the highly controversial questions which had to be thrashed out. The Lord Chancellor, Lord Elwyn-Jones, an opponent of incorporation, indicated that in his view this was not a suitable subject for a select committee. The better way forward might be a general review of the law to identify the points where domestic law fell short of the ideal of the European Convention so that they could be remedied by legislation. But the House of Lords rejected the Lord Chancellor's advice. Lord Hailsham's amendment was agreed to and Lord Wade's Bill was read a second time.[77]

[76] *Hansard*, H.L. Vol. 389, col. 973 (February 3, 1977).
[77] *Ibid*. cols. 1006–1009.

The Select Committee was established on May 17, 1977 with Lord Allen of Abbeydale, a cross-bencher, as chairman and 10 other members. Of these, four (Lords Boston, Gordon-Walker, Lloyd and Lady Gaitskell) were Labour: three (Lords Blake, Jellicoe and O'Hagan) were Conservative and two (Lords Foot and Wade) Liberal. In addition to the chairman there was a second cross-bencher, Lord Redcliffe-Maud. The Committee was re-appointed in the succeeding session of Parliament to complete its work. It held 12 public meetings to take evidence and four meetings to consider its report. The entire record of the evidence is published as a separate volume.[78]

The evidence of the witnesses fell into several distinct categories. First, there were those who favoured the incorporation of the European Convention of Human Rights into United Kingdom law. They were: Lord Hailsham, the British Institute of Human Rights, the Liberal Party, the Northern Ireland Standing Advisory Committee on Human Rights, the Scottish National Party, the National Council for Civil Liberties, and the present writer. There were two witnesses (Lord Diplock and Sir Henry Fisher) who opposed the enactment of any form of a Bill of Rights. The Law Society's Law Reform Committee was opposed to the enactment of a Bill of Rights pending a wide-ranging examination of the need for fundamental constitutional reform of the relationship between Parliament, the executive and the judiciary. In the meanwhile, it thought attention should rather be concentrated on special measures which could be taken in the short term to improve the law protecting human rights. Professor O. Hood Phillips thought that on balance the European Convention was probably too old fashioned or out of date to make it worth enacting. He preferred to see a major constitutional review — though, possibly, incorporating the European Convention would be better than nothing. Mr Cedric Thornberry, then a Lecturer in Law at the London School of Economics, also argued that the European Convention reflected too restricted a view of human rights to be worthy of incorporation into United Kingdom law. If a Bill of Rights were desirable, the European Convention was a most unsuitable draft for such a document. On balance, the status quo was probably preferable. Professor Harry Arthurs, a distinguished law professor from Osgoode Hall Law School, Toronto, testified that the Canadian Bill of Rights had had little, if any, impact. The Canadian experience suggested that enactment of a Bill of Rights in itself changed nothing. There was no reason to suppose that human rights would be better protected

[78] "Minutes of Evidence taken before the Select Committee on a Bill of Rights", House of Lords, 1977.

through the enactment of such a measure. A Bill of Rights in most Western democracies was likely to be at most a makeweight or marginal factor. It was unlikely to change a mature political culture or legal tradition, at least in the short run.[79]

The Select Committee reported on June 29, 1978.[80] The Committee said it was required to report on two separate questions: first, whether a Bill of Rights was desirable and second, if so, what form it should take. The report said it was difficult to keep the two issues apart. It was not feasible to consider the desirability of a Bill of Rights without having a broad idea of the likely contents of such a Bill. Nevertheless, it had been much easier to reach agreement on the second than on the first question. In fact, there was unanimity that "if there was to be a Bill of Rights, it should be a Bill based on the European Convention of Human Rights".[81] It had proved impossible, however, to reach agreement on whether such a Bill was desirable. On this question, six members, Lords Blake, Jellicoe, O'Hagan, Redcliffe-Maud, Wade and Lady Gaitskell (three Conservative, one Liberal, one Labour and one cross-bencher) supported the Bill of Rights. Five members, Lords Boston, Foot, Gordon-Walker, Lloyd of Hampstead and Allen of Abbeydale (three Labour, one Liberal and one cross-bencher) were against it.

But the Committee thought that even if, on balance, a Bill of Rights were desirable, too much should not be expected of it. Both the advantages and disadvantages of having a Bill of Rights had, it suggested, been put too high. In any country whatever its constitution, the existence or absence of legislation in the nature of a Bill of Rights could in practice play only a relatively minor part in the protection of human rights. What was important above all was a country's political climate and traditions.[82]

The Select Committee's report was debated in the House of Lords on November 29, 1978. The debate was opened by the Chairman of the Select Committee Lord Allen of Abbeydale who moved that the House take note of the report. However, Lord Wade, whose original Bill had resulted in the establishment of the Select Committee, moved an amendment urging the Government "to introduce a Bill of Rights to incorporate the European Convention on Human Rights into the domestic law of the United Kingdom".[83] After a debate lasting for five hours this amendment

[79] For subsequent developments on the later introduction of the Canadian Charter of Rights see however pp.127–131 below.
[80] *Report of the Select Committee on a Bill of Rights*, House of Lords, paper 176, June 1978.
[81] *Ibid*, p.20, para. 6.
[82] *Ibid*, p.29, para. 30.
[83] *Hansard*, H.L. Vol. 396, col. 1308 (November 29, 1978).

was carried by 56 to 30.[84] Those who voted with Lord Wade included Lords Bowden, Carr, Gladwyn, Hailsham, Houghton, Pitt, Plant, Redcliffe-Maud, Scarman and Wigoder. Those who were against included Lords Diplock, Elwyn-Jones, Foot, Gordon-Walker, Morris of Borth-y-Gest, Peart and Stewart.

Since 1978

In the decade after 1978 further developments consisted mainly of yet more parliamentary debates — to little political effect. But from the late 1980s support for the enactment of a Bill of Rights — especially in the form of incorporation of the European Convention (E.C.H.R) — grew significantly. Moreover, crucially, from 1993 the support for the first time came from one of the two main political parties.

In 1979, after the change of Government from Labour to Conservative, Lord Wade introduced his Bill yet again in the House of Lords, and again it was passed by the Lords and sent to the Commons.[85] It was, however, not considered by the Commons. In 1981, Lord Wade again succeeded in obtaining the Lords' approval of his Bill which was again sent to the Commons.[86] This time it was at least debated in the Commons. The Liberal M.P. Mr Alan Beith introduced the Bill and attempted to secure a Second Reading for the Bill but this attempt was defeated.[87] The Solicitor-General, Sir Ian Percival, made a non-committal speech for the Government simply saying that no decision had been taken as to the merits of the matter and that it was hoped to have discussions on the matter with the other parties.[88] But he did not give any indication that such discussions were in fact likely to take place.

The next event was two and a half years later in December 1983 when the Social Democratic M.P. Mr Robert Maclennan introduced a new (and more skilfully drafted) European Human Rights Convention Bill under the Ten-Minute Rule Bill procedure. The Bill was supported by M.P.s of all parties: Mr Donald Anderson

---

[84] *Ibid.* cols. 1395–1396.
[85] Second Reading, *Hansard*, H.L. Vol. 402, cols. 999–1038 and 1040–1071 (November 8, 1979); Committee, Vol. 403, cols. 287–295 and 297–310; Report, cols. 311 and 502–509 (November 29, 1979); Third Reading and sent to Commons, cols. 911–915 (December 6, 1979).
[86] Second Reading, *Hansard*, H.L. Vol. 415, cols. 533–561 (December 4, 1980); Committee, Vol. 416, cols. 152–155 (January 14, 1981); Report, col. 689 (January 27, 1981); Third Reading and sent to Commons, cols. 1102–1106 (February 13,1981).
[87] *Hansard*, H.C. 6th Series, Vol. 4, cols. 419–457 (May 8, 1981) and col. 1078 (May 15, 1981).
[88] *Ibid*, cols. 445–448.

and Mr Roy Mason for the Labour Party, Sir Edward Gardner, Mr Terence L. Higgins, Mr Geoffrey Rippon and Mr Norman St John Stevas for the Conservatives and Mr A. J. Beith and Mr Alex Carlile for the Liberals. Under the Ten-Minute Rule procedure the Bill was simply introduced by Mr Maclennan with a brief speech.[89] There was no debate and the Bill lapsed.

Considering that three prominent members of the Conservative Government — Lord Hailsham, Sir Keith Joseph and Mr Leon Brittan — as well Sir Michael Havers, the Attorney-General, had all expressed support for a Bill of Rights, it was perhaps surprising that the Government had shown no sign of being prepared to take action. But in June 1984 there was the first sign of serious interest from Conservative backbenchers when no less than 107 Tory M.P.s signed an early day motion calling for a Bill incorporating the European Convention into United Kingdom law. There was no indication that Mrs Thatcher's Cabinet was likely to be stirred into action by this development, but it was an unexpected signal that interest in the campaign had become widespread amongst Conservative backbenchers.

At the end of 1984, a new organisation, the Constitutional Reform Centre, emerged to promote various forms of reform of which incorporation of the European Convention was the first. Its chairman, Mr Richard Holme, writing in *The Times* on January 8, 1985 said that 1988, the last year in which the Government could call an election, would be the 300th anniversary of the Bill of Rights in 1688.

> "It would be a fitting celebration for the country which once
> led the world in constitutional democracy to have ensured the
> same standard of protection for individual rights that every
> other civilised democracy now enjoys."

In November 1985, a Conservative peer, Lord Broxbourne, (formerly Derek Walker-Smith Q.C., M.P.) introduced the Human Rights and Fundamental Freedoms Bill to incorporate the European Convention and the first Protocol into United Kingdom law. The Bill was given a Second Reading after a three-hour debate on Human Rights Day, December 10, 1985 — though it was opposed by the former Labour Lord Chancellor, Lord Elwyn-Jones and by Lord Glenarthur on behalf of the Government[90]. The Bill then

---

[89] *Hansard*, H.C. 6th Series, Vol. 50, cols. 852–854 (December 13, 1983). Mr Maclennan, who was Leader of the Social Democratic Party (SDP) 1987–88, made a second attempt as a Liberal Democrat by way of the Ten Minute Rule Bill procedure in 1992 — see *Hansard*, H.C. Vol.203, cols. 979–81 (February 12, 1992).

[90] *Hansard*, H.L. Vol. 469, cols. 156–196 (December 10, 1986).

28

passed unscathed through its Committee[91] and Report stages[92] and was given a Third Reading[93].

In December 1986, Lord Broxbourne's Bill was introduced in the House of Commons by Sir Edward Gardner. Its other sponsors included Tories (Mr Geoffrey Rippon, Dr John Gilbert, Mr Norman St John Stevas, Sir Anthony Buck), Labour (Mr Greville Janner, Mr D. Wigley, Mr Austin Mitchell) and Social Democratic Party and Liberals (Mr Robert Maclennan and Mr Alex Carlile). The Second Reading debate took place on February 6, 1987. The Bill was opposed by both the Government and by the Labour Opposition. Sir Patrick Mayhew, the Solicitor-General for the Government, said that the chief reason for opposing the Bill was that it would thrust the judges into the arena of political controversy. At present they were preserved from making policy decisions and because of that their reputation for impartiality stood so high. "My great fear", he said, "is that, if we were to pass this Bill, that reputation would seriously decline with grievously damaging results not through the fault of the judges but because of the essentially political tasks with which we would have burdened them".[94] Mr Nicholas Brown, Labour Opposition spokesman on legal affairs, said that the present judiciary was "not politically indifferent, being predominantly drawn from a narrow atypical section of the population"[95]. They could find themselves striking down legislation and creating law, but that was not the best way of making law. It was bound to lead to political controversy which could undermine support for the judiciary in their independent and impartial role. Rights should not evolve in the haphazard course of litigation. To allow the courts to question legislation would throw the law into a state of uncertainty. The vote at the end of the debate was 94 to 16 in favour of giving the Bill a Second Reading but it fell because of the technical House of Commons rule that more than 100 M.P.s have to vote on the "closure" of a Private Members' Bill. Those who voted in favour of the Bill were 58 Conservatives, 18 from the Social Democratic-Liberal Alliance, 16 Labour M.Ps. and two others.[96]

The Constitutional Reform Centre started in 1984 by Richard Holme (later Lord Holme of Cheltenham), was the genesis of

[91] *Ibid*. Vol. 472, cols. 1087–1116 (March 20, 1986).
[92] *Ibid*. Vol. 473, cols. 267–78 (April 8, 1986).
[93] *Ibid*. Vol. 474, cols. 334–342 (April 30, 1986).
[94] *Hansard*, H.C. Vol. 109, col. 1272 (February 6, 1987).
[95] *Ibid*. col. 1276.
[96] *Ibid*. cols. 1288–89.

Charter 88. Charter 88[97], which became a movement, started as a document, drafted by a small group of people[98], setting out the basis for a new constitutional settlement to protect political, civil and human rights in the United Kingdom. Signed by 243 people from all walks of life, it was first published in *The Guardian* on November 30, 1988. The first of the ten stated objectives set out in Charter 88 was to "enshrine, by means of a Bill of Rights, such civil liberties as the right to peaceful assembly, to freedom of association, to freedom from discrimination, to freedom from detention without trial, to trial by jury, to privacy and to freedom of expression". The Charter was subsequently published in *The Independent, New Statesman & Society* and *The Observer*. The initial three advertisements gathered over 5,000 signatures of supporters and from then on Charter 88 has been an influential lobby for various forms of constitutional reform including in particular for a Bill of Rights. Its current literature refers to three options in regard to the Bill of Rights. One is to draft a Bill of Rights "perhaps as part of a new constitution". The second is to integrate the UN Declaration on Human Rights into British law. The third is to incorporate the European Convention on Human Rights (E.C.H.R.) into United Kingdom law. The last is said to be "the best first step".

At the time that Charter 88 was first launched the Labour Party's attitude to the Bill of Rights proposal was distinctly frosty. Writing in *The Guardian* a few days later, Mr Roy Hattersley, then the Deputy Leader, dismissed the call for incorporation of the European Convention which he described as "the model for a written constitution which is most commonly canvassed for incorporation into British law". At best, he suggested, "a written constitution diminishes the importance of positive freedom — government action to enable more and more people to do and enjoy those things worth doing and enjoying. At worst, it actually prevents or inhibits that action from being taken". A written constitution, he opined, "has become a badly thought out counsel of despair".[99]

In December 1990, Lord Holme of Cheltenham initiated a two-hour debate in the House of Lords the purpose of which was to urge incorporation of the European Convention into United Kingdom law.[1] The Government's position was put by Lord Reay.

[97] The name was taken partly as a tribute to Charter 77, the group of writers and intellectuals who stood up for liberty in Czechoslovakia.
[98] They included Stuart Weir and Anthony Barnett (*New Statesman and Society*), Richard Holme (Constitutional Rights Centre), Mary Kaldor, Hilary Wainwright, Professor John Keane and Professor David Marquand.
[99] *The Guardian*, December 12, 1988.
[1] *Hansard*, H.L. Vol. 524, cols. 185–214 (December 5, 1990).

("It is the government's firm view that imposing on the judges a duty to interpret the Convention would add a new and undesirable dimension to their current role. The more we draw the judges into political matters the more shall we impinge on the constitutional concept of the political neutrality of the judges in terms of the public's perception of them.")[2]

Also in December 1990, Mr Frank Vibert, Deputy Director of the Institute of Economic Affairs, a Right wing think-tank, published a paper entitled "Constitutional Reform in the United Kingdom — an incremental agenda", in which he argued for a Bill of Rights "as a way to protect individuals from over-interference from governments while at the same time providing a guide to activism where action is required in order to secure liberties".[3]

In October 1991, Liberty, formerly known as the National Council for Civil Liberties, published a substantial 118-page Consultation Document entitled *A People's Charter — Liberty's Bill of Rights*. Liberty had supported the incorporation of the E.C.H.R into United Kingdom law since 1977. But this paper proposed a version of a Bill of Rights drawing not only on the E.C.H.R but on a variety of other sources including the International Covenant on Civil and Political Rights, the U.N. Standard Minimum Rules for the Treatment of Prisoners, the International Labour Organisation Convention on the Right to Organise and Collective Bargaining, the European Social Charter and the Canadian Charter of Rights and Freedoms.[4] Liberty's Bill of Rights proposed enforcement machinery involving not only the courts but also a new parliamentary committee that would scrutinise legislation for conformity with the Bill of Rights either prior to or after a review by the courts. (See further p.156 below.)

In December 1991, the Institute for Public Policy Research (IPPR) published a pamphlet entitled *A British Bill of Rights* (Constitution Paper No. 1). IPPR is an independent think tank of Left-of-Centre leanings established in September 1988 to promote discussion of social, economic and political questions. The Bill of Rights was the first part of a proposed written Constitution for the United Kingdom published by IPPR in 1991–92. The Bill of Rights

[2] *Ibid*. col. 210.
[3] Right-wing support for a Bill of Rights in the form of incorporation of the E.C.H.R. came also from Mr Ferdinand Mount, former policy adviser to Prime Minister Margaret Thatcher at No.10 Downing Street — see *The Times*, November 2, 1991 and his book *The British Constitution Now: Recovery or Decline* (1992).
[4] The latest version of Liberty's policy is available from the organisation in a 16-page document entitled *Bill of Rights*, price £1.50.

and its accompanying discussion paper were prepared by an expert committee, the Constitution Project's Judiciary Working Group.[5]

The pamphlet said that the United Kingdom was now the only member of the Council of Europe with no written constitution or enforceable Bill of Rights. Moreover the Westminster Parliament had accepted, through the Treaty of Rome and the Single European Act 1986, the supremacy of European Community Law. The British courts had become increasingly accustomed to interpreting our law in the light of E.C. law and, where necessary, overriding domestic legislation.

> "It is hardly defensible for Parliament to qualify its own sovereignty in commercial and employment matters while refusing to do so in matters of human rights."[6]

The pamphlet argued the issues and presented a draft Bill of Rights together with commentary. The text was based on a combination of the texts of the European Convention and the International Covenant on Civil and Political Rights. (A revised version of the paper was due to be published in Autumn 1996.)

In 1990 and 1991 there were several newspaper stories suggesting that Mr Hattersley and Labour had changed their minds about the undesirability of a Bill of Rights. ("Labour swings behind Euro-charter after rethink on rights safeguard"[7], "Hattersley backs charter of rights"[8]). But the reality proved less than this. Labour's *Charter of Rights*, unveiled by Roy Hattersley on January 8, 1991,[9] promised legislation on some 40 specific topics but it did not include any reference to a Bill of Rights. There was some reason to believe that Mr Hattersley had in fact been personally persuaded of the desirability of incorporation, but whether that was so or not, the Labour Party still maintained its traditional position of opposition to a Bill of Rights of any kind.

But by 1993 the Labour leadership had apparently decided to take a different view. On March 1, 1993, Mr John Smith Q.C., the then leader of the Labour Party, delivered a lecture entitled "A

---

[5] Its members were: Anthony Lester Q.C., chairman; Professor James Cornford, Director IPPR; Professor Ronald Dworkin of Oxford University and New York University; Sir William Goodhart Q.C., Chairman of the Executive Committee of JUSTICE; Patricia Hewitt, of IPPR and former Policy Coordinator for the Leader of the Opposition, Mr Neil Kinnock; Professor Jeffrey Jowell Q.C. of University College London; Nicola Lacey of New College, Oxford; Keith Patchett, Emeritus Professor of the University of Wales; and Sarah Spencer of IPPR, formerly General Secretary of the National Council for Civil Liberties.

[6] At p.6.

[7] *The Guardian*, June 11, 1990.

[8] *Independent on Sunday*, June 7, 1991.

[9] See *The Times* and *The Guardian*, January 9, 1991.

Citizen's Democracy" at Church House, Westminster under the auspices of Charter 88. Mr Smith said he wanted "a new constitutional settlement, a new deal between the people and the state that puts the citizen centre stage".

"A deal that gives people new powers and a stronger voice in the affairs of the nation . . . I want to see a fundamental shift in the balance of power between the citizen and the state — a shift away from an overpowering state to a citizen's democracy where people have rights and powers and where they are served by accountable and responsive government."

Central government, he said, was dictatorial and remote, local government was too seriously weakened after 14 years of systematic undermining by the Tories to carry out its functions effectively. Individuals felt they had no say, no voice, no influence over the decisions which directly affected their lives. One need in modernising the constitution was to revitalise local government. Another was to have a new tier of government for Scotland and Wales and for the regions of England. But a third was to strengthen people's individual rights. Britain was alone amongst major Western European nations in "not laying down in law the basic rights of its people, and in not giving its people a direct means of asserting those rights through the country's courts". The justification often offered was that in Britain the citizen was protected by the rights and freedoms established by the common law. But, important as these were, they were "incomplete, ill-defined and, perhaps most importantly of all, not immediately accessible to, or understood by, the ordinary citizen". And the extent of those rights was controlled by the judges not by Parliament. This, he suggested was a significant weakness. "The task of judges is to interpret and apply the law, not to make it. Democracy demands that fundamental rules governing citizens' behaviour, and fundamental rights protecting citizens' freedoms should be decided by Parliament and not by judges" who were "unelected and therefore unqualified to be law-makers".

"The quickest and simplest way of achieving democratic and legal recognition of a substantial package of human rights would be by incorporating into British law the European Convention on Human Rights."

Appeal to the Strasbourg machinery was intolerably slow. The need to go to Strasbourg made "the protection of basic rights appear difficult, remote, even foreign". It reinforced an atmosphere that basic rights are not that important, and that government regards them as a nuisance rather than, as it should, as a primary obligation. The European Convention was a mature statement of rights which had been interpreted and applied over many years by an expert court. Our law had been subject to it since 1950. What was needed now was to make that protection "real and accessible to our citizens, instead of a last resort available after years of struggle and litigation". Technically, an Act of Parliament could not be entrenched but effective protection of the Human Rights Act "from undermining by the courts" would be achieved by a clause requiring that any other Act that intended to introduce laws inconsistent with the Convention must do so specifically and in express terms. (On the problem of special protection or "entrenchment" see further pp.111–121 below.)

The objective was to protect individuals. Mr Smith said that the new Human Rights Act would therefore provide that its protections could not be relied on by companies or organisations. ("We do not want to repeat here the confusion and injustice that has occurred in some other countries, where companies and commercial organisations have tried to resist social legislation controlling their activities by claiming that it infringes their human rights.") The rights should be exercisable through the ordinary courts. To assist the courts there should also be an independent Human Rights Commission, along the lines of the Equal Opportunities Commission and the Commission for Racial Equality. It would monitor the operation of the Human Rights Act, provide advice and support for those who wished to assert their rights, and could, where necessary, itself institute cases. The Commission would act as a focus for human rights activities "and ensure that the protection of the public was not left to the accident of individual enthusiasm or willingness to pursue cases". Mr Smith's speech, made as leader of the Labour Party, was obviously an event of outstanding importance in the history of the campaign for a Bill of Rights.

In September 1993, Mr Smith's statement of policy was expressed almost verbatim in the Labour Party's *A new agenda for democracy: Labour's proposals for constitutional reform*, which spelled out over four pages the Party's policy regarding the E.C.H.R. and a Bill of Rights.

> "The quickest and simplest way of achieving democratic and legal recognition of a substantial package of human rights would be by incorporating into United Kingdom law the European Convention on Human Rights. That is now widely recognised, both within and outside the party, as a necessary and sensible step."[10]

[10] At p.29

The absence of incorporation meant that anyone wanting to use the Convention had to take the "intolerably slow" road to Strasbourg. The failure to incorporate the Convention had another unwelcome effect: it reinforced "an atmosphere that suggests that basic rights are not of that much importance, and that the government regards them as a nuisance rather than, as it should, as a primary obligation".[11] The Convention should be incorporated by a Human Rights Act which would be protected from being undermined by a clause that would require any intention to amend it to be stated expressly. That would make it almost impossible for judges to rule that later legislation was inconsistent with the Bill of Rights unless there was an express clause to that effect. The Human Rights Act would be expressly stated to apply to, and to override, all existing legislation. The Act would be available only to individuals. It would be enforced by the ordinary courts. But at the final appellate level, three lay members should be added to the court.

Incorporation of the Convention was however only a first step. It was desirable for Britain to have its own domestic Bill of Rights. The E.C.H.R. did not cover freedom of information, or data protection or the rights of disabled people and it was inadequate in its treatment of discrimination. Nor did it deal with economic or social rights. There should be an all-party commission charged with drafting the Bill of Rights and required to report to parliament within a limited period of time.

Yet another Human Rights Bill to incorporate the E.C.H.R into United Kingdom law was introduced in the House of Commons in January 1994 by Labour M.P. Mr Graham Allen.[12] The Bill had been prepared by Liberty. In addition to incorporating the E.C.H.R. it also sought to establish a Bill of Rights Commission whose task it would be to prepare a "draft Bill of Rights relating to all civil, political, economic and social rights in the United Kingdom". The Commission would consist of 12 persons, a mixture of lawyers and non-lawyers, appointed by the Lord Chancellor and the Lord Advocate. There was also to be a Human Rights Commission with the general function of "monitoring the workings of the Act and promoting the fundamental rights and freedoms that it contains". It received its First Reading on January 11, 1994 but there was no actual debate and the Bill did not proceed further.

The most recent parliamentary consideration of the issue was the Human Rights Bill introduced by Lord Lester of Herne Hill Q.C. in

[11] *Ibid.*
[12] It was in fact the 6th time this had happened. Mr Allen had tried to introduce a Human Rights Bill in each session from 1988–1989. None had been debated.

the House of Lords in November 1994. The Bill was a further attempt to get the European Convention incorporated into United Kingdom law. Lord Lester subsequently described it as "deliberately modest in an attempt to win a wide consensus".[13] It did not go beyond the Convention and the First Protocol. Nor did it seek to entrench its provisions against future inconsistent legislation so as to attempt to fetter Parliament. Nor did it seek to create a Human Rights Commission to take up test cases and to improve access to effective remedies.

In its original form the Bill contained two provisions which were criticised by some of the Bill's supporters and which were, in the event, dropped by Lord Lester. As first introduced, the Bill would have prevented an Act of Parliament from being relied on in legal proceedings to the extent that it was inconsistent with Convention rights. It would therefore have given similar effect to European Convention law as section 2(1) and (4) of the European Communities Act 1972 gave to European Community law. In the light of criticism by several of the Law Lords, Lord Lester moved an amendment during the Committee Stage to substitute a weaker new rule of statutory interpretation requiring that "so far as the context permits, enactments (whenever passed or made) shall be construed consistently with" Convention rights and freedoms. That provision was modelled on the New Zealand Bill of Rights 1990, s.6. (See further on this point p.114 below.) At the suggestion of Lord Taylor, the then Lord Chief Justice[14], and of Lord Woolf[15], Lord Lester also dropped the provision that would have given a right to compensation for breaches of the Convention. (On this see further p.152 below.)

As a result of these two changes, in Lord Lester's own view, his Bill became "more a mouse than a lion".[16] On the other hand, the Bill had the support of a formidable array of the senior judiciary. Lords Ackner, Browne-Wilkinson[17], Scarman, Lloyd of Berwick, Simon of Glaisdale, Slynn, Taylor of Gosforth and Woolf spoke or voted in favour of the Bill which also had the support of the then

---

[13] Lord Lester, "The Mouse that Roared: The Human Rights Bill 1995" (1995) Pub.L. 198.
[14] *Hansard*, H.L. Vol. 560, col. 1144 (January 25, 1995) — the Second Reading debate.
[15] *Hansard*, H.L. Vol. 561, col. 781 (February 15, 1995) — Committee Stage.
[16] See Lord Lester, "The Mouse that Roared: The Human Rights Bill 1995" (1995) Publ.L. 198, at 201.
[17] For a fuller expression of his views see Lord Browne-Wilkinson, "The Infiltration of a Bill of Rights" (1992) Pub. L. 397–410.

Master of the Rolls, Sir Thomas Bingham.[18] Lord Donaldson of Lymington, the former Master of the Rolls spoke strongly against the Bill and indeed went so far as to argue that the United Kingdom should withdraw from the Convention system altogether but the reason was not so much opposition to the idea of a bill of rights as to having it interpreted by European judges. Having withdrawn from the European system the text of the Convention could he thought be enacted in English law for development by English judges "in our own way".[19] According to Lord Lester[20] his Bill had the support of most other other Law Lords both serving and retired. As compared with all previous debates on the subject in the House of Lords, the broad support of the senior judiciary was an entirely new and a very significant development.

As on all previous occasions when this issue has been debated in the House of Lords, the Government opposed the Bill — here in the person of Lady Blatch. It was opposed equally by Lord Cocks of Hartcliffe (formerly Mr Michael Cocks M.P., Labour Whip). But for the first time in these debates the Labour Opposition front bench spokesmen Lord Williams of Mostyn Q.C. and Lord Irvine of Lairg Q.C. (Shadow Lord Chancellor) spoke for the Bill. During the Third Reading debate[21] it appeared that the Government might try to defeat the Bill, but in the event, possibly because it anticipated the possibility of being defeated, a division was avoided. The Bill however died in the House of Commons for lack of Parliamentary time.

Mr Tony Blair became Leader of the Labour Party in July 1994, following John Smith's untimely death that May. On February 7, 1996, Mr Blair, appropriately whilst giving the John Smith Memorial Lecture, committed himself to the same policy:

> "As a first step we should incorporate the European Convention on Human Rights . . . People in this country have access to the protection and the guarantees of basic human rights that the Convention provides yet to gain access to those rights British citizens must appeal to the Commission and the Court in Strasbourg. It is a long and expensive process and only the most diligent manage to stay the course. I believe it

[18] See T. H. Bingham, "The European Convention on Human Rights: Time to Incorporate" (1993) L.Q.R. 390. In 1996, Sir Thomas became Lord Bingham of Cornhill on appointment as Lord Chief Justice when Lord Taylor was tragically forced to retire on account of ill-health.

[19] *Hansard*, H.L. Vol.561, col.771 (February 15, 1995).

[20] See Lord Lester, "The Mouse that Roared: The Human Rights Bill 1995" (1995) Publ.L. 198, n.1.

[21] *Hansard*, H.L. Vol. 563, cols. 1271–1273 (May 1, 1995).

makes sense to end the cumbersome practice of forcing people to go to Strasbourg to hold their government to account. By incorporating the Convention into British law the rights it guarantees would be available in courts in both Britain and Northern Ireland. This would make it clear that the protection afforded by the Convention was not some foreign import but that it had been accepted by successive British Governments and that it should apply throughout the United Kingdom. Some have said that this system takes power away from Parliament and places it in the hands of judges. In reality, since we are already signatories to the Convention, it means allowing British judges rather than European judges to pass judgment."

The policy of incorporating the European Convention was also subscribed to by the Labour Shadow Lord Chancellor, Lord Irvine of Lairg[22] and the Shadow Home Secretary, Mr Jack Straw[23].

In July 1996 the issue surfaced again when the new Lord Chief Justice and the long serving Lord Chancellor, at lectures given within a few days of each other, publicly aired their sharply opposed positions regarding the incorporation of the E.C.H.R. Speaking to the Citizenship Foundation on July 8, Lord Mackay gave a variety of reasons for opposing incorporation of which the weightiest appeared to be his concern that it would "inevitably draw judges into making decisions of a more political nature". On July 17, 1996, Lord Bingham speaking at the annual dinner for H.M. Judges, again nailed his colours to the mast of incorporation.

There have of course been other important statements on the issue of incorporation of the E.C.H.R. The Liberal-Democrats have consistently supported incorporation. Their position was stated most recently in *Here we Stand* published in July 1993. The document referred back to earlier calls by the Liberal Democrats for incorporation of the European Convention.[24] The Convention however was a "very conservative document". It should be the first step, but then a Constitutional Assembly should draw up a Bill of Rights based on the European Convention and the International Covenant, as proposed in 1991 by the Institute for Public Policy Research (IPPR).[25]

[22] See for instance his essay in D. Bean (ed.) *Law Reform for All* (1996), pp.18–19.
[23] See for instance his Ambassador lecture for Community Links, *The Times*, November 8, 1995.
[24] See "We The People . . .", Liberal Democrats, Federal Green Paper 13, 1990.
[25] *Ibid*, pp.41–43.

The Guardian newspaper supports incorporation.[26] *The Times* called for incorporation in an editiorial on August 15, 1992. The leader opened with the words: "Almost unnoticed, establishment opinion is moving towards the incorporation of the European Convention on Human Rights into British law". It ended: "More than three centuries after the last bill of rights, the time has come for Britain to adopt the European Convention as its own. Without citizens' rights, a citizen's charter means little". The Council of the Law Society, rejecting its earlier view, unanimously adopted a resolution calling for incorporation on March 18, 1993. On October 22, 1995, *The Economist* in a three-page article ("Why Britain needs a bill of rights") considered the pros and cons of the arguments and came down firmly in favour. It cited opinion polls conducted by MORI in 1991[27] and 1995[28] which showed that around three-quarters of respondents were in favour of a bill of rights for all of Britain. A bill of rights, *The Economist* suggested, cannot elevate contentious political issues to an abstract plane beyond the reach of the rest of society.

> "What it can do is to nurture a culture of liberty in a society which already recognises its value, and to create a judiciary which sees the protection of liberty as one of its primary tasks."[29]

[**Note:** The Constitution Unit at University College, London was due to bring out an important and substantial report on the subject in October-November 1996 — *Human Rights Legislation*, available from the Unit, 4 Tavistock Place, London WC1H 9RA. Tel. 0171 209 1162; Fax 0171 209 1163.]

[26] See for instance its leader on March 2, 1993 the day after Mr John Smith made his speech calling for incorporation. The paper argued that incorporation was the first step toward an improved domestic Bill of Rights.
[27] See *The Independent*, October 2, 1991 — 79 per cent.
[28] *The Times*, January 27, 1995 — 73 per cent, including nearly three-quarters of Tory supporters.
[29] At p.9

2. THE ARGUMENTS FOR A BILL OF RIGHTS CONSIDERED

The principal argument for having a Bill of Rights is to give the citizen significantly more scope and power to complain about excesses or abuses of power by public authorities and to challenge unfair rules and practices. A Bill of Rights is uniquely effective in two ways. One is in respect of the nature of the remedy. The ability to sue a public authority responsible for an alleged violation of law is quite different in kind from any other form of possible remedy for grievances in a democracy. In the ordinary way public authorities can decline to respond helpfully (or indeed at all) to complaints from citizens. A writ, by contrast, cannot just be brushed aside. It requires an answer. Failure to respond will result in judgment in default. Moreover, the answer must be made in public. When a public authority decides whether to respond to a complaint it is the judge. When the matter comes before a court, the public authority is merely a litigant seeking to persuade the independent arbiter the judge.

The power to bring legal actions against the state and agencies of government of course already exists in the United Kingdom. But the second major difference lies in the opportunities for getting redress afforded under a Bill of Rights which go far beyond what is available without a Bill of Rights. This is because of the form of a Bill of Rights. At present a citizen with a grievance can only bring legal proceedings if there is already provision for his or her particular grievance in existing statute or case law. In the case of statute law this means that Parliament has already addressed itself to the matter and provided a remedy. Certainly, there is some room for expansion of the text through imaginative interpretation, but statutes are normally drafted in a precise way so that the scope for development is restricted. In the case of judicial precedents ("the common law"), there is greater flexibility. Sometimes the judges can conjure a remedy for a new grievance from the existing precedents. But the scope for this is limited.

By contrast, the open textured phrases of a Bill of Rights give far greater scope for the argument that a new grievance should be brought within the meaning of the right of freedom of speech, peaceful assembly, freedom of religion, of correspondence, family life, right to liberty and security of the person etc. Moreover, it can be used to override even existing statute law. A Bill of Rights therefore provides potentially a far richer and more fruitful source of solutions to new problems than exists without one.

These two reasons would be sufficient justification for having a Bill of Rights. But there are other subsidiary reasons.

To bring the United Kingdom into line with the rest of the world

One of the striking developments of the post-Second World War era has been the growing concern for the better protection of human rights. The annual reports of Amnesty International demonstrate that abuses of human rights occur throughout the world on a massive and deplorable scale. But both nationally and internationally this issue has received increasing attention.

The United Kingdom has played a part in these developments on the international plane but internally it has so far adhered to the historic position that there is no need either for a written constitution guaranteeing fundamental human rights nor legislation to incorporate international human rights obligations. In holding this position, the United Kingdom is now almost unique as the small number of countries that took the same position has dwindled over the past few years.[1]

The development of the concept of fundamental protection of human rights worldwide was traced in a powerful article in *Public Law* by Mr Anthony Lester Q.C. aptly entitled "Fundamental Rights: The United Kingdom Isolated?" The public philosophy inherited from Dicey, he argued, was that Parliament was sovereign and there was no need for any supreme or higher law. This remained the conventional wisdom of Westminster and Whitehall as well as of most judges and lawyers.

> "But what passes for wisdom in the United Kingdom is an ever more isolated view among the modern democracies . . . and it has become a barely tenable position for the United Kingdom to maintain as a full party to the European Convention on Human Rights and as a member of the European Community."[2]

---

[1] New Zealand adopted a Bill of Rights in 1990. Hong Kong did so in 1991. Israel adopted a Basic Law in 1992. Denmark adopted the European Convention on Human Rights in 1993. Norway has decided to do so. South Africa adopted a Bill of Rights as part of its new constitution in 1993.

[2] (1984) Pub.L. 47. – the F.A. Mann Lectures.

The United States, he wrote, had enjoyed a written constitution since the Declaration of Independence in 1776.[3] The doctrine of fundamental rights spread to the whole of Western Europe with the French Revolution and the Declaration of the Rights of Man. This was familiar to all. But what was sometimes not as well known was the extent to which the same concept became accepted by the emerging countries of the Commonwealth.

The first example was the Irish Free State Constitution of 1922 which embodied guarantees of freedom from arbitrary arrest, freedom of expression, freedom of peaceful assembly, freedom to form associations and freedom of conscience. The Irish Constitution of 1937 contained many of the same guarantees. (The Irish courts have repeatedly shown that they are prepared to uphold these fundamental constitutional rights[4] by overruling both legislation and established common law rules. Moreover, the most recent decisions of the Irish Supreme Court demonstrate a new readiness to depart from a traditional tendency to uphold a theologically based interpretation of the Constitution.[5])

But most of the important developments in this field have occurred since 1945. In December 1948 the General Assembly of the United Nations adopted the Universal Declaration of Human Rights by 48 votes to nil. The Universal Declaration[6] is not legally binding as such but it has been widely regarded as an important statement of principle. It dealt with political, civil, economic and social rights. It covered such things as the right to life, liberty and security of person; slavery; torture and cruel, inhuman or degrading treatment or punishment; arbitrary arrest, detention or exile; fair trial; privacy and protection of reputation; freedom of movement; entitlement to nationality; freedom to marry and found a family; the ownership of property; freedom of thought, conscience and

---

[3] For an elegant essay reflecting on the contrast in this respect between Britain and the USA see J. Skelly Wright, "The Bill of Rights in Britain and America: A Not Quite Full Circle" (1981) 55 Tul. L. Rev. 291. See also A. Lester, "The Overseas Trade in the American Bill of Rights" (1988) 88 Col. L.Rev.537. For the more recent view of an eminent American scholar see Ronald Dworkin, *A Bill of Rights for Britain* (1990).

[4] In Articles 40–44. See generally J. Casey, *Constitutional Law in Ireland* (2nd ed., 1992).

[5] See for instance *In the Matter of the Regulation of Information (Services Outside the State for Termination of Pregnancies) Bill 1995* (1995) 2 I.L.R.M. 81. See generally K. Boyle, C. Campbell and T. Hadden, *The Protection of Human Rights in the Context of Peace and Reconciliation in Ireland*, (1996). This report was commissioned by the Forum for Peace and Reconciliation and was published by the Government of Ireland.

[6] For the text of the Universal Declaration see I. Brownlie, *Basic Documents on Human Rights* (4th ed., 1995), p.255.

religion; freedom of assembly and association (including the right not to belong to an association); and universal suffrage by secret ballot. Many, though not all, of the rights in the Universal Declaration are to be found also in one form or another in the European Convention. (The Convention does not have any express right to freedom of movement, asylum from persecution, the right to participate in government and public life and the right to universal suffrage by secret ballot.) But the Universal Declaration includes economic and social rights which have no counter-part in the European Convention, *e.g.* covering such matters as social security, the right to work, equal pay, just remuneration, holidays with pay, public assistance with housing, etc.

The Constitution of India, which came into force in 1950, has in Part III a very full statement of fundamental rights extending to over 11 pages. The Constitution affirms the right of freedom of speech, religious freedom, the right of peaceable assembly, to form associations or unions, to freedom of movement, to hold or dispose of property and to practise any profession, occupation, trade or business. It forbids discrimination by the state on grounds of religion, caste, sex or place of birth. It also bans discrimination in public places. A remedy is provided in the Supreme Court.

In 1950, the Council of Europe adopted the European Convention for the Protection of Human Rights and Fundamental Freedoms (here referred to simply by its usual title of the European Convention on Human Rights or the E.C.H.R.). The United Kingdom played a major part in the drafting of the Convention. In fact Anthony Lester's previously cited article, drawing on then recently released Cabinet and other State papers, revealed that the actual draftsman of the Convention was Sir Oscar Dowson, former senior legal adviser in the Home Office. A prominent part was played also by Sir David Maxwell-Fyfe (later Lord Chancellor Kilmuir), who was chairman of the Consultative Assembly's Legal Committee. Within the British Government of Clement Attlee the project had the support in particular of the Foreign Secretary, Mr Ernest Bevin, and his Minister of State, Mr Kenneth Younger. It was opposed by the Lord Chancellor, Lord Jowitt, by the Colonial Secretary, Mr James Griffiths and by Sir Stafford Cripps, the Chancellor of the Exchequer.[7] In the European Consultative Assembly it was supported in particular by Sir Winston Churchill, Mr Harold Macmillan and Mr John Foster Q.C., M.P. for the Conservatives, by Lord Layton for the Liberals and by Mr Lynn

---

[7] See also G. Marston, "The United Kingdom's Part in the preparation of the European Convention on Human Rights", (1993) 42 *International and Comparative Law Quarterly*, 796.

Ungoed-Thomas, Q.C. for Labour.[8] The main issues raised by those who objected to the proposal were in regard to the suggestion that individuals should automatically have the right to petition the European Commission of Human Rights directly and over the jurisdiction of the Strasbourg Court.[9] The Convention was eventually signed by the Committee of Ministers of the Council of Europe on November 4, 1950 and on March 18, 1951 the United Kingdom became the first State to ratify the Convention. On October 23, 1953 the Conservative Government gave notice under Article 63 extending the Convention to 42 overseas territories, including Nigeria, for whose international relations the British Government was responsible. Their total population was some 97 million.

In 1957, there was a constitutional conference in London at which it was agreed that fundamental rights should be included in the constitution for the new State of Nigeria and that draft clauses should be prepared by the legal advisers to the Colonial Secretary. Clauses modelled on the European Convention were eventually included in the Nigerian Constitution of 1960. This then became the model for the codes of fundamental rights which were to be found in the great majority of independent Commonwealth countries. There were some 24 Commonwealth countries into whose independence constitutions the Convention was transplanted.[10] The constitutions of Cyprus and Malta also contained provisions deriving from the European Convention but differing in important respects from the Nigerian model. The Nigerian model was however used also for the constitutions which gave dependent territories a substantial measure of self-government: Bermuda, Gibraltar, the Gilbert and Ellis Islands and the Associated States.

As Anthony Lester observed,

> "The Parliament of Westminster has thus exported the fundamental rights and freedoms of the European Convention to the new Commonwealth on a scale without parallel in the rest of the world ... With hindsight, it is ironical to compare the Colonial Office's original hostility toward the Convention with its later use of the same Convention as the model for constitution-making in the new Commonwealth."[11]

[8] (1984) Pub.L. 47, at 49. Lester's article has a fascinating account of the exchanges between Ministers, at 49–55.

[9] The right of individual petition was subsequently made optional rather than mandatory, but it will become mandatory if and when Protocol No. 11 becomes effective — see p.62 below.

[10] In chronological order, Nigeria, Sierra Leone, Jamaica, Uganda, Kenya, Malawi, the Gambia, Guyana, Botswana, Lesotho, Barbados, Mauritius, Swaziland, Fiji, the Bahamas, Granada, the Seychelles, the Solomon Islands, Dominica, St Lucia, Zimbabwe and Belize.

[11] (1984) Pub.L. 47, at 56–57.

In December 1966, the General Assembly of the United Nations adopted the International Covenant on Civil and Political Rights and its Optional Protocol. Both the Covenant and the Optional Protocol came into force between ratifying States in March 1976. By 1996 there were some 130 States that had ratified the Covenant. The United Kingdom ratified the International Covenant in 1976, the year it entered into force — though its ratification was made subject to a number of reservations. As has been seen, the International Covenant on Civil and Political Rights[12] covers much of the same ground as the E.C.H.R. though each embodies some provisions which are not to be found in the other,[13] and to some extent the same rights are expressed in the two texts in different language. The International Covenant also has an Optional Protocol under which parties to the Covenant can allow individuals to bring cases to the Committee claiming violations of their rights under the Covenant. The great majority of the European countries that are parties to the Convention have signed the Optional Protocol[14] — though the United Kingdom has not. Judge Rosalyn Higgins D.B.E., Q.C. in the 1996 Sieghart Lecture, noted that whereas the European Convention was well known in the United Kingdom, the International Covenant was not. She explained the difference by the fact that the Government permitted the right of individual petition under the E.C.H.R. but not under the Covenant. ("Judges have a sense that cases before them may finish up in Strasbourg. The Convention becomes, incorporation or not, immensely relevant. It is the double constraints of non-incorporation and no individual application that keeps the Covenant — an instrument to which the United Kingdom is nonetheless a party — in the shadows in the United Kingdom."[15])

Although the United Kingdom ratified the International Covenant it has done little or nothing to give practical expression to this ratification and in particular it has not signed the Optional Protocol which would give British subjects the right to petition the

[12] For the text see Brownlie, *Basic Documents on Human Rights* (4th ed., 1995), p.262.
[13] Rights that appear in the Covenant but not the E.C.H.R. include minority rights, rights of aliens, rights relating to the family and to the child. Some rights, such as the right to a fair trial, are articulated in more detail in the Covenant. The Covenant has a longer list of rights that cannot be suspended in times of national emergency.
[14] In some cases the country has entered a reservation that a case may not go to the Committee if it has already been before the Strasbourg Human Rights Commission or Court.
[15] I am indebted to Judge Higgins for allowing me to quote from the unpublished manuscript of the lecture which was delivered at the London School of Economics on May 22, 1996.

U.N. Human Rights Committee. The Covenant imposes on member states the duty to report on the state of human rights in the country.[16] The U.N. Human Rights Committee, composed of 18 human rights experts, comments on these periodic reports[17] — though there is not much sign that the British Government pays great attention to the work of the Committee.[18]

In 1960, the Federal Parliament of Canada enacted a statute entitled the Canadian Bill of Rights.[19] As will be seen, this proved to be a weak vessel but two decades later in 1982 the Westminster Parliament, in passing the Canada Act negotiated by Prime Minister Pierre Trudeau, enacted a modern, strong and comprehensive Charter of Rights and Freedoms, modelled in part on the United States Bill of Rights. (See further pp.126–131 and Select Bibliography at p.165 below.)

Australia has a written constitution which is paramount and which limits the Federal Parliament and contains fundamental guarantees of freedom of religion. In summer 1984 the Australian Labour Government was in the process of preparing legislation to introduce a full scale Bill of Rights. The draft Bill was based on the International Covenant on Civil and Political Rights. The Attorney-General, Mr Gareth Evans Q.C., hoped to see the Bill of Rights legislation introduced after the General Election in November 1984. In the event, although the Labour Government was returned at the General Election, Mr Evans was moved to a different Ministerial Portfolio. The new Attorney-General, Mr Lionel Bowen, introduced the Bill in an altered form in October 1985. It passed the House, but was eventually withdrawn from the Senate in November 1986. At about the same, the Senate Committee on Constitutional and Legal Affairs produced a report entitled *A Bill of Rights for Australia?* which broadly supported federal legislation to implement the International Covenant. The Constitutional Commission 1985-88 recommended amendment of the Constitution to entrench an Australian version of the Canadian Charter. But these proposals have not so far resulted in action. In the absence of any Bill of Rights, the Australian High Court has however held that the powers of Parliament are limited by an

[16] Under Art. 40(1), member states must report within one year and thereafter every five years. The United Kingdom's Fourth Periodic Report was submitted to the Human Rights Committee in October 1994.
[17] The Committee issued its latest report on the U.K. in July 1995 — for citation see n.42 below.
[18] See Francesca Klug, Keith Starmer and Stuart Weir, "The British way of doing things: The United Kingdom and the International Covenant of Civil and Political Rights, 1976–1994" (1995) Pub.L. 505–512.
[19] See generally, W. S. Tarnopolsky, *The Canadian Bill of Rights* (2nd ed., 1975).

implied constitutional restraint which prohibits legislation under-mining freedom of expression.[20] This striking development of the common law, not surprisingly, has proved controversial.[21]

Israel has no Bill of Rights — despite numerous attempts to introduce one over the years by members of the Knesset, the Knesset Constitution and Law Committee and even the Minister of Justice. The most adamant opposition to such an initiative seems to come from the religious parties who have a principled objection to judicial review.[22] But in 1990 the Knesset passed two Basic Laws — the Basic Law: Freedom of Occupation[23] (the right to follow the vocation of one's choosing) and the Basic Law: Human Dignity and Freedom.[24] The Basic Law: Human Dignity and Freedom has many provisions of the kind ordinarily to be found in Bills of Rights. Thus it protects the person,[25] property,[26] liberty[27] and privacy.[28] There is then a general *caveat*: "The rights according to this Basic Law shall not be infringed except by a statute that befits the values of the State of Israel and is directed towards a worthy purpose, and then only to an extent that does not exceed what is necessary" (Art. 8). There is an additional *caveat* in regard to the military, the police and the security forces that the rights in the

[20] *Australian Capital Television Pty v. Commonwealth of Australia* (1992) 66 A.L.J.R. 695; *Nationwide News Pty Ltd v. Wills* (1992) 658.

[21] For critical comment see for instance K. D. Ewing "New constitutional con-straints in Australia" (1993) Pub.L. 256–62. For favourable comment see H. P. Lee, "The Australian High Court and Implied Fundamental Guarantees", (1993) Pub.L. 606–29, and Timothy H. Jones, "Fundamental Rights in Australia and Britain: Domestic and International Aspects", in C. Gearty and A. Tomkins (eds.), *Understanding Human Rights* (1996), pp.91–112.

[22] "This objection rests on the not-unfounded conviction that a bill of rights will enable the Supreme Court to exercise judicial review over legislation that was passed because of the strategic position of the religious parties in Israel's coaltion system, but that is anathema to the secular majority in the country." (David Kretzmer, "The New Basic Laws on Human Rights: A Mini-Revolution in Israeli Constitutional Law?" (1992) 26 Isr.L.Rev. 239.

[23] The law is entrenched by a provision that any amending statute has to be a Basic Law passed by an absolute majority of all Knesset members.

[24] There is no equivalent entrenchment provision as in the case of the Basic Law; Freedom of Occupation. Such a clause was included in the bill but was dropped at the second reading stage.

[25] "The life, body or dignity of any person shall not be violated" (Art. 2). "Every person is entitled to protection of his life, body and dignity" (Art. 4).

[26] "A person's property shall not be infringed" (Art. 3).

[27] "The liberty of a person shall not be deprived or restricted through imprison-ment, detention, extradition or in any other manner" (Art. 5).

[28] "(a) Every person is entitled to privacy and to the confidentiality of his life; (b) A person's private domain shall not be entered without his consent; (c) No search shall be carried out of a person's private domain, on his body, of his body, or of his personal effects; (d) The confidentiality of a person's conversations, writings and records shall not be infringed." (Art. 7)

Basic Law may not be "restricted, qualified or waived" for them "except according to law and to an extent that does not exceed what is required by the nature and character of the service."[29]

In Hong Kong, a Bill of Rights Ordinance was passed in 1991 (Ordinance No. 59 of 1991) to achieve the incorporation of the International Covenant on Civil and Political Rights into the law of Hong Kong. Part II of the Ordinance consists of section 8 which contains the 23 articles which constitute the Hong Kong Bill of Rights. Each of the articles refers in terms to the equivalent article of the International Covenant.[30]

Until very recently New Zealand, like the United Kingdom, had no fundamental law or fundamental rights. But in 1990 it enacted the New Zealand Bill of Rights Act. This was a considerably watered down version of what had originally been proposed in a White Paper issued by the Minister of Justice in 1985. It had originally been proposed as entrenched legislation with remedies and the capacity to hold legislation to be invalid. As enacted, however, there was no entrenchment provision, no remedies provision and the Act specifically stated (s.4) that no court could in relation to legislation (whether passed before or after the commencement of the Bill of Rights) "hold any provision of the enactment to be impliedly repealed or revoked, or to be in any way invalid or ineffective" by reason of inconsistency with the Bill of Rights. It states that the rights and freedoms contained in the Bill of Rights can be "subject only to such reasonable limits prescribed by law as can be demonstrably justified in a free and democratic society" (s.5). It was described during the parliamentary debate as a "totally toothless bill". But as will be seen (p.99 below) in the hands of the judges it has proved not to be quite so toothless. It is stated to be "An Act (a) to affirm, protect and promote human rights and fundamental freedoms in New Zealand and (b) to affirm New Zealand's commitment to the International Covenant on Civil and Political Rights". It is a short Act with 29 sections which briefly set out rights concerning the life and security of the person, democratic and civil rights, non-discrimination and minority rights and rights concerning search, arrest and detention.[31]

The history of recent significant developments in the protection of human rights must also include the notable Bill of Rights in

[29] For comment on the Basic Laws see Kretzmer, *op. cit.* n.22 above, at 238–246 and *Netherlands Quarterly of Human Rights* (1996) 173–183.
[30] See generally R. Wacks, *Hong Kong's Bill of Rights: Problems and Prospects* (1990); R. Wacks (ed.) *Human Rights in Hong Kong* (1993).
[31] For an early description and assessment see D. M. Paciocco, "The New Zealand Bill of Rights Act: Curial Cures for a Debilitated Bill" (1990) N.Z. Recent L.Rev., 353–81.

South Africa's post-apartheid Transitional[32] Constitution.[33] Chapter 3 of the Constitution[34] sets out rights that are deemed to be fundamental and worthy of constitutional protection during the period of transition.The rights include the main civil and political rights normally found in a Bill of Rights including an equality provision, access to information held by public authorities and the right to administrative justice.[35] But the Bill of Rights also includes various socio-economic rights, which may be a great deal more problematic to adjudicate upon.[36] In interpreting the Bill of Rights the courts are required to "promote the values which underlie an open and democratic society based on freedom and equality' and, where applicable, to have regard to public international law applicable to the protection of the rights entrenched in [Chapter 3]."[37] The court can also refer to foreign case law. Under the Constitution, the existing Supreme Court continues to operate as before but there is a new Constitutional Court whose jurisdiction is as the court of final instance over all matters concerning the

[32] The new final constitution was passed by the South African Parliament on May 6, 1996 but could only come into force when certified by the Constitutional Court under s.71(2). See Vera Sacks, "Due process in making a constitution" NLJ, August 16, 1996, 1237–1238.

[33] See H. Corder,"South Africa's Transitional Constitution: Its Design and Implementation", (1996) Pub.L. 291–308 and L. du Plessis and H. Corder, *Understanding South Africa's Transitional Bill of Rights* (1994). See also G. E. Devinish, "Human Rights in a Divided Society" in C. Gearty and A. Tomkins (eds.), *Understanding Human Rights* (1996) pp.61–90.

[34] Known officially as the Constitution of the Republic of South Africa Act, 200 of 1993.

[35] The rights protected include equality and non-discrimination (though affirmative action programmes are specifically excepted) (s.8); the right to life (s.9); human dignity (s.10); freedom and security of the person (s.11); protection against servitude and forced labour (s.12); privacy (s.13); freedom of religion, belief and opinion (s.14); freedom of expression (s.15); freedom of assembly (s.16); freedom of association (s.17); freedom of movement (s.18); freedom of residence (s.19); the right of entry and exit from the country and not to be deprived of one's citizenship (s.20); the right to take part in political life (s.21); the right to have justiciable disputes settled by a court of law (s.22); access to information held by the state to the extent necessary to exercise or protect one's rights (s.23); the right to procedurally fair administrative action and to written reasons (s.24); and rights for persons detained, arrested and accused (s.25).

[36] The right freely to engage in economic activity (s.26); the right to fair labour practices, including the right to join trade unions and to bargain collectively (s.27); the right to acquire and hold property rights which cannot be taken otherwise than in accordance with law (s.28); the right to an environment "which is not detrimental to his or her health or well-being" (s.29); various rights for children, such as the right not be neglected or abused and the right not to be exploited in the labour market (s.30); the right to use the language of one's choice (s.31); and the right to basic education and to equal access to educational institutions (s.32).

[37] s.35(1).

interpretation and enforcement of the Constitution. As at March 1996, the Court had given 14 judgments of which most have concerned matters of criminal procedure and punishment — the most important of which was the Court's unanimous decision holding the death penalty to be unconstitutional.[38] Only one of the decisions resulted in a successful challenge to the constitutional validity of an Act of Parliament.[39]

The three broad international instruments — the 1948 Universal Declaration, the European Convention and the 1966 U.N. International Covenant — all lay duties on member States affected in regard to the better protection of human rights. Article 8 of the Universal Declaration states that "everyone has the right to an effective remedy by the competent national tribunals for acts violating the fundamental rights granted him by the constitution or the law". Article 2 of the International Covenant states that:

> "where not already provided for by existing legislative or other measures, each State Party . . . undertakes to take necessary steps, in accordance with its constitutional process and with the provisions of the present Covenant to adopt such legislative or other measures as may be necessary to give effect to the rights recognised in the present Covenant."

Article 1 of the European Convention provides that State parties "shall secure to everyone within their jurisdiction the rights and freedoms defined in Section 1 of this Convention" and Article 13 provides: "Everyone whose rights and freedoms as set forth in this Convention are violated shall have an effective remedy before a national authority". At one time some commentators took the view that Article 13 of the European Convention imposed on Member States the legal duty to incorporate the European Convention.[40] This however is not the view of the European Court of Human Rights. ("Neither Article 13 nor the Convention in general lays down for the Contracting States any given manner for ensuring within their internal law the effective implementation of any of the provisions of the Convention."[41])

---

[38] *S. v. Makwanyane and another* (1995) 3 S.A. 391, C.C. As a result some 400 "death row," cases were referred back to the trial court for re-sentencing.

[39] *Executive Council, Western Cape and Others v. President of the RSA and Others* (1995) 4 S.A. 877, C.C. The case was brought by the Western Cape provincial government. The decision caused a postponement of local elections.

[40] See for instance Sam Silkin, "The Rights of Man and the Rule of Law" (1976) 28 N.Ireland Leg.Qtrly. 3.

[41] *Swedish Empire Drivers' Union Case,* E.C.H.R. Series A, Vol. 20, 1976, p.18. See also *Vilvarajah v. United Kingdom,* E.C.H.R. Series A, No. 215, p.18. For discussion of the issue see J. A. Frowein, "Incorporation of the Convention into Domestic Law", in J. Gardner (ed.) *Aspects of Incorporation of the European Convention of Human Rights into Domestic Law* (1993) pp.3–5.

The U.N. Human Rights Committee noted in 1995 that the legal system of the United Kingdom "does not ensure fully that an effective remedy is provided for all victims of violations of the rights contained in the Covenant". It was "concerned by the extent to which the implementation of the Covenant is impeded by the combined effects of the non-incorporation of the Covenant into domestic law ... and the absence of a constitutional Bill of Rights".[42] The Committee made a series of recommendations including that the United Kingdom "take urgent steps to ensure that its legal machinery allows for the full implementation of the Covenant" by examining the need to incorporate the Covenant into domestic law, or by introducing a Bill of Rights. The Committee's recommendations were rejected by the Government.[43] No doubt if the recommendation had been to incorporate the E.C.H.R. it would equally have been rejected.

Almost all the Western European members of the E.C.H.R. system in fact do make the Convention directly effective in their own law. This is the position in Austria, Belgium, Denmark, Cyprus, Finland, France, Germany, Greece, Iceland, Italy, Liechtenstein, Luxembourg, Malta, the Netherlands, Portugal, San Marino, Spain, Sweden, Switzerland and Turkey.[44] Norway was in the process of incorporating the E.C.H.R. into domestic law. In some countries the E.C.H.R. is not part of the internal law as such but all or most of its provisions are substantially reproduced in a written constitution. This is the case in Iceland, Ireland and Malta. The only member country in which there is no written constitution and the E.C.H.R. does not form part of domestic law is the United Kingdom.

On September 17, 1976, the Parliamentary Assembly of the Council of Europe adopted a recommendation that the Committee of Ministers should, *inter alia*, "urge Member States which have not yet done so to incorporate the normative provisions of the European Convention on Human Rights into their domestic law in such a way that they can be applied directly by domestic courts".

Of the various Protocols to the E.C.H.R. dealing with substantive rights (as opposed to procedure), the United Kingdom has

[42] *Comments of the Human Rights Committee: United Kingdom of Great Britain and Northern Ireland*, July 27, 1995, CCPR/C/79/Add.55.
[43] *Hansard*, H.L. Vol. 566, cols. W.A. 140–142 (October 30, 1995).
[44] For a survey of the Convention's impact in these 17 countries see J. Polakiewicz and V. Jacob-Foltzer, "The European Human Rights Convention in Domestic Law" (1991) 12 Hum.Rts.J. 65–85, 125–142.

ratified only the First (subject to a reservation about education).[45] (For a full text of the Convention and the First Protocol see Appendix, below.)

The English judges and the E.C.H.R.

Originally the English judges seemed inclined to take a very positive attitude to the E.C.H.R. In *Waddington v. Miah* in 1974, Lord Reid, referring specifically to the prohibition against retrospective legislation in Article 7 of the European Convention said, "so it is hardly credible that any Government would promote or that Parliament would pass retrospective criminal legislation".[46] The House of Lords in that case ruled that the Immigration Act 1971 was not retrospective. In *Broome v. Cassell & Co.* in 1972, Lord Kilbrandon stated that a constitutional right of free speech must be recognised in United Kingdom law at least since the date when the E.C.H.R. was ratified.[47] In *Blathayte v. Baron Cawley* in 1976 Lord Wilberforce acknowledged that a widely accepted treaty like the Convention might point the direction in which common law concepts of public policy, as applied by the courts, ought to move.[48] In 1976 in *R. v. Secretary of State for the Home Department, ex p. Bhajan Singh,* Lord Denning said that it was to be assumed that the Crown, in taking part in legislation, would do nothing which was in conflict with treaties. "So the court should now construe the Immigration Act 1971 so as to be in conformity with [the] Convention".[49] Immigration officers and the Secretary of State "in exercising their duties ought to bear in mind the principles stated in the Convention". Also in 1976, Lord Justice Scarman stated that it was the duty of public authorities in administering law — including the Immigration Act 1971 — and of the courts in interpreting and applying the law to have regard to the Convention.[50]

---

[45] Protocol No.2 dealt with the power of the Court to give advisory opinions. Protocol No. 6 concerned the death penalty. Protocol No. 7 dealt with expulsion of aliens; the right of a person convicted of a crime to have his case reviewed on appeal; compensation for victims of miscarriages of justice; double jeopardy; and equality as between spouses. Protocol No. 9 gave individuals the right to bring cases to the court. Protocol No. 10 deleted the requirement of a two-thirds majority in Article 32 for a decision by the Committee of Ministers as to whether there has been a violation of the Convention. Protocols 1, 4, 6, 7, 8 and 9 are in force.

[46] [1974] 1 W.L.R. 683, 694.

[47] [1973] A.C. 1027, 1133.

[48] [1976] A.C. 397, 426.

[49] [1976] Q.B. 198, 207.

[50] *R. v. Secretary of State for the Home Department, ex. p.Phansopkar* [1976] Q.B. 606, 626. See also *Ahmed v. Inner London Education Authority* [1978] Q.B. 36, 50, *per* Scarman L.J. dissenting.

But then in later cases the courts somewhat withdrew from this strong view. Thus in *R. v. Chief Immigration Officer, Heathrow Airport, ex p. Salamat Bibi,* Lord Denning said that his observations in *Bhajan Singh* that immigration officers ought to bear in mind the principles of the Convention had gone too far.[51] He now thought that this was asking too much of them. They could not be expected to know or to apply the E.C.H.R. They should simply follow the immigration rules laid down by the Secretary of State. Lord Denning for the Court of Appeal said that it was legitimate to refer to the E.C.H.R. so as to adopt a construction in a United Kingdom statute compatible with the E.C.H.R. if this were possible. In its 1978 Report, the House of Lords Select Committee said on this issue that the influence of the E.C.H.R. was a tenuous one:

> "It comes into operation only if a court first finds an ambiguity in an Act . . . Furthermore, there is a case for saying that even the tenuous influence the Convention does have on the construction of Acts of Parliament is confined to Acts passed since we ratified the Convention . . . . In principle it is not easy to see how the courts could justify invoking the terms of a treaty for the purpose of construing Acts passed before we ratified the treaty".[52]

In 1981, the Court of Appeal in the *Fernandes*[53] case decided that the Home Secretary, in exercising his statutory powers, was not obliged even to take the provisions of the E.C.H.R. into account since it did not have the force of law in this country.

In the decade 1974 to 1984 there were a dozen or so cases in which the E.C.H.R. was referred to in decisions of the House of Lords.[54] On several occasions the E.C.H.R. was used as a source for resolving ambiguities in legislation and some Law Lords regard the E.C.H.R. as a potential source of public policy. But the E.C.H.R. had never been used by any Law Lord as the reason for his decision.

In 1991 in *R. v. Home Secretary, ex p. Brind*[55] the House of Lords was asked to rule that the broadcasting ban imposed on statements made by representatives of the I.R.A. was unlawful as contrary to Article 10 of the E.C.H.R. guaranteeing freedom of expression. The Law Lords agreed that in construing an ambiguous provision in

[51] [1976] 1 W.L.R. 979, 984.
[52] *Report of the Select Committee on a Bill of Rights,* House of Lords, paper 176, June 1978, at para. 28.
[53] *Fernandes v. Secretary of State for the Home Dept.* [1981] Imm. A.R. 1. See to like effect *R. v. Secretary of State for Home Dept., ex p.Kirkwood* [1984] 1 W.L.R. 913.
[54] For the citations see Lester, (1984) Pub.L. 47, at 68, n.8.
[55] [1991] 1 A.C. 696.

domestic legislation the courts would presume that Parliament intended to legislate in conformity with the E.C.H.R. But there was no corresponding presumption that the courts would construe an administrative discretion on the basis that the discretion should be exercised in conformity with the Convention. The E.C.H.R., not having been incorporated into English domestic law, could not be a source of rights and obligations and, there being no ambiguity in the relevant statute, the E.C.H.R. could not be resorted to for the purposes of construction. ("It is accepted ... that ... the Convention is not part of the domestic law, the courts accordingly have no power to enforce Convention rights directly and that, if domestic legislation conflicts with the Convention, the courts must nevertheless enforce it".[56]) For the courts to introduce the E.C.H.R. "by the back door", Lord Bridge said, would be "a judicial usurpation of the legislative function".

But in the same case Lord Templeman said (at 751): "In terms of the [European] Convention, the interference with freedom of expression must be necessary and proportionate to the damage which the restriction is designed to apply". Despite the non-incorporation of the E.C.H.R., he was prepared to apply the principle to what had occurred, and having done so, he was not prepared to find that the Home Secretary had exceeded his powers.[57] In the 1987 House of Lords decision in the "Spycatcher" case four of the five Law Lords referred to Article 10 of the E.C.H.R. in the course of their speeches.[58]

In *Derbyshire County Council v. Times Newspapers Ltd* the courts had to decide whether a local authority could bring proceedings for defamation. The Court of Appeal based its decision that it could not do so primarily on Article 10 of the European Convention. Having considered the various circumstances in which the courts had previously held that they could consider the Convention, Lord Justice Balcombe said: "In my judgment, therefore, where the law is uncertain, it must be right for the court to approach the issue before it with a predilection to ensure that our law should not involve a breach of Art. 10".[59] Article 10 required a balancing

[56] *Ibid, per* Lord Bridge at 748.
[57] The concept of proportionality was approved by Lord Justice Bingham in the "Spycatcher" case — *Att.-Gen. v. Guardian Newspapers (No. 2)* [1990] 1 A.C. 219.
[58] *Att.-Gen. v. Guardian Newspapers* [1987] 1 W.L.R. 1248 at 1286, 1288, 1296–1299, 1307 *per* Lords Bridge, Brandon, Templeman and Ackner. See also *Att.-Gen. v. Guardian Newspapers (No. 2)* [1990] 1 A.C. 219, at 283, *per* Lord Goff: "I conceive it to be my duty, when I am free to do so, to interpret the law in accordance with the obligations of the Crown under this treaty" (namely the E.C.H.R.).See also in the same case the views of Lords Keith (at 256) and Griffiths (at 273).
[59] [1992] 3 All E.R. 65, at 78.

exercise to be undertaken by the court between, on the one hand, the right to freedom of expression and, on the other, such restrictions as are necessary in a democratic society for the protection of the reputation of a non-trading corporation which is also a public authority. He found the balance to fall in favour of the newspaper largely because of the "chilling effect" which the ability to sue for libel would have on criticism of public authorities. Lord Justice Gibson and Lord Justice Butler-Sloss agreed in separate judgments.[60] The House of Lords unanimously affirmed the decision in a single judgment delivered by Lord Keith.[61] In his speech Lord Keith said he reached his conclusion on the basis of the common law "without finding any need to rely upon the European Convention".[62] But he quoted Lord Goff's dictum in "Spycatcher No. 2" that in the field of freedom of expression there was no difference in principle between English law and Article 10 of the Convention[63] and said that he could only add his satisfaction that this was so.[64]

In *R. v. Chief Metropolitan Magistrate, ex p. Choudhury*[65] the Divisional Court had to decide whether to grant a remedy under the law of blasphemy to stop the publication of Salman Rushdie's *The Satanic Verses*. In determining this it considered whether the common law of blasphemy was discriminatory in protecting Christianity but not Islam, making detailed reference to the provisions of Articles 9, 10 and 14 of the E.C.H.R. In *Rantzen v. Mirror Group Newspapers*[66] the Court of Appeal considered whether damages of £250,000 awarded by a jury in libel proceedings to T.V. presenter Esther Rantzen were excessive. The court said that it should take into account guidance given both by the House of Lords and by the European Court of Human Rights interpreting and applying Article 10 of the Convention.[67]

At the time of writing the most recent case to raise the issue was *R. v. Khan* decided by the House of Lords on July 2, 1996.[68] The appellant was convicted of unlawful importation of heroin as a result of evidence obtained by a bugging device unlawfully placed on the exterior of his house by the police. He lost his appeal. In the course of their speeches three of the law lords referred to the

[60] *Ibid*, at 83–90 and 90–97.
[61] [1993] 1 All E.R. 1011.
[62] *Ibid*, at p.1021.
[63] [1990] 1 A.C. 109, at 283–284.
[64] *Ibid*.
[65] [1990] 3 W.L.R. 986.
[66] [1993] 4 All E.R. 975.
[67] *Ibid*, at 994.
[68] [1996] 3 All E.R. 289, H.L.

contention that the appellant's rights under Article 8 of the E.C.H.R. had been infringed. The leading judgment by Lord Nolan said that this was the first case to raise the question whether a criminal court in considering whether to exclude evidence under section 78 of the Police and Criminal Evidence Act was required to have regard to the E.C.H.R. and to the jurisprudence of the Strasbourg Court. He cited with approval what had been said in this regard in the Court of Appeal by Lord Taylor, the Lord Chief Justice.[69] Lord Taylor acknowledged that on the authorities[70] "it is clear that it is permissible to have regard to the Convention, which is of persuasive assistance, in cases of ambiguity or doubt". But in this case "the position is neither ambiguous nor doubtful: nor is it incumbent on us to consider whether there was a breach of Article 8, and we do not propose to do so". Lord Nolan, whilst approving that passage, nevertheless went on, "That is not to say that the principles reflected in the Convention on Human Rights are irrelevant to the exercise of the section 78 power". The principles could hardly be irrelevant "because they embody so many of the familiar principles of our own law and of our concept of justice". If there had been a breach of Article 8, that could be taken into account by the trial judge when exercising his discretion under s.78 of PACE. But on the facts the judge had been fully entitled to hold that the exclusion of the evidence was not required even if there had been a breach of Article 8.

Lord Nicholls said that the discretionary powers of the trial judge to exclude evidence "march hand in hand with" Article 6.1 of the E.C.H.R.. "Accordingly, when considering the common law and statutory discretionary powers under English law the jurisprudence on Article 6 can have a valuable role to play". He cited *Schenk v. Switzerland*[71] and concluded that E.C.H.R. case law on this issue "leads to the same conclusion as English law". Lord Slynn too said that in exercising his powers under section 78 the trial judge could have regard to Articles 6 and 8 of the E.C.H.R. and to their application by the Court of Human Rights.[72]

It is clear from the recent cases therefore that the English judges at the highest level are now prepared to have the E.C.H.R. and the case law of the Strasbourg Court of Human Rights cited to them in

---

[69] [1995] Q.B. 27, at 40.
[70] He cited *Chundawadra v. Immigration Appeal Tribunal* [1988] Imm.A.R. 161 and *Pan-American World Airways Inc. v. Department of Trade* [1976] 1 Lloyd's Rep. 257.
[71] (1988) 13 E.H.R.R 242.
[72] See also Sir John Laws, "Is the High Court the Guardian of Fundamental Constitutional Rights?" (1993) Pub.L. 59.

argument and to consider its application.[73] (Much of the credit for bringing the judges to this point rightly belongs to Anthony Lester Q.C., who has played an especially notable role over many years in deploying the E.C.H.R. argument in the course of his court-room advocacy.) It is clear too that the judges will apply their interpretation of the E.C.H.R. where they find that there is no conflict between English law and the E.C.H.R. or where the law is uncertain or there is a discretionary power to exercise. But where there is a total void in English law, the E.C.H.R. cannot fill the gap — for instance to provide the basis for a right to privacy.[74] Nor can the E.C.H.R. be used to override clear English law to the contrary.[75]

The E.C.H.R. and Community Law

A limited qualification to the proposition that the E.C.H.R. is not part of United Kingdom law arises through membership of the European Community. There are some pronouncements of the Court of Justice of the European Court at Luxembourg (the court responsible for the interpretation of Community Law), to the effect that the human rights matters in the European Community Treaty will be interpreted by reference to the jurisprudence of the Strasbourg Court.[76] The European Court in Luxembourg looks to

[73] See generally N. Bratza, "The Treatment and Interpretation of the European Convention on Human Rights by the English courts", in J. P. Gardner (ed.) *Aspects of Incorporation of the European Convention of Human Rights into Domestic Law* (1993) Chap. 6. For consideration of the comparable issue in Scotland see J. L. Murdoch, "The Europe n Convention on Human Rights in Scots Law" (1991) Pub.L. 40–51.

[74] *Kaye v. Roberston and Another* [1991] F.S.R. 62, at 70, *per* Bingham L.J. In *R. v. Khan* [1996] 3 All E.R. 289 the House of Lords said *obiter* that, even if English law could be said to have a right to privacy by virtue of Art.8 of the E.C.H.R. and even if it had been breached by the placing of the bug, the trial court had correctly exercised its discretion to exclude the evidence.

[75] But see Deryck Beyleveld,"The Concept of a Human Right and Incorporation of the European Convention on Human Rights"(1995) Pub.L. 577–598. His argument is that despite *ex p.Brind* the E.C.H.R. is part of English law even without legislative incorporation. See also Lester, "Government compliance with international human rights law: a new year's legitimate expectation" (1996) Pub.L. 187. Lord Lester argues that there could be said to be a "legitimate expectation" that ministers and civil servants will comply with the international human rights treaties to which the U.K. is party. He finds this legitimate expectation in the publication *Questions of Procedure for Ministers* and the new Civil Service Code which expressly place ministers and civil servants under a duty to comply with the law "including international law and treaty obligations".

[76] See especially Case 29/68, *Stauder v. City of Ulm* [1969] E.C.R. 419, [1970] 9 C.M.L.R. 112, 119; Case 11/70, *International Handelsgesellschaft* [1970] E.C.R.1125, [1972] C.M.L.R. 263; and Case 4/73, *Faj Nold AG v. E.C. Commission* [1974] E.C.R. 491, [1974] 14 C.M.L.R. 338, 354.

the Human Rights Court in Strasbourg for guidance on human rights matters. It will also itself use the E.C.H.R. where it impinges on Community law. Thus in *R. v. Kirk* there was a United Kingdom statutory instrument regarding fishing which operated retroactively. This retroactive effect was authorised by a Community rule which was itself retroactive. Captain Kirk, a Dane, was arrested for unlawful fishing in breach of the retroactive rule and was fined £30,000 by a magistrates' court. The European Court held that the prohibition on retroactivity enshrined in Article 7 of the E.C.H.R. prohibited retroactive imposition of penalties.[77] Community Law, as declared by the Luxembourg Court, is automatically part of English law — by virtue of the terms of the Treaty as translated into English law by the European Communities Act 1972.[78] The result is that rulings of the Luxembourg Court on human rights problems such as equal pay do become English law directly.[79]

Consideration has been given to the question whether the Community itself could accede to the European Human Rights Convention.The European Commission proposed this in a report published in 1979.[80] But in April 1996, the Luxembourg Court held that this was not possible without an amendment to the Treaty. While respect for human rights was a condition of the lawfulness of Community acts, accession to the Convention would entail a substantial change in the present Community system for the protection of human rights in that it would entail the entry of the Community into a distinct international institutional system as well as integration of all the provisions of the Convention into the Community legal order. This would be a fundamental change which would require amendment of the Treaty.[81]

Although the scope of Community Law is wide and growing it is nevertheless limited. If the European Convention is to play its full part in the United Kingdom the only realistic route is through its formal incorporation into domestic law as a statute.

---

[77] Case 63/83, [1984] E.C.R. 2689.
[78] See especially *R. v. Secretary of State for Transport, ex p.Factortame (No. 2)* [1991] A.C. 603 (ECJ) Case C213/89.
[79] See generally N. Grief,"The Domestic Impact of the European Convention on Human Rights as Mediated Through Community Law" (1991) Pub.L. 555–567.
[80] "Accession of the Communities to the European Convention on Human Rights", E.C. Bull.Supp. 2/79.
[81] Opinion No. 2/94 — see *The Times*, April 16, 1996. On the issue of the relationship between Community Law and the Convention see generally T. Hartley, *The Foundations of European Community Law* (3rd ed., 1994) pp.139–149.

The procedure for the enforcement of human rights in Strasbourg is far too slow

It can fairly be said that Britain has in reality had a Bill of Rights since December 1965 when the then Labour Government accepted the right of individual petition under the European Convention.[82] Since that date, any person or corporation, whether a national or not, who complains of a breach of the Convention by United Kingdom authorities can take the complaint to Strasbourg. Given the major significance of this step it is remarkable that at the time the issue was not thought sufficiently important for discussion either by the Cabinet or even by a Cabinet sub-committee. The issue was dealt with simply by correspondence between Ministers.[83] To use Anthony Lester's phrase: "Thus was the substance, if not the form, of parliamentary sovereignty over fundamental rights transferred from London to Strasbourg, not with a roar but a whisper".[84]

Over the years a large number of complaints emanating from the United Kingdom have been brought to Strasbourg and a considerable number have ended with judgments of the Strasbourg Court.[85] By 1996, there had in fact been over 60 substantive judgments of the Strasbourg Court in cases brought against the United Kingdom They have raised a wide variety of issues concerning, for instance, suspects, unconvicted defendants, convicted prisoners, asylum seekers, immigrants, mental patients, children in care, censorship, transsexuals, homosexuals, and litigants in civil proceedings. Over half of the judgments resulted in a finding of a breach of the Convention.[86]

Many of the judgments have required action by the United Kingdom Government including action in the form of legislative

---

[82] Acceptance of the right of individual petition has been extended from time to time — most recently in December 1995 for five years — see *Hansard*, H.L. Vol. 567, W. A. col. 117 (December 14, 1995). This will, however, no longer be necessary when the new machinery provided for by Protocol 11 becomes operative.

[83] Lester, (1984) Pub.L. 47, at 60.

[84] *Ibid*, at 61.

[85] See generally A. W. Bradley,"The United Kingdom before the Strasbourg Court 1975–90" in W. Finnie, C. M. G. Himsworth and N. Walker (eds.) *Edinburgh Essays in Public Law* (1991), pp.85–214; F. J. Hampson, "The United Kingdom before the European Court of Human Rights" (1989) 9 Yrbk. of European L. 121–173.

[86] In 1995 it was stated in the House of Lords that there had been 35 cases against the U.K. in which at least one breach of the Convention had been found — compared with 82 against Italy, 29 against France, 27 against Austria, 23 against Holland, 21 against Sweden, 20 against Belgium, 14 against Switzerland and 11 against Germany. (*Hansard*, H.L. Vol. 563, W.A. col. 43–44 (April 18, 1995).

changes in the law. Though there has sometimes been room for argument as to whether such action has been sufficiently speedy or complete, broadly, the United Kingdom Government has complied with judgments of the Strasbourg Court. This, therefore, is a system that is functioning.

But to get a remedy in Strasbourg takes an unconscionable time. The machinery is extremely ponderous. The first stage is for the Commission to decide whether or not the claim is admissible. This may take anything up to a year. If the claim is admissible the Commission attempts a friendly settlement between the complainant and the respondent Government. Normally many months will again elapse for this process. If this fails, the Commission moves to consider the substantive issue. Argument can be both written and oral and can again take many months. Then comes the Commission's decision. If the Commission finds a breach of the Convention, the matter goes either to the Committee of Ministers or to the Court. If it goes to the Court, again there is both written and oral argument before eventually the Court gives its considered, written decision. According to the Council of Europe itself "it takes on average over five years for a case to be finally determined by the Court or the Committee of Ministers"[87]. However dilatory English courts may be, they do not take nearly as long as that to reach their decisions.

The problem of the unacceptable length of proceedings at Strasbourg has been a serious issue already for many years. In autumn 1984, the Steering Committee for Human Rights of the Council of Europe prepared a draft new Protocol to the European Convention on Human Rights designed to expedite proceedings before the Commission. This became Protocol No. 8 which was ratified by the United Kingdom in April 1986 and which entered into force on January 1, 1990. This allowed the Commission to divide into chambers for certain cases, thereby permitting an increase in its working capacity. It also provided for a new procedure whereby the Commission could establish small committees empowered to reject petitions that were manifestly inadmissible.

But the problem of serious delays continued — and as membership of the E.C.H.R. system expanded to include many Eastern European, formerly Communist countries it was clear that the situation would go from bad to worse. In January 1994 the number

---

[87] Council of Europe, "Protocol No. 11 to the European Convention on Human Rights and Explanatory Report", May 1994, (H (94 5), p.19, para. 21). For discussion and explanation see A. Drzemczewski, "The need for a radical overhaul", N.L.J., January 29, 1993, p.126.

of pending cases stood at 2,672, almost 1,500 of which had not even been looked at by the Commission. In 1985 the number of countries in the E.C.H.R. system was 21 — all Western European. But recently there has been a dramatic expansion in numbers resulting from the changes in Eastern Europe.[88] By 1996 the number of countries in the system had increased to 33. Countries whose membership has recently become effective (in alphabetical order) are Bulgaria (1992), the Czech Republic (1993), Estonia (1996), Finland (1990), Hungary (1992), Lithuania (1995), Poland (1993), Roumania (1994), Slovakia (1993) and Slovenia (1994).[89]

On May 28, 1993, during a special meeting of the Council of Europe's Committee of Ministers, a decision was taken to ask the principal human rights experts advising the organisation to prepare a draft amending Protocol "with the aim of improving efficiency and shortening the time taken for individual applications".[90] This initiative led eventually to Protocol No. 11 which was signed on May 11, 1994 by 33 countries.

Protocol No. 11 is the most radical reform of the E.C.H.R. machinery since its inception. Under it the Commission is abolished altogether and the Committee of Ministers only retains jurisdiction in regard to supervision of compliance and enforcement under Article 50. The main feature of the reform is to create a single court system. Instead of a part-time Commission and Court the new court will be full-time. There will be three categories of proceedings — those dealt with by *Committees* of three judges, those dealt with by *Chambers* of seven judges and *the Grand Chamber* consisting of seventeen judges. Committees would only have the power to declare cases inadmissible or to strike them from the list. Chambers would have the power to deal with substantive hearings and would deal with most cases that reach that stage. The Grand Chamber would operate in inter-state cases and in the cases raising the most important questions of Convention law.[91]

---

[88] In 1950, David Maxwell-Fyfe (later Lord Chancellor Kilmuir) described the E.C.H.R. as "a beacon to the peoples behind the Iron Curtain, and a passport for their return to the midst of the free countries" — quoted by Anthony Lester in (1996) Pub.L. 5.

[89] In addition Russia, Albania, Latvia and the Ukraine have each signed but not ratified the Convention.

[90] For the background see, for instance, Alistair R. Mowbray, "Reform of the Control System of the European Convention on Human Rights" (1993) Pub.L. 419–426.

[91] For a more detailed explanation of Protocol 11 see Andrew Drzemczewski, "Putting the European House in Order" N.L.J. May 13, 1994, p.644; and Alastair R. Mowbray,"A New European Court of Human Rights" (1994) Pub.L. 540–552.

The Protocol will come into force when ratified by all member states. By July 1996 it had been ratified by 21 countries (including the United Kingdom); twelve countries have yet to ratify. By the time that it does come into effect the backlog of cases will be even more crushing and the volume of new applications will certainly have grown even greater. It would therefore be a miracle if the new reformed system manages to stay abreast of the problem of delay — let alone makes any significant dent on it. For the foreseeable future, a remedy under the E.C.H.R. in the national courts system is likely to be a great deal speedier than one obtained from Strasbourg.

The absence of adequate machinery for the enforcement of human rights in Britain means that "dirty laundry" is washed unnecessarily abroad to the detriment of Britain's good name

Every time that a case is brought against the United Kingdom in the European forum the country's reputation is in some sense and to some extent brought into international disrepute. The argument has frequently been made that incorporation of the Convention would prevent Britain's "dirty laundry" being washed abroad instead of being dealt with more discreetly at home. It is of course true that an action brought in the English courts might also redound to the discredit of the United Kingdom but the degree of international opprobrium would normally be less than where the same action was brought in the European forum.

Between 1975 and 1996, as has been seen, over 60 cases brought against the United Kingdom under the E.C.H.R. reached the Strasbourg court. They involved a very wide range of issues. More than half resulted in a finding of one or more breaches of the Convention. If these actions could have been brought in the courts of this country, it is likely that some at least would have been dealt with in such a way as to avoid the need for action in the Strasbourg system — with resulting benefit to the good name of the United Kingdom.

The argument should not, however, be taken too far. It cannot plausibly be argued that incorporation of the E.C.H.R. into United Kingdom law would stop cases being brought to Strasbourg. That view is plainly untenable given the fact that incorporation has not stopped such proceedings against other European countries. Thus Italy incorporated the E.C.H.R. into domestic law in 1955 but it has been the country with the largest number of cases brought against it of any in Europe.[92] The number of E.C.H.R. cases brought against a country obviously depends on a host of factors including the extent to which civil liberties are protected in the country and the availability of lawyers familar with the E.C.H.R. able to take up cases. If the E.C.H.R. were incorporated and the United Kingdom judges rejected large numbers of complaints brought under the Bill of Rights, the number of cases coming to Strasbourg by way of appeal from unsuccessful litigants could in theory actually be *higher* than it is today.

A British Bill of Rights would take decisions on matters of importance away from foreign judges

There is a strong body of opinion in the United Kingdom that deplores the influence of Europe — whether it is through the Community or through the E.C.H.R. For them the European Court of Justice in Luxembourg and the European Court of Human Rights in Strasbourg are fundamentally the same — foreign courts, foreign judges.

Some who hold this opinion would wish the United Kingdom to pull out of the E.C.H.R. system and to establish our own Bill of Rights instead. This view has been expressed only rarely — though one who has done so, as has been seen (p.37 above), is Lord Donaldson, formerly Master of the Rolls.

For Britain to withdraw from the E.C.H.R. system would obviously be a very serious step both for the system and for Britain. It is doubtful whether many civil libertarians would regard it as a welcome development. If Britain enacts its own Bill of Rights whilst retaining the right of appeal to Strasbourg, a person who complains of a breach of the Convention has two chances. If he succeeds in the home courts he has won and there is no right of appeal for the Government; if he loses in the home courts, he can still pursue the matter on to Strasbourg. The establishment of the opportunity of trying to get a remedy in the home courts is a benefit to the complainant — apart from the time and money he

[92] In 1994 Italy accounted for no less than 51 per cent of all applications to the European Commission that were declared admissible (298 out of 582) and in 1995 the proportion was 56 per cent (453 out of 807). France and Greece were other countries with a high number of cases declared admissible in 1994 and 1995, notwithstanding the fact that the E.C.H.R. is given precedence over domestic law by the municipal courts in those countries. In 1994, France had 63 and Greece 103; in 1995, France had 108 and Greece had 27. The U.K. had 16 in 1994 and 24 in 1995. The figures are stated annually in the Council of Europe's *Survey of activities and statistics* regarding the European Commission of Human Rights.

would then have to spend in "exhausting his local remedies" as international law calls the requirement to use any remedies available internally before complaining on the international level. The European system created by the E.C.H.R. remains in place. If, on the contrary, the United Kingdom were to withdraw from the E.C.H.R. system, the complainant could only test the issue by action in the United Kingdom courts.

The argument regarding incorporation as a way of reducing the influence and effect of foreign judges is however usually advanced without any reference to a proposed withdrawal from the E.C.H.R. system.[93] This is obviously based on a misunderstanding of the true position. If the United Kingdom stays within the E.C.H.R. system, the domestic Bill of Rights is in addition to, not in substitution for decision-making by "foreign judges". It is not always clear that those who advance the argument are aware of this.

A Bill of Rights is a flexible and adaptable tool

One of the criticisms advanced against Bills of Rights is that they are vague and general. But this is the whole point of having a Bill of Rights. It is true that Bills of Rights typically take the form of broad principles, though these principles can be stated to be subject to broad qualifying clauses. The European Convention is of this kind. The consequence is that the solutions to concrete problems have to be left to the courts to work out as they arise. The answer to the problem does not necessarily appear on the face of the text: the meaning of the text and its application to the facts of the case in question can only be revealed by the decision of the court. So, one can say with certainty that the E.C.H.R. forbids torture, because Article 3 specifically says so. But one cannot be sure by looking at the text whether and to what extent it protects the suspect's "right to silence" because that is not specifically covered. It has to be established by putting the issue to the test in legal proceedings regarding the scope of the phrase in Article 6(2) which protects everyone's right to be presumed innocent until proved guilty. This at present requires the case to be brought in Strasbourg. If the E.C.H.R. were incorporated into United Kingdom law it could also be raised in proceedings in legal proceedings within the country.

The possibility of such proceedimgs has the unfortunate effect that a measure of uncertainty is created as to the scope and

---

[93] Thus Mr Robert Jackson, Conservative M.P.: "What reason do we have to believe that a Turkish or Icelandic judge sitting in Strasbourg is better qualified to make the type of judgment which the Convention requires in a case arising out of the United Kingdom?" (*Hansard*, H.C. Vol. 109, col. 1268 (February 6, 1987).

meaning of the law at any given time. On the other hand, the advantage is that it gives persons with felt grievances the chance to argue their case for a remedy in the courts and the response of the judges will reflect the changing *mores* of society. The history of decisions given by the United States Supreme Court over the years has demonstrated the adaptability of a Bill of Rights to the changing needs of society.

But what is the point of giving rights in the form of broad statements of principle[94] and then seemingly cancelling them by broad qualifying clauses[95]? The point is that both the broad principle and the qualifications have value. The broad principle provides a potential platform for the grievance to be aired in a court. The qualifications direct the court as to the issues that need to be weighed. Unless the respondent can show that the restrictions were "necessary", the claimant wins. This provides the right context for the matter to be considered by the courts — and the burden of proof lies on the respondent not on the claimant which is of great importance.

A Bill of Rights is an opportunity for developing law and practice beyond what would be likely to occur if left to the executive and the legislature

The vested interest of all government is to preserve the normal ways of doing things and to resist pressure for change. Government, of whatever political complexion, is usually moved to change things only when the pressure to do so become greater than the convenience of leaving things as they are. Legitimate pressure can be generated through litigation under a Bill of Rights. Unlike the executive or the legislature, a court cannot say that the time is unripe for a decision on the issue, or that it is politically awkward to alter existing rules or policy. Legislation or executive action on human rights matters is frequently affected by the political exigencies of the moment. Often it cannot be achieved at all, or only partially. Litigation to enforce the Bill of Rights may be easier to mobilise than either legislation or executive action.

On some issues judges may be readier to find a remedy for a grievance than politicians or civil servants. So, for instance, civil

[94] *e.g.* "Everyone has the right to freedom of expression" (Art. 10).
[95] Thus, the Art. 10 right can be restricted if it be "necessary in the interests of national security, territorial integrity or public safety, the prevention of disorder or crime, the protection of health or morals, for the protection of the reputation or rights of others, for protecting confidentiality or for maintaining the authority and impartiality of the judiciary".

65

liberties lawyers in the United States in the 1960s and 1970s made more progress in the courts on behalf of blacks and prisoners than they could make in either state or federal legislatures. A court may be readier to respond to an appeal advanced in the name of principle from an unpopular litigant than would the political machine. In other words, part of the reason for having a Bill of Rights is to protect the individual against the illiberal action or inaction of the legislature or of the executive branch and to provide a remedy where they cannot or will not act.

A Bill of Rights may, therefore, have an important function in defusing political grievances. The role of the courts generally is to provide a forum for the resolution of disputes. Sometimes the point at issue relates simply to the parties; sometimes it has wider importance. Litigation under a Bill of Rights frequently affects large sections of the community. Far preferable that grievances be met than that they be allowed to fester. The late Professor Stanley de Smith, for instance, expressed the view that:

> "If the constitution of Northern Ireland had been equipped from the outset with more detailed guarantees against religious discrimination, coupled with efficacious machinery for their enforcement, it is just conceivable — one cannot put it more highly — that the worst of the recent troubles might have been averted".[96]

A Bill of Rights would be needed if there is any significant measure of devolution of legislative powers to regional assemblies

The Conservative Party is currently opposed to devolution, but both New Labour under Mr Tony Blair and the Liberal Democrats propose a measure of devolution to Scotland and Wales.

In the 1970s, when devolution proposals were last seriously on the agenda, the Government accepted the advice of the Kilbrandan Royal Commission on the Constitution[97] that no bill of rights should be included in the Scotland and Wales Bill, and later in the

---

[96] S. de Smith. *Constitutional and Administrative Law* (4th ed., 1981), pp.447–448.

[97] *Devolution within the United Kingdom*, Cmnd. 5460, 1973, paras. 746–755. The reasons were partly to do with Bills of Rights generally, and especially the wide discretion given to the judiciary and the resulting uncertainty in the law until case law has developed. But the Royal Commission also thought there would be little point in having a Bill of Rights for the regions if there was not one for the national system — and that issue was beyond its terms of reference. Also, it said, "there is no evidence that the public conscience, as made effective through our existing democratic institutions is not adequate to provide the protection called for" (para. 755).

separate Scotland and Wales Acts. Now that it is again under consideration, neither Labour nor the Liberal Democrats have as yet signified an intention to include a Bill of Rights in the legislation creating devolved assemblies. But that may change.

Lord Scarman and Lord Hailsham have emphasised the need for a Bill of Rights in the context of devolution. According to Lord Scarman, the Report of the Kilbrandon Royal Commission underestimated the problems that would be created by devolution. Problems, he thought, would arise between regional and central legislatures. Such local assemblies would be likely to explore the extent of their legislative powers and to seek the independent decision of the courts if they found themselves at variance with the central Parliament in their interpretation of the extent of their powers. There would also be a severe problem of providing machinery to ensure equal social, economic and personal rights throughout the *de facto* independently governed regions of the United Kingdom.[98]

Lord Hailsham said that if the powers of the devolved assemblies for Scotland and Wales are to be adequately controlled and policed on the one hand, and protected from the central government and legislature on the other, some measure of judicial control seems to be inevitable, and if this is right, some definition of the rights of individuals and minorities against both central and local authority would seem to be desirable and perhaps essential.[99]

In its summary of the arguments for a Bill of Rights, the House of Lords Select Committee Report in 1978 said one was that a Bill of Rights would constitute a framework of human rights guaranteed throughout the United Kingdom. This would have special value

> "If Scottish and Welsh Assemblies are established with powers devolved from Westminster, to ensure the exercise of such powers (*e.g.* those respecting local government and education) by the Assemblies with due regard to the United Kingdom's international commitments under the [European] Convention."[1]

The Scottish Constitutional Convention[2] in its 1995 report *Scotland's Parliament. Scotland's Right* said:

---

[98] Scarman, *English Law — The New Dimension* (1974), pp.65–68.
[99] *The Times*, May 19, 1975.
[1] *Report of the Select Committee on a Bill of Rights,* House of Lords, paper 176, June 1978, at p.31, para. 32(g).
[2] For an account of the Scottish Constitutional Convention see a note in (1995) Pub.L. 215–223.

"The Convention expects Scotland's Parliament to provide for special protection for fundamental rights and freedoms within Scots law. This is best achieved through adoption of a Charter, advancing clear principles and specifying the rights and freedoms held to be inviolable. The Convention expects the Charter to encompass and improve on prevailing international law and convention (the European Convention on Human Rights, the International Covenant on Civil and Political Rights and the European Parliament Declaration of Fundamental Rights and Freedoms)."

A Bill of Rights may assist a willing Minister to achieve needed reforms

Not infrequently, the stumbling block to progress is not the Minister or his senior officials but those at a lower level. A decision from a court which demands change and which seems, to that extent, to be contrary to the interests of the government department concerned may in fact be welcomed by those concerned with running it. The *Golder* case (the first involving the United Kingdom to reach the Strasbourg court), might be an example. The decision of the European Court required the Home Office to liberalise its rules about access of prisoners to lawyers. Clearly such a change would not be likely to be welcomed by the Prison Officers' Association but it might be acceptable and sensible to Ministers and their senior advisers. If it were left to the Department itself, such changes might never be achieved, or only with Herculean efforts. The Minister would not be able to bring his lower echelon officials or the "hard liners" along. If he can simply point to the court's decision and disclaim any personal responsibility, his position may be greatly eased. The changes can then be made without any equivalent tension being generated.

A Bill of Rights places the power of action where it belongs — with those who claim to be aggrieved

One of the chief weaknesses of the argument that grievances should be remedied, if at all, only by Parliament on a topic-by-topic basis is that it places effective control and power in the hands of those who administer the system. Human nature being what it is, this means that the system will always be slow to respond to grievances. If individuals can raise their complaints before an impartial tribunal where they can be heard, where they can publicly contest the arguments put by the authorities and from which they can obtain an actual decision, the system to that extent becomes more responsive and politically accountable.

A Bill of Rights is a major educative force

A Bill of Rights by no means guarantees either the establishment or the enforcement of human rights. There is much bitter experience in a variety of countries showing that Bills of Rights, like treaties and other solemn commitments, can be mere scraps of paper. On the other hand, there can be little doubt that a Bill of Rights may play a major role in raising the level of consciousness about human rights. Summarising the arguments for a Bill of Rights the House of Lords Select Committee in its 1978 report said that the E.C.H.R. "seems likely to have far more practical effect on legislators, administrators, the executive, citizens as well as legislators if it ceases to be only an international treaty obligation and becomes an integral part of the United Kingdom law".[3] Much the same point was made vividly by Harold Laski when he wrote of the real value of Bills of Rights which it was "both easy and mistaken to underestimate":

> "Granted that the people are educated to the appreciation of their purpose, they serve to draw attention . . . to the fact that vigilance is essential in the realm of what Cromwell called fundamentals. Bills of Rights are, quite undoubtedly, a check upon possible excess in the Government of the day. They warn us that certain popular powers have had to be fought for, and may have to be fought for again. The solemnity they embody serves to set the people on their guard. It acts as a rallying point in the State for all who care deeply for the ideals of freedom."[4]

---

[3] *Report of the Select Committee on a Bill of Rights,* House of Lords, paper 176, June 1978, at 31–32.
[4] Harold Laski, *Liberty and the Modern State* (3rd ed., 1948), p.75.

3. THE ARGUMENTS AGAINST A BILL OF RIGHTS CONSIDERED

A Bill of Rights is an "un-British" way of doing things

This argument is difficult to sustain in view of the fact that we virtually invented Bills of Rights with Magna Carta 1215 and the Bill of Rights 1689.

Magna Carta was a code of reforming laws passed against the will of the sovereign and may in that sense be seen, as has been said, as "the germ of the root principle that there are fundamental rights above the State, which the State . . . may not infringe". Amongst the provisions of Magna Carta were: a guarantee of freedom of overseas travel (save in time of war); provisions against confiscation of property without payment; against selling or delaying justice, against excessive fines disproportionate to the offence or so heavy as to deprive a man of his livelihood, against public prosecutions unsupported by the evidence of independent witnesses and finally the famous clause declaring that no one's life, liberty or property should be taken "except by the lawful judgment of his peers or by the law of the land".[1]

Magna Carta also provided a form of enforcement machinery. First the "liberties" were declared to be permanently binding.[2] Secondly, it was given supremacy over any other law in the stipulation that anything "by which any part of these concessions or liberties [might be] revoked or diminished . . . shall be null and void".[3] The Charter was, in a sense therefore, "entrenched". Moreover, its terms were to apply not only to the king but also to the barons. The king proclaimed that "all those aforesaid customs and liberties which we have granted to be held in our realm as far as it pertains to us towards our men, shall be observed by all men

---

[1] J. Holt, *Magna Carta* (1965), Chap. 9, p.327. I am indebted to Judge Skelly Wright in his article in (1981) Tul.L.Rev 291 for the references to Magna Carta.
[2] *Ibid*, Chaps. 1, 61, 63, pp.317, 333–337.
[3] *Ibid*, Chap. 61, p.337.

of our realm, both clerk and layman, as far as it pertains to them, toward their own people".[4] Moreover, a committee of 25 barons was established to deal with complaints and they were specifically authorised "to distrain and distress [the King] in every way they can . . . until in their judgment, amends have been made".[5] All subjects were stated to be permitted to swear allegiance to those engaged in righting a violation of the Charter — with force if necessary.[6]

In the following two centuries Magna Carta was reissued or confirmed almost 50 times. Thus in 1369 Edward III ordered that "the Great Charter . . . be holden and kept in all Points; and if any Statute be made to the contrary, that shall be holden for none".[7] Two and a half centuries later, Coke remarked: "Magna Carta is such a fellow, that he will have no sovereign". But in the seventeenth century Magna Carta in effect lapsed. It played no part in the constitutional battles involving the Stuart Kings, or Cromwell. Since that time Parliament has reigned supreme.

The other great constitutional document apart from Magna Carta was the Bill of Rights of 1689. The offer of the throne to William and Mary by the Convention Parliament was subject to conditions set forth in the Declaration of Right which then became the Bill of Rights. After dealing with limitations on the prerogative and the dispensing power, it restated certain fundamental principles as they were then conceived. These included the right to free elections and debate in Parliament, the levying of taxes only with the consent of Parliament, the right to petition, the right (for Protestants) to bear arms, and freedom from excessive bail, fines and punishments. As a statement of the limitation on government and the corresponding rights of citizens, the Bill of Rights is a direct ancestor of several provisions in the Constitution of the United States. Moreover, the recognition of certain basic and inviolable rights in the 1689 Bill of Rights may be said to have presaged not only the American Declaration of the Rights of Man (1789), but also the United Nations Universal Declaration of Human Rights and the European Convention on Human Rights.

Admittedly, neither Magna Carta nor the Bill of Rights would prevail over contrary more recent authority in an English court but they are still referred to with respect verging on veneration. They are major historic relics and reflect a significant part of the cultural

[4] *Ibid*, Chap. 60, p.333.
[5] *Ibid*, Chap. 61, pp.333–337.
[6] *Ibid*.
[7] F. Thompson, *Magna Carta: Its Role in the Making of the English Constitution, 1300–1629* (1948) p. 16.

and political-legal tradition of Britain. To say therefore that Bills of Right are "un-British" is to show an ignorance of history. The notion that fundamental constitutional documents are "nonsense on stilts" derives from the nineteenth century and in particular the work of Dicey. Moreover, as has already been seen, the British may have been slow to establish a modern Bill of Rights for themselves but they showed no reluctance in bestowing Bills of Rights on the emerging countries of the Commonwealth.

Certainly it is the case that a Bill of Rights couched in broad and general language would be different from the precise and detailed form of existing English legislation. Equally the ordinary processes of the English common law tradition are to work empirically and slowly from case to case developing principles in a gradual way. Under a Bill of Rights the courts would start with principles of wide generality and the courts would have a very free hand in deciding how to apply the principles to the facts of cases before them. Even though in recent years the courts have become familiar with a broader form of legal text in the form of Community law, this would be something new.

A Bill of Rights is not needed — human rights are adequately protected in Britain

It is, of course not the case that the absence of a written constitution means that we have no protection of human rights. Indeed there may be truth in the widely held belief that civil liberties are as well, or better, protected in Britain than in most other countries.[8]

This essentially is the position adopted by the United Kingdom Government in its continuing dialogue with the United Nations Human Rights Committee. In the United Kingdom's Third Periodic Report to the Committee (October 1989) it was claimed that the United Kingdom has a long history of concern for human rights but that it had not felt the need for a written constitution or a comprehensive Bill of Rights since "the principle has been that the rights and freedoms recognised by other systems are inherent in the United Kingdom's legal system and are protected by it and

---

[8] This point has been made by many critics of the Bill of Rights. See for instance the late Professor Lord (Dennis) Lloyd, a member of the House of Lords Select Committee *Hansard*, H.L. Vol. 396, cols. 1322–1324 (November 29, 1978).

by Parliament" (para. 1).[9] The Report went on to note that the rights and freedoms protected in that way had at various times been reinforced by legislation to deal with specific problems as they arose. It also claimed that the European Commission and Court of Human Rights had increased in influence in domestic courts and that "The Government routinely scrutinises draft legislation and proposals for administrative change to see whether they are compatible with the international human rights instruments to which the United Kingdom is a party" (para. 5). In the Fourth Report to the United Nations Human Rights Committee in 1994 the same theme was repeated. There was still no need for the incorporation of international human rights instruments into domestic law because,

> "The United Kingdom's human rights obligations are rou-
> tinely considered by Ministers and their officials in the
> formulation and application of government policy, whilst
> judgments of the House of Lords have made clear that such
> obligations are part of the legal context in which the judges
> consider themselves to operate." (para. 5)

It is revealing that this submission presents the matter entirely as if it only concerned the Government and official agencies and makes no reference to the position of the citizen seeking a remedy for a grievance.

If statutes and judicial decisions in the areas covered by Bills of Rights were collected and codified it would be found that Britain has an elaborate system of remedies rather than of rights. But there are many gaps and the law does not lay down general principles. The effect of this is to place severe restrictions on the issues covered and on the scope for development of the law. The system lacks the flexibility and capacity for growth that is poten-tially inherent in broad, general statements. Thus, a general phrase such as "the right to liberty and security of person", "freedom of

[9] The position in Northern Ireland is different. There is first a written constitution — the Northern Ireland Constitution Act 1973. This Act has provisions (ss.17 and 19) invalidating legislation or government action which discriminates on the grounds of religion or political belief. But this protection covers only devolved matters. For discussion of the limited impact of the sections see Standing Advisory Commission on Human Rights, *Second Report on Religious and Political Discrimi-nation*, Cm. 1107 (1990), Chap. 4. The Westminister Parliament has unrestricted power to suspend the Northern Ireland Constitution and to introduce emergency powers — see Government of Ireland Act 1920, s.75. This power has been used frequently. Northern Ireland is the only part of the United Kingdom with a permanent official commission — the Standing Advisory Commission on Human Rights with responsibility for monitoring the effectiveness of human rights protection — see s.20 of the 1973 Act.

thought conscience and religion", or "the right to peaceful assembly" provides a peg on which an argument can be hung. It enables issues to be litigated which cannot even be argued in a system that merely provides remedies for a limited range of situations. The one system is more closed, where the other is more open-ended.[10]

Certainly even the most sanguine apologist for Britain can hardly suggest that there is no room for improvement. The very fact that so many significant persons and bodies have in recent years supported the call for some form of Bill of Rights suggests an unease about the present state of civil liberties in Britain. The fact that the European Court of Human Rights has decided several dozen cases against the United Kingdom suggests that this unease may be justified.

The existing ways of getting remedies — the free press, complaints raised through one's M.P.,[11] pressure groups,[12] the Ombudsman,[13] the Citizen's Charter[14] and the operation of the ordinary courts all have their limitations. It is true that in recent years the judges have been readier than in the past to review and check the actions of Ministers and civil servants.[15] But it certainly could not be said that they provide a complete system for the remedying of all genuine grievances.

The United Nations Human Rights Committee has repeatedly expressed scepticism about the Government's claim that there was no need for legislation to guarantee human rights.[16] As has been seen, in its 1995 Report,[17] the Committee said that "the legal

---

[10] See generally Louis Jaffe, *English and American Judges as Lawmakers* (1969).

[11] See R. W. Rawlings, "The M.P.'s Complaints Service", (1990) M.L.R. 22–42, 149–169.

[12] See C. Harlow and R. W. Rawlings, *Pressure through Law* (1992).

[13] See on this subject P. Giddings and R. Gregory,"Auditing the auditors: Responses to the Select Committee's Review of the United Kingdom's Ombudsman system 1993" (1995) Pub.L. 45–51; and A. W. Bradley, "The Parliamentary Ombudsman again — A positive report" (1995) Pub.L. 345–350.

[14] See, for instance, Anne Barron and C.Scott, "The Citizen's Charter Programme" (1992) 55 M.L.R. 526–546; G.Drewry, "Mr Major's Charter:empowering the customer" (1993) Pub.L. 248–256; Norman Lewis, "The Citizen's Charter and Next Steps: A New Way of Governing" (1993) Pol.Qtrly. 316–26.

[15] The leading authority is the late Stanley de Smith's magisterial *Judicial Review of Administrative Action*, substantially revised in its 1995 edition by Lord Woolf and Professor Jeffrey Jowell. See also commentary on the civil servants's guide *The Judge Over Your Shoulder* — Mark I in (1987) Pub.L. 485; Mark II in (1994) Pub.L. 514. See further pp.92–93 below.)

[16] For extracts from the Committee's Reports and revealing quotations from the exchanges between Committee members and the U.K. representatives, see F. Klug, K. Starmer and S. Weir, "The British way of doing things: The United Kingdom and the International Covenant of Civil and Political Rights, 1976–94" (1995) Pub.L.504, 506–509.

[17] At p.51 above.

74

system of the United Kingdom does not ensure fully that an effective remedy is provided for all violations of the rights contained in the Covenant" and that implementation of the Covenant's protection of human rights was impeded by "the combined effects" of the non-incorporation of the Covenant into domestic law, the refusal to allow British subjects to petition directly to the Committee, and the absence of a domestic Bill of Rights (para. 9). It urged the Government either to incorporate the Covenant into domestic law, or to introduce a Bill of Rights "under which legislative or executive encroachments on Covenant rights could be reviewed by the Courts" (paras. 9 and 20).

Not that a Bill of Rights would solve all problems or even *necessarily* improve our way of handling such problems. But every country — even one with an outstanding record in the field of civil liberties — always has room for improvement. The question therefore is whether the network of systems that exists in the United Kingdom for responding to problems in the field covered by a Bill of Rights would on balance be strengthened by the enactment of a Bill of Rights. This turns on an overall evaluation of all the advantages and disadvantages of taking such a step.

It has been suggested, by no less a person than the new Lord Chief Justice, Lord Bingham (at a time when he was still Master of the Rolls), that the burden of proof in this regard lies on those who oppose the introduction of a Bill of Rights. The case for entrenchment of rights was so strong that the burden lay "on the opponents to make good their ground of opposition."[18] I incline to the opposite view — that the burden of proof lies rather on those who propose a change, especially where the change is as fundamental as this one.

A Bill of Rights is suitable for a primitive or unsophisticated system of law but is not appropriate to a modern, complex society

In his 1975 *Times* article, Lord Hailsham said he had always thought a Bill of Rights was a sign of an undeveloped legal system. But, as he himself later admitted, this depends entirely on the nature of the Bill of Rights, on the methods of enforcement, and on the character and style of its operation. A Bill of Rights which is simply a pious declaration of high sounding principles, with no true enforcement procedures, is of little value and may indeed be counter-productive in that it creates the illusion of progress

---

[18] T. H. Bingham, "The European Convention on Human Rights: time to incorporate", (1993) L.Q.R. 390, at 399.

without actually achieving anything. Common law judges developing the law from precedent to precedent may provide better
protection against the abuse of power than a Bill of Rights which
lacks teeth.

But a Bill of Rights which does have enforcement procedures,
and which exists in a climate favourable to the protection of legal
rights, is a very different matter. There is much wrong with
American society but it could not be said that the U.S. Supreme
Court lacks authority to redress grievances. Sometimes the effect of
decisions is dramatic and far-reaching. A decision that criminal
cases require legal representation results in the release of hundreds
of prisoners convicted without the benefit of a lawyer.[19] A judge
holds prison conditions to be so inhumane as to require that the
prison be altogether closed by a named date.[20] The court strikes
down the country's entire educational system as not conforming
with the requirement of equal opportunity for black and white
citizens.[21] The voting system is declared void as giving undue
weight to rural as against urban votes.[22] Decisions of such broad
import are hardly the signs of a primitive legal system. On the
contrary, they show a degree of confidence in the strength of the
legal order quite beyond what has been traditional in this country.

Sometimes, of course, this confidence is misplaced. There may
be a gap between the aim of the court's decision and its realisation:
or it may take many years to implement the decision.[23] But the
same is true of legislation. A statute is not a magic wand. The
balance of functions between what can and what ought to be
achieved by legislation, and what by the courts, is for each society
to work out for itself. But it is wrong to dismiss Bills of Rights as
feeble instruments unworthy of serious believers in the rule of law.
Everything depends on how the system is established and operated.
It can be totally useless — mere window dressing — acceptable to

---

[19] *Gideon v. Wainwright,* 372 U.S. 335 (1963).
[20] *Holt v. Sarver,* 309 F. Supp. 362 (1970); affirmed 442 F. 2d (8th Cir. 1971). This
decision related to the notorious Alabama system. In Philadelphia the court
found that conditions in the city prison were so bad as to require it to be
condemned. "Conditions in the prison constitute cruel and inhuman punishment." *Byrant v. Hendrick,* Philadelphia Court of Common Pleas, August 11,
1970. In New Mexico a court ordered that a prison reduce the number of
prisoners: *Curley v. Gonzales,* U.S. District Court, New Mexico, February 12,
1970. In New York, the U.S. District Court ordered the prison authorities to
make major improvements in conditions at the Tombs or close the prison —
Rhem v. Malcolm, 371 F. Supp. 594 (1974).
[21] *Brown v. Board of Education,* 347 U.S. 483 (1954).
[22] *Baker v. Carr,* 369 U.S.186 (1962).
[23] For scepticism about the capacity of judicial decisions to achieve results see
nn.19–21 and accompanying text pp.130–131 below.

the most repressive regime, or it can be a quite effective means of providing remedies even in highly sensitive areas of public policy.[24] Experience over the past three decades with the decisions of the European Court of Human Rights suggests that the E.C.H.R. is in the latter rather than the former category.

A Bill of Rights is too powerful a tool to be entrusted to judges and is incompatible with democratic principles

This argument is roughly the reverse of the previous one. It is based on the view that in democratic countries difficult, controversial or important social policy issues ought generally to be decided by the legislature rather than the courts. This is especially the case where the existence of a Bill of Rights gives the judges the power to strike down legislation.

Before looking at the argument in detail it is important to acknowledge that in a democracy the legislature should generally have the final word on matters of major political significance. A Bill of Rights is not intended to prevent the legislature from doing what needs to be done — providing only that what the government thinks "needs to be done" is consistent with the requirements of the Bill of Rights. Thus, when in January 1991 the Labour Party unveiled its Charter of Rights, it was presented as a substitute for a Bill of Rights. The Charter of Rights contained a list of some 40 items for a legislative programme in the area of civil rights and civil liberties. The topics included freedom of information, new rules on privacy, the security service, equal opportunities, immigration, citizenship, asylum, children, criminal justice, employment rights and the right to assembly. Such a legislative programme is, however, not a substitute for a Bill of Rights. It is something quite different — not worse, but different. If the next Labour Government were to legislate to incorporate the E.C.H.R. into United Kingdom law it could and should also tackle a whole raft of problems by way of individual statutes targeted on specific topics. Such a programme is wholly consistent with having a Bill of Rights.

But the argument considered here is that a Bill of Rights is misconceived because powers that properly belong to the legislature are transferred to judges. It concerns legitimacy of decision-making. In its pure form this argument does not depend on the content of actual judicial decisions. It is founded rather on the

---

[24] In 1995 the European Court of Human Rights published *Survey of Thirty-five years of activity, 1959–1994*. This included a rather impressive 14 page report on action taken by respondent States in response to decisions of the court — see pp.70–83.

formal or theoretical point that, because the judges are not elected, they lack legitimacy in deciding the kinds of important issues that may occur in litigation under a Bill of Rights and, above all, in striking down legislation.

The argument does not proceed from the premise that the government represents the statistical majority of the electorate. In modern Britain it is rare for the government to have a majority of the popular vote.[25] Professor Keith Ewing and Professor Conor Gearty of King's College, London, who with Professor John Griffith are the most important exponents of the argument, put weight rather on the fact that a Bill of Rights would undermine what they suggest are three fundamental attributes of democracy — participation, representativeness and accountability.

> "In the first place it is properly assumed that a fundamental requirement of a democracy is that every adult person should be entitled to participate in the system of government . . . Secondly, the transfer of political power to the judges would undermine the principle that those who exercise political power should be representative of the community they serve . . . Thirdly, the introduction of a Bill of Rights would violate the principle that those who wield political power should be accountable to the community on whose behalf they purport to act when they exercise this power."[26]

"Participation" would be confined to "a handful of lawyers rather than be open to the community as a whole."[27] Worse, since access to law requires money and power "those who would be best able to play this game would be those, such as corporations, with lashings of both."[28] Judges are not representative either in the "strong" sense of being elected, or in the "weak" sense of being broadly typical of the composition of the community. The judges tend to be drawn disproportionately from a narrow social class, they are almost all male and white and they are of mature years. So far as concerns accountability "the judges are accountable to no one."[29]

> "So no matter how insensitive judges are in rape cases, no matter how politically hostile they are to trade unions, and no

[25] In 1979 the Conservatives won the General Election with 43.9 per cent of the vote. In 1983 and 1987 they won again with 42.4 per cent and 43.3 per cent of the vote. In 1992 they won with 41.9 per cent.

[26] K. D. Ewing and C. A. Gearty, *Democracy or a Bill of Rights* (1991), p.5–6. See also K. D. Ewing, "Human Rights, Social Democracy and Constitutional Reform" in C. A. Gearty and A. Tomkins, (eds.) *Understanding Human Rights* (1996) pp.40–59.

[27] K. D. Ewing and C. A. Gearty, *Democracy or a Bill of Rights* (1991), p.5.

[28] *Ibid.*

[29] *Ibid*, p.6.

matter how indifferent they are to the cause of liberty and freedom they are secure in their tenure — and this is regardless of whatever public outrage their performance might provoke ... The judges would operate as a kind of juristocracy, a body with extraordinary power without any political responsibility."[30]

If participation, representativeness and accountability are essential aspects of democracy and if decision-making on important social issues in a democracy should be in the hands of persons who have legitimacy in those terms, then plainly judges will not do at all. But the argument seems, to this writer at least, to be too simplistic. The contrast drawn between the unacceptable judges and the acceptable legislature is drawn in comic-book caricature style. Thus there is little reality in the notion that all adult persons participate in the system of government. All adults do not even participate in the sense of voting once every five or so years. But voting has little or nothing to do with governing. The process of government is in the hands of ministers and civil servants. Even M.P.s have little effective voice in the process of government. For the most part they are merely lobby-fodder who vote as they are told by the party Whips. If backbench M.P.s of the party in government have only a marginal role in the process of government, opposition M.P.s have none. The role of non-elected civil servants in the legislative process, through their work preparing the Bill and seeing it through all its stages in Parliament, is considerably greater than that of elected backbench M.P.s even on the government side.[31].

The fact that ordinary citizens cannot participate in the process of decision-making by judges is therefore a poor reason for not having a Bill of Rights. The reality is that a citizen is better able to activate the judicial than the legislative process. For the relatively modest fee required to issue a writ one can force even a Minister of the Crown to respond to one's grievance in a court of law. The political process affords the citizen no equivalent effective access to the Minister and decision-making. The gibe that "access to law requires money and power"[32] leaves out of account the availability of legal aid,[33] pro bono work for disadvantaged litigants by

---

[30] *Ibid.*
[31] See generally M. Zander, *The Law-Making Process,*(4th ed., 1994), chaps.1 and 2.
[32] Ewing and Gearty, *Democracy or a Bill of Rights* (1991), p.5.
[33] The future of the legal aid scheme is in doubt following Lord Mackay's dramatic White Paper, *Legal Aid Striking the Balance*, Cm 3305, July 1996. But despite all the uncertainties, it seems certain that there will still be very substantial sums of taxpayer's money available for supporting legal proceedings, including those brought under the system for multi-party actions.

practising lawyers[34] and the support of organisations like Liberty, JUSTICE, MIND, the Commission for Racial Equality, the Equal Opportunities Commission and other organisations able to sponsor and support test case litigation. Many of the cases that have reached Strasbourg have been brought with the help and support of such bodies. They would be likely to be involved in a significant number of cases brought under a Bill of Rights. The extensive use made of lobbyists by powerful interest groups suggests that it is access to legislation even more than access to the courts that requires money and power.

On the issue of "representativeness", it is true that judges are not representative of the community either in the sense of being elected or in the sense of reflecting the make-up of the community. But again the importance of the distinction is considerably over-drawn. Ministers are elected but most members of the electorate play no part whatever in the process of selection of candidates for General Elections. The electorate therefore has no real say in what particular individuals (as compared with the political Party) form the government. With the exception of the party leader and perhaps a few prominent party members, the vote in constituencies is rarely much affected by the strengths and weaknesses of individual candidates. The vote tends to reflect national trends in regard to policies and the "feel-bad factor", rather than what the electorate thinks of the candidates either individually or in aggregate. Also, to the extent that governmental decision-making is actually in the hands of non-elected civil servants, they are open to precisely the same objection of being as unrepresentative as the judges.

As to "accountability", it is perfectly true that judges cannot be dismissed because of their decisions. But that is broadly true of politicians as well — at least if one means dismissed or forced to resign as a result of what they do in their official capacity.[35] The fact that every five or so years the government has to face the electorate may or may not weigh on the minds of ministers in the context of day-to-day decision making. One suspects that for the most part it is a consideration that plays little or no part in their

[34] In June 1996, the Bar launched a new Pro Bono Unit. The unit holds the names of barristers willing to offer up to three days per year of their time to deserving cases in any field of law. At the launch it was stated that there were already some 300 barristers who had put their names on the register.

[35] In lectures given after publication of his Arms for Iraq Report, Sir Richard Scott has said that the only resignation in recent years arising out of what could be called Ministerial accountability of which he was aware was that of Lord Carrington after the outbreak of the Falkands War — and most people considered that it had not been required.

decisions. But even when the electorate exercises its power to "kick the rascals out", it seems more likely to be a judgment about their overall stewardship during a period of years rather than a comment on any particular decision.

Moreover, as has already been seen, insofar as worry about the views of the electorate does weigh, it is by no means necessarily a strength. The politician who is concerned about what the electorate may think will often trim on principle, whereas the judge who does not have to worry about being elected can act on principle without having to concern himself with the political consequences. When the Court of Appeal holds that the Minister acted unlawfully in depriving asylum seekers of their social security benefits, it is acting without regard to political consequences.[36] In other words, it is the unaccountable judge not the accountable minister who is better able to give a decision responsive to the principled issue of civil liberties. Since a high proportion of issues raised under a Bill of Rights are of just that kind — an unpopular minority affected by a decision of the authorities — this relative freedom of the judge by comparison with the constraints on the politician is not a trivial matter.

Professor Ewing and Dr Gearty make their point above all in regard to the possibility that under a Bill of Rights judges have a power to strike down legislation — which they suggest is unacceptable. This issue will be discussed below in the context of the argument about entrenchment — pp.111–112. But it is appropriate to indicate here that this point loses much of its force as soon as it is conceded that even under a Bill of Rights *ultimate* power internally should lie with the legislature. This is the position adopted under the Charter in Canada and seems to the writer to express the right balance between the proper respective role of the judges and of the legislature. However, it is also important to note in that regard that most cases brought under Bills of Rights do not raise the issue of striking down legislation. They pose not the question whether legislation is consistent with the Bill of Rights but whether the actions of ministers, civil servants and other public bodies and authorities are consistent with the Bill of Rights. When clashes between the courts and the legislature occur they are of course of importance, but to place so heavy an emphasis on one relatively small category of Bill of Rights litigation is to get its true significance out of perspective.

Plainly, whatever system one has will give rise to plenty of unsatisfactory results. The present system certainly does. Civil

---

[36] *R. v. Secretary of State for Social Security, ex p.Joint Council for the Welfare of Immigrants*, *The Times*, June 22, 1996, N.L.J. Law Reports, N.L.J. July 5, 1996, p.985.

libertarians in England who contemplate almost twenty years of Conservative Party rule from Mrs Thatcher's first victory in 1979 onwards are in considerable difficulties in arguing that the legislature is to be preferred to the judges as protector of civil liberties. The record over that period gives little comfort to anyone minded to advance such a proposition.

Ewing and Gearty in their book, *Freedom under Thatcher: Civil Liberties in Modern Britain,*[37] devote the first two hundred and fifty pages to telling what they paint as a dismal story. They start the final chapter: "It should by now be clear that civil liberties are in a state of crisis".[38] The chief reason, they suggest, "is a political system which has allowed the concentration of power in the hands of the executive (and the Prime Minister in particular) and the absence of any effective checks and balances".[39] They consider ways of addressing the problem — improved parliamentary scrutiny, a Human Rights Commission and a Bill of Rights. They concede that "there is indeed much to be said"[40] for incorporating the European Convention on Human Rights into United Kingdom law.

> "Apart from the fact that it could impose a major limitation on the arbitrary power of government, it would at the same time permit individuals to take steps to protect their political freedoms without having to take the long and tortuous road to Strasbourg."[41]

They concede that it was tempting to believe that the proposal should be adopted but, having considered the pros and cons, they come down against it. One reason is that it would leave "the final political decision, on say a woman's right to abortion, to be determined by a group of men appointed by the Prime Minister from a small and unrepresentative pool".[42] Another is that these appointed people, the judges, are not accountable. The third is that, because of the loosely drafted nature of a Bill of Rights the judges would have excessive freedom to determine the limits and scope of their own power.[43] They argue that the crisis in civil liberties "is much too serious to be met by glib proposals for the introduction of a bill of rights".[44] The need was for reforms that

[37] (1990).
[38] *Ibid*, p.255.
[39] *Ibid*.
[40] *Ibid*, p.263.
[41] *Ibid*.
[42] *Ibid*, p.268.
[43] Ewing and Gearty, *Freedom under Thatcher: Civil Liberties in Modern Britain,* (1990), p.268.
[44] *Ibid*, p.275.

would redress the balance of political power — electoral reform, devolution, an elected second chamber, reform of the judiciary and freedom of information — rather than cosmetic changes such as a Bill of Rights.

It is remarkable that, having analysed civil liberties as being in a state of crisis, Ewing and Gearty reject the potential of judicial decision under a Bill of Rights on the abstract, theoretical ground that the judges are unrepresentative and unaccountable — even though they concede that a Bill of Rights, in their words "could impose a major limitation on the arbitrary power of government". Given their principled objection to incorporation of the E.C.H.R. it is also odd that they (like Professor John Griffith) raise no objection to the fact that Britain can be made subject to proceedings brought in Strasbourg. If it is undemocratic and therefore unacceptable to allow English judges to decide matters of consequence, why is it not even more undemocratic and therefore even more unacceptable to allow such matters to be decided by judges from a variety of European countries?

As for Ewing and Gearty's preference for electoral reform, devolution, an elected chamber, reform of the judiciary and freedom of information, I would gladly exchange them all for a domestic Bill of Rights. A Bill of Rights, has a far better prospect of delivering worthwhile results.

It is not appropriate for judges to be deciding what laws are "necessary in a democratic society"

This issue, a variant of the previous topic, is one frequently addressed by Professor John Griffith. In its simplest and most direct form it comes down to the statement, "I do not want judges to have the power to decide what laws are necessary in a democratic society."[45] The phrase "necessary in a democratic society" appears repeatedly in the E.C.H.R.[46] and Griffith's point at first sight has considerable force. All persons of sound judgment must surely agree that what laws are necessary in a democratic

---

[45] J. A. G. Griffith, "Judicial Decision-Making in Public Law" (1985) Pub.L. 564, at 582.

[46] Thus Art.8 dealing with the right to respect for private and family life says that there shall be no interference by a public authority with this right "except such as is in accordance with the law and is necessary in a democratic society in the interests of national security, public safety or the economic well-being of the country, for the prevention of disorder or crime, for the protection of health or morals, or for the protection of the rights and freedoms of others". See also Arts. 9, 10, 11 in the Appendix below.

society is a matter for the legislature, not the courts. It sounds unanswerable.

But when examined the statement is less impressive. If the word "laws" is taken to mean statute law, the proposition is trite. Clearly only the legislature can pass statutes. No one suggests otherwise. If, however, the proposition refers to rules of law, it is obvious that the judges have an important role to play in the development of the common law. They have been playing this role for centuries and will continue to do so. In the process of deciding issues of law that come before them the judges unavoidably have to make value judgments. They do so in deciding whether to treat an earlier decision binding,[47] whether to follow precedent that is not binding[48] and generally in the fashioning of the rules of law. They do so equally in deciding on the interpretation of statutes.[49] When a point of law comes up for decision the court has to decide what the law "is", not what it ought to be. But to the extent that the court has freedom to decide what the law is (for instance because the precedents are not binding), the decision is likely to include an assessment by the court of what the law ought to be.[50] In other words, the judge is permitted to take into account, amongst many other things, what he personally thinks the law on that point should be. The phrase "what laws are necessary[51] in a democratic society" is essentially the same as the question "what laws are sensible in the society we happen to live in". That question is considered by judges every time they have to decide a point of law where there is enough to be said on both sides of the argument to give the court a real choice.

The judges cannot be trusted to get it right

There is a related but different issue which is focussed not so much on issues of general principle or on the specifics of actual judicial decisions. That is the argument either that judges (or at least British judges) are too executive or Establishment minded or that they are insufficiently sensitive to the real issues. The first is a concern traditionally voiced in Britain by the political Left. The

---

[47] See M. Zander, *The Law-Making Process* (4th ed., 1994), Chap. 4 and pp.259–274.
[48] *Ibid*, 274–279 and Chap. 7.
[49] *Ibid*, Chap. 3.
[50] *Ibid*, pp.346–350.
[51] So, for instance, the United Kingdon lost the *Golder* case [1975] 1 E.H.H.R. 524 about the rule restricting access to a solicitor for prisoners because it could not show that such a rule was "necessary". Several European countries seemed to manage without such a rule.

second is a concern expressed most often by civil servants and politicians.

Until recently it has been an article of faith of the political Left that judges were not to be trusted with any important issues affecting the fate of the ordinary man.[52] The intellectual foundation for this view was provided by Professor John Griffith, then of the London School of Economics, in his book *The Politics of the Judiciary*, first published in 1977.[53] He argued that careful analysis of the case law in fields such as police powers, race relations, immigration and deportation, industrial relations, conspiracy laws, students and property matters showed that the judges generally tended to take "the wrong side". He criticised the bench for its "tenderness toward private property and dislike of trade unions, strong adherence to the maintenance of order, distaste for minority opinions, demonstrations and protests, the avoidance of conflict with Government policy even where it is manifestly oppressive of the most vulnerable, support of governmental secrecy, concern for the moral and social behaviour to which it is accustomed."[54] This was not, however, because the judges were products of a capitalist system — rather it was a function of the role of judges in any society. ("In both democratic and totalitarian societies, the judiciary has naturally served the prevailing political and economic forces".[55]) His thesis, he said, was that governments represent stability and had a considerable interest in preserving it. This was true of all governments of all political complexions, democratic and authoritarian alike.

"Whenever governments or their agencies are acting to preserve that stability — call it the Queen's peace, or law and

[52] See for instance, the speech Mr Michael Foot, then Lord President of the Council, made to the Union of Post Office Workers at its weekend conference on May 14, 1977. "If the freedom of the people of this country — and especially the rights of trade unionists — had been left to the good sense and fair-mindedness of judges, we would have precious few freedoms in this country" — *The Guardian*, May 16, 1977. When the Labour Prime Minister was asked for his reaction on May 16 in the House of Commons, Mr Callaghan replied that he did not think that Mr Foot had been criticising the judges. Rather he had engaged in a historical exegesis. "Frankly I do not think that he went far enough. What he should have said is that trade unionists are enmeshed, harassed, worried and checked at every turn by all kinds of legal decisions." If only Mr Foot had used these words of Sir Winston Churchill he would have been more in agreement with him. (See, similarly, Sir Winston Churchill's view cited in n.28, p.106 below.)
[53] See now 4th ed., 1991. A new edition is due to be published in 1997.
[54] *Ibid*, p.319. In the 2nd edition the list included also "indifference to the promotion of better race relations" (p.230) — but this has been dropped, presumably because Professor Griffith no longer thinks that it applies.
[55] *Ibid*, p.328.

order, or the rule of law, or whatever — the judges will lend their support and will not be over concerned if to do so requires the invasion of individual liberty".[56]

Professor Griffith's view that the judges will too often tend to favour the Establishment or the authorities is shared by Professor Ewing and Professor Gearty:

"Many of the restrictions on political freedom which have taken place in the 1980s have not been as a result of legislation but have been judge-made initiatives authorising the extension of executive power. Some of the most significant restrictions on the freedom of assembly, freedom of movement and the freedom of the press were imposed by the courts."[57]

But this pessimistic view pays insufficient regard to factors pointing in a different direction. First, it ignores the extent to which the record of the English judges is far from uniform. Secondly, in each of the four editions of his book, Professor Griffith has argued that his basic thesis applies to the way judges perform their role in *any* society. If that is so, he does not explain how it was that over a period of several decades the federal judges in the United States used both the Bill of Rights and the common law to develop significantly better protection of many disadvantaged groups including blacks, the poor, prisoners, civil rights demonstrators and other minority interests. The record of the United States federal judiciary from the 1960s, though mixed, has nevertheless been quite impressive. No doubt the Supreme Court under Chief Justice Earl Warren was more "liberal" than that of Chief Justice Burger, which may in turn have been more liberal than the Rhenquist court. To this extent, the thesis that judges, by definition, are broadly unsympathetic to civil liberties issues is shown to be false.[58] There is therefore evidence that judges *per se* are not beyond redemption. It obviously does not follow that English judges would "do well" on civil liberties problems but the *a priori* position adopted by John Griffith on the basis of the innate characteristics of the function of judging does not seem convincing.

The view that English judges would be likely not to do well with civil liberties cases finds much support in the cases going back over

---

[56] *Ibid*, p.323.

[57] Ewing and Gearty, *Freedom under Thatcher: Civil Liberties in Modern Britain* (1990), p.270 and generally pp.271–274.

[58] Ewing and Gearty, by contrast, concede that "in some countries, the courts have, on some issues, played a helpful role in the development of social progress and in the safeguarding of civil liberties", *ibid*, at p.270. They cite in particular the decisions of the Warren Supreme Court.

the past few decades. But there are also many cases that suggest the contrary.[59] In recent years the judges' "civil liberties record", especially perhaps in the important field of judicial review, has been healthier[60] — which is no doubt one of the reasons why important bodies that previously opposed the idea of a Bill of Rights changed their mind. Liberty and the Labour Party are the most significant examples. During the years of Conservative Government from the time of Mrs Thatcher's election in 1979, the Left came to appreciate the importance of the judicial role, as over and over again judges struck down decisions of Tory Ministers. Dr Robert Stevens, Master of Pembroke College, Oxford, has referred to the recent "expansion of judicial review to provide an extensive

[59] The 3rd edition of this work had several pages (pp.52–57) setting out a brief account of some of the more celebrated cases pointing in both directions. They have been dropped here simply to economise on space.

[60] See, however, John Griffith's letter to the *London Review of Books* (LRB), May 9, 1996 responding to an article by Anthony Lester in the same publication of April 18, 1996 in which Lester said that the senior judiciary and their case law "have changed beyond recognition over the past thirty years" and that they were to be trusted. Griffith cited as evidence to the contrary a number of recent cases on freedom of expression: "In *British Steel Corporation v. Granada Television* (1980) the Law Lords ruled that journalists' sources must be revealed. In *Schering Chemicals* (1981) the Court of Appeal injuncted the showing of a film on Thames Television. In *Home Office v. Harman* (1982) the Lord Lords held the legal officer of the National Council for Civil Liberties to be in contempt of court for showing a journalist material that had already been disclosed in open court. In *Defence Secretary v. Guardian Newspapers* (1984) the Court of Appeal ordered the disclosure of journalists' sources about the date when Cruise missiles were to be delivered, leading to arrest and imprisonment of Sara Tisdall. The Law Lords upheld the order. There followed the *Spycatcher* saga and the refusal of the Law Lords to lift the injunction on publication although the book was readily available in this country. In 1986–87 the BBC programmes *Out of Court, The Secret Society, Rough Justice* and *My Country Right or Wrong* were the subject of judicial injunction or criticism. Finally in the most blatant invasion of free speech this century, the Law Lords upheld the Court of Appeal's refusal to review the Home Secretary's decision to ban from the BBC and independent broadcasting words spoken by representatives of legitimate political organisations in Northern Ireland: *ex parte Brind*."

In his reply (LRB, August 1,1996), Lord Lester said he agreed with Professor Griffith's criticism of those cases but suggested that his list was "seriously incomplete"

He cited: cases like *Spycatcher* on the merits (1990), *Derbyshire County Council v. Times Newspapers* (1993), *Esther Rantzen v. Mirror Group* (1994), *Elton John v. MGN* (1995) and *George Blake* (1996).

Lord Lester also said he did not understand how Professor Griffith could both object to the decision in *ex p.Brind* and oppose incorporation of the E.C.H.R. In *ex p. Brind* the Law Lords decided that they could not incorporate the E.C.H.R. through the back door when Parliament had refused to do so through the front door. If the House of Lords had applied the E.C.H.R. to the broadcasting ban, it would have usurped the powers of Parliament by making the E.C.H.R. part of United Kingdom law.

87

power for the courts to intervene in procedural due process over a wide range of public and quasi-public matters, and, by subtle use of the so-called *Wednesbury* doctrine, to provide a hint of control of substantive due process".[61] Many different Government departments felt the impact of these decisions but:

> "Once again, the Home Secretary has borne the brunt of this assault — where he found his efforts to reform sentencing,[62] the criminal injuries compensation programme,[63] barring the Moonie leader[64] and attempting to deport a Saudi dissident thwarted by the judges.[65] John Major has had a speech to Scotland banned from television by Lord Abernathy and the Foreign Secretary was forced to restructure the Foreign Aid programme after the judges found he had taken into account inappropriate criteria in the *Pergau Dam* case."[66]

In June 1996, the Court of Appeal struck down the regulations introduced by the Secretary of State for Social Services depriving asylum victims of social security entitlements[67] — a ruling that the Government reversed almost immediately.[68] In July 1996 the Court of Appeal held that the Home Secretary had acted unfairly in the way that he set the tariff sentence for the two killers of James Bulger.[69]

In his lecture and subsequent published paper, Dr Robert Stevens cited the claim in the Beaverbrook Press that there was "a

[61] Originally delivered as the 1996 Hardwicke Building Lecture, the text was subsequently revised for publication in the forthcoming *festschrift* in honour of Don Harris of the Oxford Socio-Legal Centre. I am indebted to Dr Stevens for supplying me with copies of both texts and for allowing me to quote from them.

[62] See also the excitement when the appeal courts refused to allow him to extend the sentence of the child murderers of James Bulger. "Howard acted unlawfully over Bulger sentences" and "Ruling further weakens minister's powers over judiciary", *The Times*, May 3, 1996; "Howard furious at Bulger ruling", *The Independent*, May 3,1996. "Mr Howard is playing with fire" (editorial), *ibid*.

[63] *R. v. Secretary of State for the Home Department, ex p.Fire Brigades Union* [1995] 2 A.C. 513.

[64] *R. v. Secretary of State for the Home Department, ex p.Moon*, 1 November 1995; "Judicial Moonshine: Howard was right to refuse Moon entry to Britain", *The Times*, November 3, 1995.

[65] "Judge tells Howard to reconsider Masari case", *The Independent*, March 6, 1994.

[66] *R. v. Secretary of State for Foreign and Commonwealth Affairs, ex p.World Development Movement Limited* [1995] 1 W.L.R.386 D.C.

[67] *R. v. Secretary of State for Social Security, ex p.Joint Council for the Welfare of Immigrants*; and the same *ex p.B* — see NLJ Law Reports, N.L.J., July 5, 1996, p.985.

[68] The new rules introduced by the Government were defeated in the House of Lords but the Government insisted and reversed the House of Lords amendment - see *The Times*, July 16, 1996.

[69] *R. v. Secretary of State for the Home Department, ex p.Venables and Thompson*, *The Times*, August 7, 1996.

sickness sweeping through the senior judiciary — galloping arrogance,"[70] singling out Mr Justice Dyson ("While European Human Rights Judges, some from countries which once sent political prisoners to Siberia, are venting their spleen on Britain, legal weevils here at home are practising their own brand of mischief."[71] The *Daily Mail* joined in: "Now it seems that any judge can take it on himself to overrule a minister, even though Parliament might approve the minister's action. This is to arrogate power to themselves in a manner that makes a mockery of Parliament" and the *Daily Mail* suggested that the judges were "acting on a political agenda of their own."[72]

There were of course still plenty of decisions that civil libertarians could deplore, but the overall balance seemed to have shifted and in the mid-1990s the current "mood music" seemed to derive more from the Right's concern that the judges were overreaching themselves and being too interventionist than from the Left's concern that the judges were too supine in the face of the executive.[73]

If the Left's worst fears were proved correct and the judges did consistently decide Bill of Rights cases so as to benefit the strong against the weak, sooner or later the Bill of Rights would be scrapped. The experiment would have failed. What seems more likely, however, is that the pendulum would swing somewhat from period to period. If it were felt to have swung too far in one period, it would probably tend to correct itself in the next. Corrective pressure would come from both outside and inside the system — from lay and professional criticism, appointment of new judges, test cases brought on behalf of the discontented and the general climate of opinion.

Also, whatever was the prevailing judicial attitude regarding the Bill of Rights at the outset, it is inevitable that the process set in train by its enactment would be a major force for educating the judges in the values implicit in a more "civil liberties" oriented approach to the law. It would not happen overnight, nor would it be true at all times or for all judges. But there would be a better

[70] *Daily Express*, November 4, 1995.
[71] *Sunday Express*, October 1, 1995.
[72] *Daily Mail*, November 2, 1995.
[73] See Andrew Le Sueur, "The Judicial Review Debate: From Partnership to Friction" (1996) 31 Govt. and Opp.8–26. See also Nicola Lacey, "Are Rights Best Left Unwritten?", (1989) 60 Pol.Qtrly.433. Writing from a socialist perspective, Lacey states that she found herself "on balance in favour of a Bill of Rights" (p.434). "The central preoccupation of the Left must be with gaining democratic political power. But it does not destroy the case for the modest improvements to the lot of the disadvantaged that a Bill of Rights might make"(p.440).

hope of such a development with the Bill of Rights than without it. Also, unfortunate decisions rendered by the judges could be set right in the first instance by the legislature by whatever method was prescribed for amendments to the Bill of Rights. There would also continue to be the monitoring and controlling influence of the right of further appeal to the Strasbourg court.

The suspicions about the Bill of Rights project on the part of some of those on the Left are, to some extent, based on a view of the world that is simply inconsistent with the protection of human rights. This element in radical thinking proceeds on the basis that the individual must, if necessary, be sacrificed to the greater good of Society or the People — with a capital "S" or "P". Democracy, of course, recognises the potency of a majority. But the traditional liberal democratic view, if true to itself, should not countenance oppressive conduct by the majority against the minority.

Professor H. L. A. Hart said democracy did not mean that the majority have a moral right to dictate how all should live.[74] Hart said that the central mistake was the failure to distinguish the acceptable principle that political power is best entrusted to the majority from the unacceptable claim that what the majority do with that power is beyond criticism and must never be resisted. Anthony Lester made this point at the outset of his 1968 pamphlet:

> "When democracy degenerates into populism, it becomes a weapon of arbitrary power against individuals and minorities, the 'tyranny of the majority' about which John Stuart Mill gave his celebrated warning: 'the will of the people . . . practically means the will of the most numerous or active of the people: . . . the people, consequently may desire to oppress a part of their number: and precautions are as much needed against this as against any other abuse of power. The limitation, therefore, of the power of government over individuals loses none of its importance when the holders of power are regularly accountable to the community, that is, to the strongest party therein.' "[75]

Democratic socialists, Mr Lester said, were especially vulnerable to the populist fallacy in an age of mass communications and opinion polls. Without being in any way opposed to strong government or collective power "there is no reason why a government which is accountable to the popular will or expeditious in despatching its business should not also be fair to the individual citizen".[76] This principle commands overwhelming support in most Western democracies, including our own.

[74] H. L. A. Hart, *Law, Liberty and Morality* (1963) p.79.
[75] Lester, *Democracy and Individual Rights,* (1968), p.1.
[76] *Ibid,* p.2.

Also, although a Bill of Rights would transfer significant power to the judges, it would leave much more significant powers in the legislature. The precise limits of the subject matter of the Bill of Rights obviously are a matter for discussion. But however wide, most of the major economic and social issues of the day would remain, for decision by the legislature.

The European Convention on Human Rights, for instance, guarantees to all the peaceful enjoyment of his possessions.

> "No-one shall be deprived of his possessions except in the public interest and subject to the conditions provided for by the law and by the general principles of international law. The preceding provision shall not, however, in any way impair the right of a State to enforce such laws as it deems necessary to control the use of property in accordance with the general interest or to secure the payment of taxes or other contributions or penalties."[77]

Some have suggested that enactment of a Bill of Rights would prevent a Government from enacting legislation providing for, say, compulsory purchase of housing, or slum clearance or steep rates of taxation. But there is nothing in the European Convention to justify such views. There is ample protection for a government concerned to nationalise industries or redistribute income, say, by a wealth tax,[78] to do so consistently with the E.C.H.R. What might not be permitted, however, is nationalisation of the property of aliens without compensation,[79] or the seizure of accrued rights to social security payments at least under a system where contributions are related to benefits.[80]

The question, therefore, is not whether the courts will sometimes arrive at interpretations that are unacceptable to this or that group in the community — governors or governed — but whether any group or groups will be especially and consistently victimised. Will the overall balance be tolerably fair, or will it not? Will the benefits to be derived from a Bill of Rights outweigh the disadvantages? Will the judges persistently decide cases under the Bill of Rights to the disadvantage of minority interests? There are undoubtedly those who fear that this may be so. The judges, they say, are broadly middle and upper class. They share many of the values

---

[77] First Protocol, Art. 1, see Appendix below.
[78] See case 511/59, *Gudmundson v. Iceland Human Rights Yearbook* (1960) 394.
[79] It is ironical that Article 1 of the First Protocol appears to condone seizure without compensation from nationals whilst clearly condemning such seizure from aliens, who are covered by existing international law.
[80] See 4288/69, *Human Rights Yearbook*, 13, p.892; 4130/69 European Convention, *Collection of Decisions*, 38, p.9.

typically held by those in government and in senior positions in the civil service. Minority rights are uncongenial to judges, especially when they are those of groups who are thought to represent dissident or disaffected groups — students, squatters, demonstrators, prisoners, drug addicts, gypsies, mental patients. If these fears were realised the position of such groups would be worse rather than better under a Bill of Rights. This would be the more so since adverse decisions given in the course of interpreting a Bill of Rights would have even more than the usual authority — simply because of the special aura surrounding a Bill of Rights.

The belief that "the judges cannot be trusted to get it right" is held, as has been said, not only by some on the political Left, but, from a different vantage point, in the civil service and amongst government ministers. When judges strike down acts of the executive it is not uncommon for those in Whitehall to feel that they rather than the judges know best. Such feelings are understandable given that it is the job of ministers and civil servants to run things. It is hardly surprising that they may come to believe that they are the people best able to reconcile conflicting interests and to devise the most effective solutions to problems. Judges, by comparison, are largely ignorant of crucial matters such as the availability and disposition of resources, and the implications of choosing one solution over another. But it does not follow that giving the judges the referee's whistle is wrong.

The civil servant's guide to judicial review — *The Judge Over Your Shoulder* — written by the Treasury Solicitor's Department in conjunction with the Cabinet Office, suggested in its 1987 first edition that judicial review was not simply mysterious and complicated but a nuisance which unnecessarily got in the way of administrative processes. It seemed almost to be suggesting that the right approach was to do what one could get away with. However, the second edition, published in 1994, adopted a more positive tone, placing strong emphasis on the role of law in promoting good administration: " . . . judicial review and the principles of administrative law that underlie it is a part of the whole process of good administration". The judge was there "to ensure that those affected by our decisions are treated fairly: there are no shortcuts or magic formulae to evade the Court's supervision and to attempt to give any would not be in the spirit of the principles of good administration that the citizen has the right to expect from us". The pamphlet refers to European Community law and urges that immediate legal advice be taken on any issue raising such questions. But, curiously, there is no mention of the European Convention on Human Rights.

There can be no doubt that dealing with the litigation in Strasbourg creates many difficulties for Whitehall, especially when

the court rules against the government. Incorporation of the
E.C.H.R. into United Kingdom law would create many more
problems. It is therefore not to be expected that civil servants and
ministers will ever come to regard the introduction of a domestic
Bill of Rights as a blessing. Its main purpose, after all, is to limit
and control decision-making by all manifestations of public authority, of whom civil servants and ministers are the most important
exemplars. They are unlikely to welcome this.

*The professional outlook of judges regarding law-making is not
conducive to good decision-making under a Bill of Rights*

There is a view that the English judiciary is temperamentally and
professionally not fitted to the demands of a Bill of Rights. A Bill
of Rights demands a capacity to handle broad statements of
principle. The tradition of English judges is to hug closely to the
shores of literal meanings and to eschew the "unruly horse" of
public policy. This objection is founded on a number of related
arguments:

(a) English judges carry to extremes the tendency to write
    their judgements in such a way as to make it seem that
    the decision is the result either of inexorable logic or of
    the self-impelling momentum of the precedents. In either
    case, the judge seems to say he has had little or no
    control over the outcome. But this is mere pretence or
    form. The reality is that, as has been said above, the
    judges exercise considerable discretion in performing the
    law-making function.[81]

(b) Some English judges object if counsel tries to argue
    openly what the law should be ("We are here to decide
    what the law *is*, not what it ought to be"). Judges who put
    forward this view reveal their own ignorance of the
    nature of the judicial process.[82] The belief that judges do
    not *make* law was described by Austin over a hundred
    years ago as a childish fiction. Today it is impossible to
    sustain, if only in light of the statement in 1966 by the
    House of Lords that it would, in appropriate circum-
    stances, decline to follow its own decisions.[83] If the House
    of Lords changes its mind on a rule of law it must be
    because it has fashioned a new rule. The fact that two

[81] See generally M. Zander, *The Law-Making Process* (4th ed., 1994) especially
Chap. 7.
[82] *Ibid*, pp.346–350.
[83] Practice Statement (Judicial Precedent)[1966] 1 W.L.R. 1234.

sides, represented by lawyers, have come to court to contest a point of law means, almost by definition, that there is an arguable issue which could go either way. It may be that the court is bound by a precedent or that the weight of technical reasoning strongly suggests the answer, but frequently, if not normally, the court could quite respectably decide the question either way. Which way it goes will often then be influenced by its (conscious or unconscious) preferences. Once this fundamental point is appreciated it becomes impossible to pretend that judges do not exercise choice and value judgments in reaching their decisions.

(c) The English situation is made the worse where the courts are reluctant to go outside the narrow confines of the technical question. In interpreting statutes, for instance, the judges traditionally refused to look not merely at Parliamentary debates, but even at the reports of law reform bodies which propose and often prepare the legislation.[84] But this attitude has recently been transformed — notably by the House of Lords' decision in *Pepper v. Hart*[85] holding that the courts can look at Parliamentary debates at least when there is a clear statement by a Minister on the point of statutory interpretation at issue.

(d) The traditional, literal approach to interpretation is another example. In the past the dominant approach to statutory interpretation was to construe an ambiguous text (whether in a statute or a will, contract or other document) as if the use of language was almost like mathematics, capable of right and wrong answers.[86] If the draftsman has been inept, the court rejects his effort and tells him to try to do better next time. ("It is not for the court to write the document". "We can see what was meant but the words used failed to give it expression".[87] "If Parliament had meant that, it would have said so".)

---

[84] See especially *Black-Clawson International Ltd v. Papierwerke Waldhof-- Aschaffenberg AG* [1975] A.C.591.

[85] [1993] 1 All E.R.42 and M. Zander, *The Law-Making Process* (4th ed., 1994), at pp.147–157.

[86] *e.g. Fisher v. Bell* [1961] 1 Q.B. 394 in which the Divisional Court managed to hold that a flick knife in a shop window had not been "offered for sale" because under the technical law of contract it was only an "invitation to treat".

[87] See, for instance, *Re Rowland* [1963] Ch. 1 in which a majority of the Court of Appeal refused to give the commonsense interpretation to a provision in a will because, *although they agreed on the intended meaning*, the words used were not quite apt to express it!

In applying the literal approach, the court often denies the existence of any ambiguity even when the existence of an ambiguity is obvious from the very fact that there are two opposing parties before the court. Sometimes, even more absurdly, several judges say that the meaning of the words used is so clear as not to require interpretation — yet they disagree as to what the clear, obvious or literal meaning is.[88] But in recent years this traditional approach has begun to change. Increasingly the courts speak of adopting the "purposive approach" to statutory interpretation, giving effect to what may be assumed to have been the legislature's intention. The search for the purpose of the statute fuelled the House of Lords 6-1 decision in *Pepper v. Hart*:

> "The days have long passed when the courts adopted a strict constructionist view of interpretation which required them to adopt the literal meaning of the language. The courts now adopt a purposive approach which seeks to give effect to the true purpose of legislation and are prepared to look at much extraneous material that bears on the background against which the legislation was enacted."[89]

(e) Another example is the virtual absence in English courts of arguments on points of law based on factual data — economic, social, or other relevant material. In the United States such argument has been a familiar part of legal disputation since the famous "Brandeis brief" in 1907. The later Supreme Court Justice argued the constitutionality of Oregon legislation limiting hours of work for women by producing data drawn from hundreds of reports designed to show that as a matter of fact long hours were dangerous to women's health, safety and morals and that shorter hours resulted in social and economic benefits. The strictly legal argument took less than two pages, the factual data occupied over a hundred pages of Brandeis' brief. The court accepted the argument and based its decision on his reasoning.[90]

---

[88] See, for instance, *London & Northern Eastern Ry Co. Ltd v. Berriman* [1946] A.C. 278 in which Lord Macmillan and Lord Wright reached opposite conclusions on the fair and ordinary meaning of the word "repairing". For criticism of the literal approach generally, see the Law Commission, *Interpretation of Statutes*, 1969 and M. Zander, *The Law-Making Process* (4th ed., 1994), pp.121–129.

[89] [1993] 1 All E.R. 42, *per* Lord Griffiths at 50.

[90] Alpheus Thomas Mason, *Brandeis* (1956), pp.248–251 — excerpted in M. Zander, *The Law-Making Process,* (4th ed., 1994), p.277.

In English courts such argument would simply not be presented[91] — partly because the court would deny its relevance, partly because counsel would in any event find it difficult to marshal the data. Argument in an English case is normally limited to discussion of the statutes and precedents, and what counsel on either side can add, through reasoning by analogy, "common sense" and assertion of the consequences of adopting alternative views. ("The result of following the view urged by my learned friend would, in my submission, be inconvenient, unjust, or wrong, whereas if the courts adopt our client's approach the law will be cast in sensible terms.")

(f) A final example of the alleged inappropriateness of English judicial procedures to a Bill of Rights is the reluctance of English courts to accept argument save from the parties. It is a familiar part of United States judicial argument that interested and expert bodies may, with the permission of the court, participate in litigation between third parties by submitting written arguments. The *amicus* brief from, say, the National Association for the Advancement of Coloured People, the American Civil Liberties Union, the American Legion or other similar groups has played a major seminal role in the development of the law.[92] The concept of the *amicus* is known to English procedure mainly as a means of permitting the Attorney-General to argue "the public interest" in rare cases, and then often at the instance of the court. Interested private bodies, however expert and however much they might be able to contribute to the court's understanding of the problem before it, are not normally permitted to intervene — though there are cases in which bodies like the Law Society, the Equal Opportunities Commission or the Commission for Racial Equality have been allowed or even invited to appear as *amicus*.[93] In *R. v. Khan (Sultan)*[94] the House of Lords

---

[91] For a rare exception, see *Hanning v. Maitland* (No. 2) [1970] 1 Q.B. 580 in which the Court of Appeal reversed its interpretation of the Legal Aid Act 1964, largely it seems because of statistics regarding the result of its previous view.

[92] See Ernest Angell, "The Amicus Curiae: American Developments of English Institutions" (1967) 16 I.C.L.Q. 1017.

[93] See for instance *Woodard v. Woodard and Curt* [1959] 1 All E.R. 641; *Re S.L. (Infants)* [1967] 1 W.L.R. 1379 and other cases cited in *Matthews and Oulton on Legal aid and Advice* (1971), p.447, n. 20. See also *E. Coomes (Holding) Ltd v. Shields* [1979] 1 All E.R. 456; *Nasse v. Science Research Council; Vyas v. Leyland Cars Ltd* [1979] Q.B. 144; and M. Zander, *The Law-Making Process* (4th ed., 1994), pp.359–360.

[94] [1996] 3 All E.R. 289.

permitted Liberty (formerly the National Council for Civil Liberties) to intervene with a 40-page submission drafted by a Q.C. regarding the relevance of the E.C.H.R. to section 78 of the Police and Criminal Evidence Act.

At least one reason is that the English courts have only recently begun to see the value of written argument to supplement oral advocacy. But today skeleton written argument on points of law presented by the parties have become the rule,[95] and it would not be a giant step to allow third party intervention with permission of the court (and perhaps the parties[96]) through written briefs.

The above objections amount to a strong case and it would be wrong to pretend that there are any easy answers to the doubts they raise.

To give English judges the responsibility for interpreting a broad Bill of Rights would unquestionably be a risk. There have been too many examples of their adopting a needlessly restrictive approach both to legislation and to developing the common law. Nevertheless, there are reasons for thinking that the risk may be worth taking.

First, a Bill of Rights has to be judged over the long run — decades or even longer. What happens in the first few years is only of real importance if it has a significant impact on the eventual course of events. In the United States, it was a very long time before the Supreme Court gave expression to many of the rights enshrined in the Bill of Rights, which itself dates from the end of the eighteenth century.[97] Judge Skelly Wright has indicated the date of the decisions in which the Supreme Court vindicated some of the most significant express guarantees of the Bill of Rights — free exercise of religion (1940); freedom of speech (1927); freedom of the press (1931); freedom of assembly (1937); freedom of petition (1939); speedy trial (1955); public trial (1948); right to counsel (1932), etc.[98] Until well into the twentieth century, the

---

[95] See M. Zander, *The Law-Making Process* (4th ed., 1994), pp.364–372.

[96] In *R. v. Khan* [1996] 3 All E.R. 289 both sides had stated that they had no objection to Liberty submitting a written argument as *amicus*.

[97] The Bill of Rights was not part of the original Constitution of the United States which dates from 1789. But the first ten articles of the Bill of Rights were adopted in 1791 as the first ten amendments to the Constitution, as a *quid pro quo* for States' acceptance of the remainder of the Constitution — See further Justice Brennan of the Supreme Court giving the H. L. A. Hart Lecture "Why Have a Bill of Rights?", Oxford, May 24, 1989. Further significant additions were the thirteenth Amendment in 1865 (abolition of slavery), the fourteenth Amendment in 1870 (votes for black persons), and the nineteenth Amendment in 1920 (votes for women).

[98] Skelly Wright, "The Bill of Rights in Britain and America: A Not Quite Full Circle" (1981) 55 Tul.L Rev. 291, 311–312.

record of the United States judges under the Bill of Rights was less than distinguished.

Obviously, one would hope that it would not take English judges several decades to warm to a Bill of Rights. If that were to be so it is safe to predict that the project would be doomed to failure. But the recent history of the Charter of Rights in Canada and of the Bill of Rights in New Zealand suggest that there is reason to suppose that that would not be the case. As will be seen the experience in both Canada and New Zealand is that the judges there have been very ready to use the new tools. Even Ewing and Gearty, who vigorously oppose the whole Bill of Rights project, concede that the Canadian Charter "has been enthusiastically embraced by the courts"[99] — but they predict that the same would not happen here. In Canada, the Charter was adopted after a lengthy period of political preparation as part of the very popular package of constitutional reform introduced to general acclamation by Prime Minister Pierre Trudeau. The process has recently been described by Professor Roland Penner Q.C., former Attorney-General of Manitoba:

> "During nationally televised hearings of a joint parliamentary committee, over 1,000 individuals and 300 groups petitioned for changes and additions to the draft Charter of Rights and Freedoms. The Committee, after 60 days of hearings, successfully proposed to Parliament some 65 substantial amendments to the Government draft."[1]

Commentators had noted that "the widespread public response to the Charter's composition amazed government and opposition alike"[2] Professor Penner continued:

> "When Madam Justice Beverley McLachlin of the Canadian Supreme Court suggested in September 1994 in an unpublished speech that from the beginning the people took the Charter up and the judges gave it real substance, it seems to me she was saying in effect the judges gave it real substance *because* the people took it up. And this may well be the most important lesson to be learned from the Canadian experience. A minimalist bill of rights passed quietly, purely as a parliamentary measure without popular backing and substantial consensus, may not be given its full weight by a cautious judiciary."[3]

[99] Ewing and Gearty, *Freedom Under Thatcher: Civil Liberties in Modern Britain*, (1990), p.266.
[1] Roland Penner, "The Canadian Experience with the Charter of Rights: Are there Lessons for the United Kingdom?" (1996) Pub.L. 104, 107.
[2] R. Sheppard and M. Valpy, *The National Deal* (1982) p.135.
[3] Penner, *op. cit.*, 107.

In New Zealand the process was, however, very different. First, in 1985, a broadly based Bill of Rights was proposed by the government in a White Paper . The proposal was referred to the Justice and Law Reform Parliamentary Select Committee. The Committee received 304 written and 107 oral submissions. Its report[4] stated: "A clear majority of submissions were opposed to the bill of rights proposal" (page 8). As a result, the Government eventually introduced a considerably watered down version of a Bill of Rights which became the New Zealand Bill of Rights Act 1990.

But despite its attenuated form the judges have shown themselves ready to give it teeth. Thus the 1990 Act provides for no entrenchment and no remedy for a breach of the Bill of Rights. In the first case argued under the Act the District Court judge said: "In the absence of constitutional entrenchment and the omission of any remedies clause it would be inappropriate for this Court to provide a prosthesis for a statute that is more crippled than debilitated".[5] But in the succeeding four years there was a major sea-change of opinion. According to Justice Silvia Cartwright of the New Zealand High Court, "The Court of Appeal has seized this Act, rescued it from imminent oblivion and emphasised its significance for the general body of New Zealand law".[6] The court had emphasised that "the Bill of Rights is intended to be woven into the fabric of New Zealand law";[7] and that "it is to be construed generously" and in a manner "suitable to give to individuals the full measure of fundamental rights and freedoms referred to"[8]. The Court of Appeal, she said, had "resoundingly supported the development of the law where it relates to fundamental rights and freedom and has declared that "primacy be given to the vindication of human rights"[9]. This, she said, was despite the fact that "this was not at all what was contemplated during the political debate which led to the enactment of the New Zealand Bill of Rights Act".

If the next Labour Government were to legislate to incorporate the European Convention on Human Rights, it might introduce such legislation relatively quickly after coming into power and with little previous public debate. It has to be said that the final year or two of Mr Major's Government was not the ideal climate to

---

[4] Interim Report of the Justice and Law Reform Select Committee *Inquiry into the White Paper — a Bill of Rights for New Zealand*, (1986).
[5] *Ministry of Transport v. Noort*, Porirua District Court, 7 May 1991, Hobbs, D.C.J.
[6] "Bills of Rights at Work", an unpublished paper given at a Liberty Human Rights Convention held in London, June 16, 1995.
[7] *R. v. Goodwin* [1993] 2 N.Z.L.R.153 at 156, *per* Cooke P.
[8] *Flickinger v. Crown Colony of Hong Kong* [1991] 1 N.Z.L.R. 439.
[9] *R. v. Goodwin* [1993] 2 N.Z.L.R. 153, at 194, *per* Richardson J.

promote public acceptance of an increase of power for judges. There were too many occasions when Ministers and M.P.s protested about decisions of English judges, of judges in the European Court in Luxemburg and of judges of the European Court of Human Rights in Strasbourg. The media did what it could to stir the pot. In June 1996 things had got to such a pass that Lord Irvine of Lairg Q.C., the then Labour Shadow Lord Chancellor, initiated a House of Lords debate on relations between the judiciary, the legislature and the executive.[10]

Nevertheless, my hunch is that if the E.C.H.R. were to become available to them, the English judges would not be slow to use it — and that they would not be unduly deterred by a lack of popular support for incorporation. So many senior judges have recently spoken publicly in favour of incorporation of the E.C.H.R. that it seems improbable that they would feel hindered in applying it by a fear of popular disquiet. If their decisions became the subject of fierce public controversy and criticism they might be forced to reconsider, but I believe that most of the senior judiciary would embark on a new Bill of Rights era in a spirit of wanting to make it work powerfully rather than feebly.

For one thing senior judges are these days alive to the main currents of opinion in other countries. They fly about the world attending conferences and lecturing. They meet fellow judges and engage in comparative debate. In the field of human rights, an important role has been played in this respect by Interrights (the International Centre for the Legal Protection of Human Rights in London), which for almost a decade has organised a series of high level colloquia for senior Commonwealth and American judges on international human rights issues. The first, in 1988 in Bangalore, produced what have been called "the Bangalore Principles". These noted that in most common law countries, international human rights conventions were not directly enforceable unless their provisions had been incorporated by legislation into domestic law. However they welcomed the growing tendency of national courts to have regard to these international norms where the domestic law was uncertain or incomplete. They expressed the wish that the norms in the international human rights codes should be still more widely recognised and applied by national courts, taking into account local laws, traditions, circumstances and needs.[11] The

[10] See *Hansard*, H.L., Vol. 572, cols. 1254–1313 (June 5, 1996). See also Lord Irvine, "Judges and Decision-Makers: The Theory and Practice of *Wednesbury* Review", (1996) Pub.L. 59–78.
[11] Information supplied by Lord Lester, who first established the centre and has played a major role in its management.

Bangalore Principles were adopted in five successive similar colloquia.[12] Better protection of human rights has become one of the leading intellectual concepts of the age. English judges will want to play their part in this developing story.

One way of assisting the necessary broadening of approach would be to alter the procedure of the courts to permit intervention by qualified third parties (with the consent of the court), and by the admissibility of written arguments by parties and others. This would encourage the fuller development of argument on relevant aspects of problems before the courts, as has occurred in Canada under the Charter. Justice Beverley McLachlin of the Canadian Supreme Court wrote:

> "A Charter tends to transform the debate from an adversarial debate between two parties to a polycentric inquiry, where effects on persons not before the court become relevant. This poses new challenges for the litigation process. How do we hear from unrepresented parties? One answer which the Canadian Supreme Court has adopted is to receive the submissions of intervenors, who in some cases have changed the course of the law".[13] Such an innovation might, in the first instance, be restricted to litigation arising out of the Bill of Rights, but, if helpful, it could be extended generally.

A Bill of Rights would inevitably increase participation in human rights matters by lawyers, politicians, the press, and academic commentators as well as judges. To the extent that the present judges were resistant to the new style of approach, the next generation might be more amenable.

The risks of incorporation would be also be limited by the fact that the European Court would remain as "long stop". The complainant in the United Kingdom would have a right of appeal from the decisions of the English judges to Strasbourg just as does the complainant in any other country where the E.C.H.R. is part of internal law. Moreover, the English judges could look to the jurisprudence of the E.C.H.R. for guidance.[14]

In fact, interpretation of Bills of Rights or written constitutions is not entirely unfamiliar to English judges. The Judicial Committee of the Privy Council has, in recent years, had a number of

---

[12] The fifth such colloquium was held in 1992 at Balliol College, Oxford. Judges from 16 Commonwealth countries, as well as from the U.S.A., Ireland, and Hungary took part. Lord Mackay, the Lord Chancellor, convened the meeting which was attended by several senior British judges and the President of the E.C.H.R. (Information supplied again by Lord Lester.)

[13] "The Canadian Charter and the Democratic Process" in C. Gearty and A. Tomkins (eds.) *Understanding Human Rights* (1996) p.33.

[14] For an example of a Northern Ireland case in which this occured see *R v. McCormick* [1977] N.I. 105.

such cases and it has dealt with at least some of them in a manner that was far from timid. In the third edition of this work the writer here set out details of five such cases[15] and concluded:

"All these decisions exhibit a strong concern for fundamental rights and a willingness to defy legislative or Government authority in the name of higher principles of constitutionality. They suggest that those who prophecy that English judges are temperamentally not equipped to handle a Bill of Rights may be taking an unduly pessimistic view (at page 64)."

This passage was quoted critically in 1991 by Keith Ewing, a strong critic of incorporation. After reviewing a number of other Privy Council cases decided between 1967 and 1990, Ewing (very plausibly on the basis of the cases discussed by him), suggested that they hardly bore out the claim made in my third edition.[16] In order to test the question further I checked all Privy Council cases reported in the All England Law Reports in the years 1992 to 1995. In those three years there are a dozen or more cases that do justify my original contention — which I hereby accordingly reaffirm.[17] The contention is not that the Judicial Committee invariably deals with such cases in a splendid way. It is simply that there is sufficient evidence to suggest that it deals well with them in a fair proportion of such cases.

The English judges have equally shown their ability to handle effectively the broad and open textured phrases of European Community law in regard to equal pay and sex discrimination. In the view of Anthony Lester, one of the leading experts in the field,

"English judges have interpreted and applied these general

[15] *Liyanage v. R.* [1967] 1 A.C. 259; *Oliver v. Buttigieg* [1967] 1 A.C. 115; *Akar v. Att.-Gen. of Sierre Leone* [1970] A.C. 853; *Hinds v. R.* [1977] A.C. 195; *Att. Gen. of St Christopher, Nevis and Anguilla v. Reynolds* [1980] A.C. 637.
[16] "A Bill of Rights: Lessons from the Privy Council", in W. Finnie, C. M. G. Himsworth and N. Walker (eds.) *Edinburgh Essays in Public Law* (1991) p.231 at 231, 246.
[17] *Phillip v. Director of Public Prosecutions of Trinidad and Tobago, Phillip v. Commissioner of Prisons* [1992] 1 All E.R.665; *Ali v. R., Rassool v. R.* [1992] 2 All E.R.1; *Att.-Gen. of Trinidad and Tobago* [1992] 2 All E.R.924; *Berry v. R.* [1992] 3 All E.R.881; *Kunnath v. The State* [1993] 4 All E.R. 30; *Commissioner of Police v. Davis* [1993] 4 All E.R.476; *Pratt v. Att.-Gen. for Jamaica* [1993] 4 All E.R. 769; *Prebble v. Television New Zealand Ltd* [1994] 3 All E.R. 407; *Vasquez v. R., O'Neil v. R.* [1994] 3 All E.R. 674; *Att.-Gen. of Trinidad and Tobago v. Philip* [1995] 1 All E.R. 93; *Sankar v. The State of Trinidad and Tobago* [1995] 1 All E.R. 236; *Dunkley v. R.* [1995] 1 All E.R. 279; *Reckley v. Minister of Public Safety and Immigration* [1995] 4 All E.R. 8; *Burut v. Public Prosecutor of Brunei* [1995] 4 All E.R. 300; *Guerra v. Baptiste* [1995] 4 All E.R. 583. See also *Ministry of Home Affairs v. Fisher* [1979] 3 All E.R. 21, 25 and *Att.-Gen. of Gambia v. Momodou Jobe* [1984] A.C. 689, 700.

principles in a manner which recognises their fundamental nature and which gives full effect to the underlying aims. The English judicial contribution of clear, coherent reasoned decision-making in this area is a model which might be followed with advantage elsewhere in the European Community. Those sceptics who doubt the ability of English judges to protect the fundamental rights of the Convention should consider their impressive record in translating the fundamental rights of Community law into practical reality."[18]

It is obviously true that a Bill of Rights is not as familiar to English judges as other forms of legislation, but there have been judges prepared to uphold the individual against the executive. The conventional view, frequently espoused by the judges themselves, is indeed that they are the citizen's chief bulwark against the State. A Bill of Rights would take the judges at their word and give them better tools to do the job.

A Bill of Rights would politicise the judges

This argument is based on the fear that a Bill of Rights would necessarily involve the judges in controversial issues and would, to that extent, result in some loss of the reputation for impartiality which characterises the English judiciary.[19] As was seen in Chapter 1, this view has often been expressed by Tory Ministers in rejecting the argument that the E.C.H.R. should be incorporated into United Kingdom law. It was made by Lord Mackay, for instance in July 1996 in a lecture to the Citizenship Foundation:

"Incorporation of the European Convention or a Bill of Rights as the yardstick by which Acts of Parliament are to be

---

[18] Lester, (1984) Pub.L. 47, at pp.70–71. He cited a dozen or more cases which illustrate his point — p.70, n. 20. See, for instance, *Snoxell v. Vauxhall Motors Ltd* [1978] Q.B.11; *Shields v. E. Coomes (Holdings) Ltd* [1978] 1 W.L.R. 1408; and *Clay Cross (Quarry) Services Ltd v. Fletcher* [1978] 1 W.L.R. 1429. For a more recent example see *Equal Opportunities Commission v. Secretary of State for Employment* [1994] 1 All E.R. 910 in which Community law was invoked successfully to challenge the discriminatory provisions of U.K. statutes against the yardstick of proportionality.

[19] For a forceful statement of this view, see Lord Devlin. "Judges and Lawmakers" (1976) 39 M.L.R. 1. Lord Devlin's main thesis was that the prime virtue of the independence of the judiciary would be squandered if they were to devote themselves to law reform, at least if they moved ahead of the consensus achieved in the larger community. See to same effect Lord Denning, *Hansard*, H.L., Vol. 369, col. 797 (March 25, 1976) and Lord Diplock *Hansard*, H.L., Vol. 396, cols. 1364–1365 (November 29, 1978).

measured would inevitably draw judges into making decisions of a far more political nature, measuring policy against abstract principles with possible implications for the development of broad social and economic policy which is and has been accepted by the judiciary to be properly the preserve of Parliament."[20]

The same argument was made a decade ago by the distinguished Scottish judge Lord McCluskey in the course of his Reith Lectures entitled *Law, Justice and Democracy*[21]. "Everyone", he said, "agrees that judges should stay out of politics . . . the principle is not in dispute".[22] The greater the latitude allowed to judges, "the greater is the risk of their appearing arbitrary, capricious and biased".[23] The judge should be confined to resolving disputes by applying the law. He continued:

> "Lawmaking should be left to lawmakers, policymaking to responsible policy-makers. And that's just the problem with a constitutional Bill of Rights. It is inevitably a charter of enduring super-rights, rights written in delphic words but in indelible ink on an opaque surface. It turns judges into legislators and gives them a finality which our whole tradition has hitherto professed to withhold from them. It makes the mistake of dressing up policy choices as if they were legal choices. It asks those whose job it is to know and apply the law to create and reform the law . . . If legislators don't tell us precisely what the words mean, then the words will mean what the judges say they mean."[24]

In the United States, he said, the Supreme Court was the "dignified cauldron" in which the essentially political questions of race, civil liberties, economic regulation, abortion, contraception, freedom of speech, pornography, capital punishment and the powers of the President were decided. To give judges the task of interpreting a vaguely worded Bill of Rights would draw them into the political arena "in a way that neither they nor many others would welcome".[25] One consequence would be that the cast of mind of judicial appointees would become of importance, as it had in the U.S.A.

---

[20] "Parliament and the Judges — A Constitutional Challenge", Lecture on July 8, 1996 at the Saddlers Hall. On the related question whether a Bill of Rights would entail a different method of selecting judges, see pp.145–151, below.
[21] (1987).
[22] *Ibid*, p.32.
[23] *Ibid*.
[24] *Ibid*, p.34.
[25] *Ibid*, p.54.

It is of course correct that English judges observe the convention that they should not take part in ordinary public life. Thus if judges speak in the House of Lords or on other public platforms, it is normally on issues of lawyers' law reform rather than general economic, social or political questions. This reluctance to get involved in political controversy is based on the widely held view, shared by the writer, that a judge's main task is to decide disputes in court between litigants and that it is important that the community should feel confidence in the fairness of such decision-making. There are some who regret the tendency of Governments of both political persuasions to use judges as chairman of controversial committees of inquiry.[26] But whilst it is true that controversy surrounded all these reports, there is no evidence that they led to any diminution in respect for the judiciary. Although under Lord Mackay there has in recent years been a welcome relaxation of the Kilmuir Rules, which previously prohibited judges from appearing on radio or television, they still are very cautious about media appearances and hardly ever write in the newspapers.[27]

A Bill of Rights would unquestionably require the judges to show themselves more openly as law-makers. It would be apparent that the broad words of the Bill of Rights permitted alternative interpretations that could be associated with particular viewpoints. If the judges favoured one interpretation, they might be accused of promoting the "conservative" approach; if they adopted the alternative, they might be said to be following the "liberal" or "progressive" school. In either event, they would be targets for criticism from the supporters of the losing faction.

There can be no doubt that English judges do enjoy an unusually high reputation for impartiality and fairness. The one significant exception, perhaps, is in the field of industrial relations where, as has been seen, there is a body of opinion which holds that the

[26] The clearest example was perhaps the tribunal chaired by Lord Wilberforce in 1972 on miners' pay. Other examples were Lord Widgery's inquiry into events on "Bloody Sunday" in Londonderry (H.C. 220, HMSO 1972); Sir Leslie Scarman's inquiry into Violence and Civil Disturbance in Northern Ireland in 1969 (1974, Cmnd. 566); and the same judge's inquiry into the Red Lion Square fracas (1975, Cmnd. 5919) and the Brixton riots (1981, Cmnd. 8427). Lord Justice Roskill chaired the inquiry into the sitting of London's third airport. Lord Devlin chaired the investigation of the constitutional settlement in Nyasaland (1959). Recent examples are Sir Richard Scott's inquiry into the Arms for Iraq scandal (*Report of the Inquiry into the Export of Defence Equipment and Dual-use Goods to Iraq and Related Prosecutions*, H.C. 115, 1995–96) and Lord Nolan's ongoing Committee on *Standards in Public Life* (First Report Cm. 2850–1, May 1995).

[27] See Joshua Rozenberg, *The Search for Justice* (1994) pp.61–68.

judges are not free from bias.[28] (It is far from clear that this view is based on solid foundations.[29]) But, broadly, English judges are generally believed to be even-handed and apolitical in deciding cases. Partly, this belief is based on an insufficient appreciation of the degree to which judges can and do exercise choice in their decision-making on questions of law. Most judges spend most of their time deciding disputed questions of *fact* and in such cases they are usually impeccably fair. But when it comes to deciding a disputed point of law, as has been seen, there may be scope for the judge's own preferences to influence the way he marshals the precedents and the competing arguments. Even the intelligentsia are probably unaware of the extent to which this does occur. The educated layman probably tends to assume that when the court declares the law it is performing a largely technical function — equivalent to that of the oracle pronouncing on the condition of the entrails. In other words, the judges' reputation for impartiality is greater than the facts could justify.

If the full process of decision-making were exposed to the gaze of the populace, the public would have a more realistic view. Research, for instance, has shown the extent to which the leading nineteenth-century decisions in the field of landlord-tenant relations, tended to a marked degree to favour the landlord class.[30] Fifty years ago, conflicts between the revenue and the taxpayer tended to be resolved in favour of the taxpayer, where today the judges, being more sympathetic to the basic objectives of the welfare state, would decide the same cases the other way. In the nineteenth century, male judges tended to rule that women were not persons within the meaning of statutes that gave persons the

[28] For a surprising source of such opinion, see a sharp attack on the impartiality of the judges in industrial affairs from Mr Winston Churchill, then Home Secretary, in debates in 1911 on the Trade Union (No. 2) Bill, to make it legal for unions to collect funds for political purposes. The Bill was introduced to cancel a judicial decision. Churchill said that "the courts had, justly, a high, and I think unequalled prominence in respect of the world in criminal cases, and in cases between man and man, no doubt they deserve and command the respect and admiration of all classes in the community, but where class and party issues are involved . . . it is impossible to pretend that the courts command the same degree of general confidence. On the contrary, they do not, and a very large number of our population have been led to the opinion that they are, unconsciously no doubt, biased" (*Hansard*, H.C. Vol XXVI, col. 1022 (May 30, 1911)).

[29] For a report of a survey of judicial decisions over a long time period see M. Zander, *The Law-Making Process* (4th ed., 1994), pp.304–305

[30] See J. I. Reynolds, "The Slum Tenant and the Law: A Comparative Study", Ph.D. thesis 1974, London University, unpublished. For an application of the same analysis to modern cases on the landlord's duties, see J. I. Reynolds "Statutory Covenants of Fitness and Repair: Social Legislation and the Judges" (1974) 37 M.L.R. 377.

right to vote or to exercise other civic functions.[31] In other words, in a variety of contexts the judge's "political" preconceptions may, and in fact do, influence his judicial decisions. The pretence that this does not occur is merely naive.[32]

There can be no doubt that a Bill of Rights would increase this tendency and as has been said, it would be more visible, since a Bill of Rights is cast in general terms which patently lend themselves to differing interpretations. Would the greater scope for law-making in areas of controversy, combined with the greater visibility of the process, be harmful? Even if the judges' reputation for even-handedness is partially undeserved, it is mostly a reality — and such a reputation should not lightly be squandered. Would introduction of a domestic Bill of Rights put this reputation at risk?

Predictions that English judges would be politicised are usually made by reference to the experience of the United States and to the nature of the Supreme Court. But this example may be somewhat misleading. First, part of the Supreme Court's particular character is undoubtedly due to the fact that the court has the power to strike down legislation as unconstitutional. A constitutional amendment to override such a judicial decision requires a two-thirds majority in the Congress and ratification by three-quarters of the States. This is exceedingly difficult to achieve. As will be seen below, amendment of a Bill of Rights so as to override a decision of the courts would only require a simple parliamentary majority. The power of the English courts would therefore be significantly less than that of the courts in the USA.

Secondly, differences between the two systems suggest why the Supreme Court is more political than would be likely of any English court even with a Bill of Rights. Judges in the United States are selected from more varied backgrounds — academics, politicians and office lawyers in addition to advocates. The doctrine of precedent is weaker than in this country and courts feel freer than ours to deviate from past decisions. Legal education in America produces lawyers who are more policy orientated than does our own. Lawyers are more dominant in society generally than in England and feel less diffident than here in offering their techniques to solve society's problems.

Thirdly, the belief that the American judiciary is political in the sense discussed here is not usually applied to the main body of the

---

[31] See generally Albie Sachs and Joan H Wilson, *Sexism and the Law* (1978).
[32] The point was made powerfully by Nicola Lacey from a Left perspective in her article "Are Rights Best Left Unwritten?" (1989) Pol.Qtrly.433 at 438:"Cases which involve just the issues touched upon by Bills of Rights come to the courts every week . . . Do left-wing commentators really want to participate in the liberal fiction that these cases involve legal interpretation and not political discretion?"

federal judges around the country. It applies principally to the Supreme Court, notwithstanding the fact that all the federal judges have the task and role of interpreting the constitution.

Nor does the experience of other countries with Bills of Rights or written constitutions appear to justify the view that they necessarily result in unacceptable politicisation of the judiciary. English judges are, by tradition, more conservative than most. It is likely that they would tend to under-use rather than to over-use powers of law-making implicit in a Bill of Rights. There is, for instance, no evidence that the Law Lords have over-used the power to depart from their own previous decisions which they granted to themselves in 1966.[33] To the extent that the Bill of Rights produced greater public familiarity with the true nature of the judicial process and its scope for judicial law-making, this would in itself be a gain. If the emperor has fewer clothes than had previously been thought, it is not necessarily a bad thing for this to be understood.

Can the judges give expression to "fundamental human rights" in defiance of statute law?

The view has been expressed by no less a person than Lord Woolf, in a lecture given before he became Master of the Rolls, that, despite the absence of a Bill of Rights, judges could, *in extremis*, hold invalid an Act of Parliament in order to give expression to fundamental principles of the common law. Lord Woolf said that if Parliament did the unthinkable and abolished judicial review, in his view the courts would not be obliged to give effect to the legislation. The courts would recognise legislation which controlled how the courts exercised their jurisdiction. But he saw a distinction

> "between such legislative action and that which seeks to undermine in a fundamental way the rule of law on which our unwritten constitution depends by removing or substantially impairing the entire reviewing role of the High Court on judicial review, a role which in its origin is as ancient as the common law, predates our present form of parliamentary democracy and the Bill of Rights."[34]

Mr Justice Laws expressed much the same view:

---

[33] See M. Zander, *The Law-Making Process* (4th ed., 1994) 192–198.
[34] Lord Woolf, "Droit Public-English Style" (1995) Pub.L.57 at 68. The article was based on his F. A. Mann lecture given at Lincoln's Inn in November 1994. He cited as authority Sir Robin (now Lord) Cooke, "Fundamentals" (1988) N.Z.L.J. 158.

"The democratic credentials of an elected government cannot justify its enjoyment of a right to abolish fundamental freedoms . . . The need for higher order law is dictated by the logic of the very notion of a government under law . . . the doctrine of Parliamentary sovereignty cannot be vouched by Parliamentary legislation; a higher-order law confers it and must of necessity limit it."[35]

Lord Irvine of Lairg Q.C., in a lecture in October 1995, doubted whether these propositions could be sustained.[36] First, they were contrary to the established laws and the constitution of the United Kingdom. Secondly, an assault on the basic tenets of democracy which could arguably justify such a rescue mission by the judges was inconceivable. If it did occur, he wondered whether "it is not extra-judicial romanticism to believe that judicial decisions could hold back what would, in substance, be a revolution". Thirdly, he considered it to smack of "judicial supremacism".[37]

In the writer's view, if there is no Bill of Rights enshrined in United Kingdom law it is improbable that the judges would ever have the occasion to put Lord Woolf's theory to the test. The doctrine of legislative supremacy is so powerful in the United Kingdom that, as Lord Irivine suggested, it is "inconceivable" that Parliament would pass legislation so profoundly and so obviously contrary to fundamental principle that the courts would feel able to declare such a statute invalid in the name of some higher law. Whether, in theory, there is such a principle, though a nice question for speculation, therefore lacks credibility as one likely to resolve real issues.

Bills of Rights prevent the government from taking necessary emergency action

It is of course the case that a Bill of Rights may prevent the legislature from doing something it otherwise might do. But this is

---

[35] Laws J., "Law and Democracy" (1995) Pub.L. 72, 84, 85, 87. See also Laws J., "Is the High Court the Guardian of Fundamental Constitutional Rights?" (1993) Pub.L. 59–79.

[36] "Judges and Decision-Makers: The Theory and Practice of Wednesbury Review" (1996) Pub.L. 59 at 77.

[37] *Ibid.* See to like effect what Lord Irvine said in introducing a debate in the House of Lords on "The Judiciary, Legislature and the Executive", *Hansard*, H.L. Vol. 572, col. 1255 (June 5, 1996)): "I regard as equally unwise a number of recent extra-judicial statements by distinguished judges that in exceptional cases the courts may be entitled to hold invalid statutes duly passed by Parliament. This causes ordinary people not only to believe that judges may have got over and above themselves but that perhaps they are exercising a political function in judicial review cases instead of simply upholding the rule of law".

only to say that from time to time a Bill of Rights may be effective. That however does not mean that a Bill of Rights would necessarily impede proposed legislative action which the government of the day considered essential to meet some emergency situation. For one thing the Bill of Rights itself may state that there are circumstances in which its provisions can be waived or suspended. The Indian Constitution, for example, provides in Article 359 that the Fundamental Rights guaranteed by Part III of the Constitution can be suspended in an emergency declared by the President where he is satisfied that the emergency threatens the security of the state through external aggression or internal disorder. It was this that, rightly or wrongly, Mrs Indira Gandhi used in moving against her political opponents in the Emergency of July 1975.

The E.C.H.R. too makes provision for emergencies. Article 15 permits a Member State to take measures derogating from the obligations under the Convention "in time of war or other public emergency threatening the life of the nation". Such action must be limited to that strictly required by the exigencies of the situation and must be consistent with international law. In 1978 the European Court of Human Rights held in a case brought against the United Kingdom by the Irish Government that the United Kingdom's derogations from Article 5 because of the emergency situation in Northern Ireland were not in breach of the E.C.H.R.[38] That was in regard to actions taken in Northern Ireland. In 1988 the British Government conveyed to the Council of Europe a derogation in regard to the period of time for which terrorism suspects could be held without charges. On November 29, 1988, in the case of *Brogan and Others,*[39] the European Court of Human Rights had held that there had been a violation of the E.C.H.R. where a terrorism suspect had been held for four days and six hours. The United Kingdom Government's derogation related to the provisions permitting detention of terrorism suspects without charges for up to seven days. In May 1993, the Strasbourg Court held that this derogation was not contrary to the E.C.H.R.[40]

Article 15(2) of the E.C.H.R. states that no derogation is permitted, even in time of emergency, from guarantees of the right to life, save through lawful acts of war (Art. 2), from guarantees against torture or inhuman or degrading treatment or punishment (Art. 3), from the guarantee that no one shall be held in slavery or servitude (Art. 4) or the guarantee against retrospective legislation in the criminal law (Art. 7).

[38] *Ireland v. U.K.* [1978] E.H.R.R 25, 90–97.
[39] Series A, 145-B.
[40] *Brannigan and McBride*, Series A, 258-B.

If a power of derogation for exceptional circumstances exists, who is to decide whether conditions are sufficiently exceptional? Both the Northern Ireland Standing Advisory Commission and the House of Lords Select Committee recommended that the courts should not have the power to determine whether the declaration of a state of emergency was justified. The Northern Ireland report proposed that this be a matter for determination by Parliament (*e.g.* that the Government would declare an emergency and that this would be subject to Parliamentary approval).[41] The House of Lords Select Committee thought that a Royal Proclamation should establish the fact of an emergency and that this should be conclusive in the courts.[42]

Lord Lester's Human Rights Bill, introduced in the House of Lords in November 1994, (p.36 above) provided for recognition by English judges of derogations only if they had been validly made by the United Kingdom government under the E.C.H.R. (clause 2(1) and clause 3(2)). It also stated that any such derogation had to be made by statutory instrument after a draft order had been approved by affirmative resolution in each House of Parliament (clause 3(2)(3)). The effect of such provisions is that the English judges would not be permitted to go behind such a statutory instrument to consider whether the conditions had been fulfilled, but the Strasbourg court would of course be able to do so. That seems the right balance.

A Bill of Rights would need to be protected against amendment or repeal and would thereby restrict Parliament's freedom to legislate

In his 1974 Hamlyn Lectures, Lord Scarman urged that the rights expressed in a Bill of Rights should be "protected against all encroachments, including the power of the state, even when the power is exerted by a representative legislative institution such as Parliament".[43] This, he said, called "for entrenched or fundamental laws protected by a Bill of Rights"[44] by which he meant a provision that the Bill of Rights could not be amended or repealed save by some special procedure. The problem of the entrenchment of a proposed Bill of Rights has been one of the most vexed issues in the whole Bill of Rights debate — and it is one that has given rise to much confusion, even though in practice the issue is probably much less important than is often realised.

[41] Northern Ireland Report, *op. cit.* at p.68, para. 7.12.
[42] House of Lords, "Select Committee Report", *op. cit.* at p.38, paras. 44–65.
[43] Leslie Scarman, *English Law — The New Dimension* (1974), p.15.
[44] *Ibid*, p.20.

Whether a Bill of Rights is buttressed by any special protective rules or not, and what those rules happen to be, does not necessarily make a great difference to what subsequently transpires. If there were what is sometimes called "full entrenchment" in the form of a requirement of a special majority in the legislature for amendment or repeal, that would not necessarily prevent the legislature from amending or even repealing the Bill of Rights. Lord Scarman called for a Bill of Rights to protect the individual citizen "from instant legislation, conceived in fear or prejudice and enacted in breach of human rights".[45] But when legislation is passed in that way it tends to go through with little or no opposition often in an unseemly rush. Thus the Official Secrets Act 1914[46] and the Commonwealth Immigrants Act 1968 both passed through all their parliamentary stages in a single day. The Prevention of Terrorism (Temporary Provisions) Act 1974, passed in the wake of the I.R.A. Birmingham bombings, went through all its parliamentary stages in the House of Commons on November 28, 1974 and all its stages in the House of Lords on the following day with the complete agreement of almost all who spoke in the debates.[47] The requirement of a two-thirds majority would have made no difference to the outcome in any of these cases.

Conversely, the total absence of any special formal protection for the Bill of Rights does not mean that the government of the day will easily or frequently introduce legislation to amend its provisions. A Bill of Rights clothed only in the special aura created by its title has a significant measure of entrenchment through the mere fact of its existence. Experience suggests that even when procedures exist that permit them quite easily to circumvent or negate the Bill of Rights, governments typically choose not to make use of them[48], presumably because they are reluctant to attract the political odium that would be involved. In other words, entrenchment by what might be called "strings and mirrors" may be entrenchment as powerful as any formula laid down in the enacting statute.

But although political scientists would bear witness to this phenomenon, before and at the time of enactment, the issue of

[45] *Ibid.*
[46] For a description see M. Zander, *The Law-Making Process* (4th ed. 1994), 58–59.
[47] For another instance, again involving terrorism, see the Prevention of Terrorism (Additional Powers) Act 1996 — *Hansard*, H.C. Vol. 275, cols. 152–298 (April 2, 1996) *Hansard*, H.L. Vol. 571, cols. 290–343 (April 3, 1996). The debate in the Commons lasted from 3.43 p.m. to 1.21 a.m.; the debate in the Lords lasted from 12.31 p.m. to 4.30 p.m.
[48] As will be seen, this, broadly,has been the experience to date in the case of the Canadian Charter.

special protection is commonly and understandably regarded as being of capital importance. Special protection for a Bill of Rights is desirable to mark its unusual importance and to give it higher authority than is available to ordinary statutes. A Bill of Rights is not like an ordinary statute and it is appropriate to make this clear to all — to the legislature, to the courts, to the public, to the government — and, most of all, to future governments. One purpose of such special status is to make it more difficult for the government of the day to legislate to amend or repeal the Bill of Rights. Not that a Bill of Rights is, or should be, beyond politics or beyond change. But in giving some form of special status to the Bill of Rights the legislature marks it out as different and to an extent above or beyond the day-to-day business of party politics. So a Bill of Rights that becomes a kind of political football, amended and re-amended in the spirit of narrow party politics of the kind familiar in all democratic countries is unlikely to be a Bill of Rights that is performing the role envisaged for it.

There are a variety of techniques for protection of a Bill of Rights that might be adopted[49]:

(1) A special majority requirement One adopted in many constitutions is that any amendment is only valid if passed by a specified parliamentary majority — such as two-thirds or three-quarters. There seems to be general agreement amongst constitutional writers that such a provision could not be made to operate in Britain under the present constitutional system[50] because of the well-established constitutional rule that one Parliament cannot bind its successors. Each Parliament is sovereign. This is regarded as a kind of *grundnorm* of the British constitution.[51] It was expressed by Dicey in Chapter 1 of his *Law of the Constitution:* — "The principle of Parliamentary sovereignty means neither more nor less than this that Parliament . . . has under the English constitution, the right to make or unmake any law whatever".[52] If, therefore, Parliament were to lay down a requirement that a particular statute could only be amended or repealed by a, say,

[49] The writer follows here the schema set out in a very helpful article by A.W.Bradley, "The Sovereignty of Parliament-in Perpetuity", in J.Jowell and D.Oliver (eds.) *The Changing Constitution* (3rd ed., 1994) pp.80–197, see especially pp.102–103.

[50] A special procedure for amendment was however part of the complete constitution proposed in 1991 by the Institute for Public Policy Research *The Constitution of the United Kingdom*, ss.69, 70.

[51] In *Ellen Street Estates Ltd v. Minister of Health* [1934] 1 K.B. 590,597 Maugham L.J. said, 'The legislature cannot, according to our constitution, bind itself as to the form of subsequent legislation . . ." See to like effect *Vauxhall Estates v. Liverpool Corporation* [1932] 1 K.B. 733.

[52] Dicey, *Law of the Constitution* (9th ed.), p.38.

two-thirds majority in both Houses of Parliament, and then passed an act to repeal the prior statute which passed by a bare majority, the courts would recognise the validity of the repeal.

Even if it were technically possible, it is clear that neither of the two main political parties would espouse such a strong form of "full entrenchment".[53] Since modern governments rarely have anything like a two-thirds majority such a provision would transfer effective blocking power over future legislation to the opposition.

(2) A rule of interpretation The Bill of Rights could provide that legislation should be interpreted to be consistent with the Bill of Rights so far as the context permits. This was the formula ultimately adopted in the amended version of the Human Rights Bill introduced in the House of Lords by Lord Lester in 1994.[54] It is also the formula adopted in the New Zealand Bill of Rights Act 1990.[55] Lord Lester has suggested that this rule of interpretation at least undoes the restrictive ruling expressed by the House of Lords in *ex parte Brind*[56] that where Parliament confers unambiguously broad statutory powers on Ministers and public authorities, there is no presumption that Parliament intended that those powers should be exercised in accordance with the E.C.H.R. It would also incidentally ensure that regard was had to the E.C.H.R. in Scottish courts.[57] But most commentators are agreed that this form of protection is too weak. If there were an apparent conflict between

---

[53] For a different "strong" form of protection for a Bill of Rights see Liberty's proposal for what it calls "democratic entrenchment": Francesca Klug and John Wadham, "The 'democratic' entrenchment of a Bill of Rights: Liberty's proposals" (1993) Pub.L. 579–88. As conceived by Liberty, democratic entrenchment would operate through a new specialist joint committee of both Houses of Parliament. Its main function would arise if primary legislation were struck down by the courts for infringing the Bill of Rights. It would be asked to determine whether the legislation conformed to the meaning, intention and spirit of the Bill of Rights. If so, it would so certify and thereby enable Parliament to re-enact the legislation. The Committees decisions would be by a two-thirds majority and would then have to be confirmed by a simple majority of each House of Parliament. For a fuller statement of the proposal see *A People's Charter: Liberty's Bill of Rights*, (1991), pp.24–29.

[54] "So far as the context permits, enactments (whenever passed or made) shall be construed consistently with" E.C.H.R. rights and freedoms. For the history see Lord Lester, "The Mouse that Roared: the Human Rights Bill 1995" (1995) Pub.L. 198 at 199.

[55] "Wherever an enactment can be given a meaning that is consistent with the rights and freedoms contained in this Bill of Rights, that meaning shall be preferred to any other meaning"(s.6).

[56] *R. v. Secretary of State for the Home Department, ex p. Brind* [1991] A.C. 696, H.L.

[57] The Court of Session held in *Kaur v. Lord Advocate* (1981) S.L.T. 322 and *Moore v. Secretary of State for Scotland* (1985) S.L.T.38 that the E.C.H.R. had no effect in Scottish municipal law even as a mere aid to construction of ambiguous legislation.

the new statute and the Bill of Rights Act, the court would have to give effect to such an implied amendment — even though the issue was never addressed in Parliament.

(3) Overriding earlier Acts plus a rule of interpretation The Bill of Rights could provide that the courts would not apply any existing Act of Parliament inconsistent with its provisions (save for any specifically excluded) and that in regard to future legislation the courts should apply the same rule of interpretation as in (2) above. This hybrid form of protection was that adopted in the Hong Kong Bill of Rights Ordinance 1991.[58]

(4) Overriding all past and future legislation by transferring authority to European bodies The formula adopted in the European Communities Act 1972 gives precedence to Community law until such time as Parliament expressly changes its mind. Section 2(1) of the 1972 Act provided that all directly effective Community law in whatever form is to be given legal effect in the United Kingdom.[59] Section 2(4) requires of the courts in the United Kingdom that "any enactment passed or to be passed, other than one contained in this Part of this Act shall be construed and have effect subject to the foregoing provisions of this section". Section 3(1) states that any question as to the "effect" of any of the Treaties or of Community legislation must be decided "in accordance with the principles of any relevant decision of the European Court".

The Specialist Adviser to the House of Lords Select Committee on the Bill of Rights doubted whether such provisions would be effective.[60] It seemed likely, he thought, that if faced with an irreconcilable conflict between an Act of Parliament and an earlier provision of directly applicable Community law the court would apply the ordinary principle of Parliamentary supremacy and give effect to the Act of Parliament. The argument to the contrary would have to be based on the view that the passage of the

---

[58] Section 3(1) states that all pre-existing legislation that admits of a construction consistent with the Ordinance shall be given such a construction. Section 3(2) states that previous legislation that does not admit of such a construction "is, to the extent of the inconsistency, repealed". Section 4 states that all subsequent legislation shall be construed, "to the extent that it admits of such a construction", so as to be consistent with the International Covenant as applied to Hong Kong. See James Allan, "A Bill of Rights for Hong Kong" (1991) Pub.L. 175.

[59] "s.2(1) All such rights, powers, liabilities and restrictions from time to time created or arising by or under the Treaties [of the European Community], and all such remedies and procedures from time to time provided for . . . as in accordance with the Treaties are without further enactment to be given legal effect or used in the United Kingdom shall be recognised and available in law, and be enforced, allowed and followed accordingly."

[60] *op. cit.* p.26, n.80 at p.9, para. 27.

European Communities Act coupled with our accession to the EEC had involved a transfer of legislative sovereignty in regard to Community matters from Parliament to the Communities. This was indeed the view taken by the European Court in the cases in which it has laid down the supremacy of directly applicable Community law. But, even if this were so, he thought that it provided "no precedent for suggesting that Parliament could effectively entrench a Bill of Rights".[61]

We now know, however, that the Specialist Adviser was wrong in his view. If there is a conflict between Community law and even a later statutory provision, the English courts must give effect to the Community law. That was established by the series of decisions in *Factortame* concerning the rights of Spanish fishermen to stop enforcement of the Merchant Shipping Act 1988 which they successfully claimed was passed in breach of the EEC Treaty provisions prohibiting discrimination on grounds of nationality. At first the House of Lords ruled that it had no power to set aside a statute pending a reference to the European Court and, in any event, the courts had no jurisdiction to grant an injunction against the Crown.[62] The dispute was then referred to the European Court of Justice in Luxemburg which ruled that

> "Community law must be interpreted as meaning that a national court which in a case pending before it concerning Community law, considers that the sole obstacle which precludes it from granting interim relief is a rule of national law must set aside that rule."

The House of Lords accepted the ruling.[63] This invalidated the Specialist Adviser's advice to the House of Lords Select Committee.[64]

It may be suggested that the *Factortame* decision derived from the particular set of arrangements that govern the Community. The

[61] *Ibid*, para. 28.
[62] *Factortame Ltd v. Secretary of State for Transport* [1989] 2 All E.R.692 H.L. As will be seen, the rule prohibiting injunctions against the Crown was later changed by the House of Lords — see p.151, below.
[63] *Factortame Ltd v. Secretary of State for Transport (No. 2)* [1991] 1 All E.R., H.L. 70, 111 *per* Lord Goff. For discussion see Dawn Oliver, "Fishing on the Incoming Tide" (1991) 54 M.L.R. 442. The ruling was applied in *Equal Opportunities Commission v. Secretary of State for Employment* [1994] 1 All E.R. 910, H.L. in which the House of Lords held that equal pay provisions of the Employment Protection (Consolidation) Act 1978 were incompatible with Community law.
[64] In the third edition of this work I said : "This view would naturally be strengthened if contrary to the prediction of the Specialist Adviser, the courts interpreted Section 2(4) of the European Communities Act 1972 so as to invalidate a later statutory provision in the face of an earlier directly applicable Community law. In the meanwhile one can only say that the matter is uncertain." (p.73)

English courts are required to give effect to Community Law even when it conflicts with later statutes by virtue of the combination of section 2(4) of the 1972 Act and the rulings of the Luxemburg Court interpreting the Treaties and developing Community Law.

The European Communities Act 1972 could be expressly repealed by Parliament and if this were to happen in the form of open and clear withdrawal from the Community, the English courts would undoubtedly recognise such legislation. This was clearly expressed by Lord Denning M.R. in *Macarthys Ltd v. Smith*[65]:

> "If the time should come when Parliament deliberately passes an Act with the intention of repudiating the Treaty or any provision in it or intentionally of acting inconsistently with it and says so in express terms then I should have thought that it would be the duty of our courts to follow the statute of our Parliament. I do not however envisage any such situation . . . Unless there is such an intentional and express repudiation of the Treaty, it is our duty to give priority to the Treaty."

But any legislation inconsistent with Community law short of full withdrawal would run afoul of the principle in *Factortame*. Whether it was implied or express amendment of Community law would make no difference.

The E.C.H.R. is different, however, in that there is no equivalent of the ruling of the Luxembourg Court in *Factortame*. The Strasbourg Court has not laid on Member States a duty to give effect to the E.C.H.R. in internal law.[66] Nor is there any equivalent to the machinery for seeking a ruling from the Luxemburg Court on a Community law point that has arisen in the course of litigation. Could Parliament achieve the same effect with a Bill of Rights Act which enacted the E.C.H.R. equivalent of sections 2(1) and 2(4) of the 1972 Act?

Even to pose the question ignores political realities. Given the current negative British attitude to Europe it seems exceedingly unlikely that any foreseeable future Labour Government would be prepared openly and avowedly to give the jurisprudence of the E.C.H.R. exactly the same status as that of Community law.[67] It is of course true that ultimately decisions as to the meaning of the E.C.H.R. are for the Strasbourg court, but that is not the same as

---

[65] [1990] 2 A.C. 85.

[66] The E.C.H.R. itself however lays on Member States the duty to provide an "effective remedy before a national authority" (Art. 13).

[67] But see Dawn Oliver, *Government in the United Kingdom: The search for Accountability, Effectiveness and Citizenship*, (1991), p.159 where she proposes the enactment of a "notwithstanding clause" (see below) together with a provision like s.2(1) and 2(4) of the 1972 Act.

saying that the Bill of Rights Act should import the jurisprudence of the E.C.H.R. wholesale into United Kingdom law. It would be sufficient for the Act to state that United Kingdom courts should take account of the jurisprudence of the Strasbourg Commission and Court[68]. That is the formula that has in fact been adopted in many of the Bills introduced to incorporate the E.C.H.R. into United Kingdom law. It recognises the reality that under the E.C.H.R. system Contracting States are to an extent permitted to achieve results in different ways. The Convention for the most part lays down standards of conduct rather than detailed rules, which gives a range of choices to national authorities. They are held to be in breach of the Convention only if they have gone beyond this range — outside the "margin of appreciation".

(5) Recognising amendments of the Bill of Rights if done expressly by a "notwithstanding clause" The technique that seems most likely to be adopted is the formula used in the Canadian Charter. This permits amendment of the Bill of Rights providing that it is express in the form of what is known as a "notwithstanding clause".[69] (Amendment would occur through use in the amending Act of the words "notwithstanding the provisions of the Charter/ Bill of Rights Act . . . "). The "notwithstanding clause" formula was adopted in the Private Members' Bills introduced in 1983-84 by Mr Robert MacLennan M.P. (p.27 above) and in 1985/86 by Lord Broxbourne (p.28 above. It was also the formula originally adopted in Lord Lester's Human Rights Bill of 1994 — until it was watered down in deference to the Law Lords).[70]

The Specialist Adviser to the House of Lords Select Committee thought that this was not possible under the British constitution but he relied for his authority on authorities the relevance of which to this question are at least open to question.[71] In fact the Specialist Adviser's view was questioned at the time by Lord Hailsham. In evidence to the Select Committee he said that the

---

[68] For literature on the jurisprudence of the Strasbourg Court see Select Bibliography — p.165 below.

[69] The Canadian Charter is governed by s.52(1) of the Constitution Act which states, in part: "The Constitution of Canada is the supreme law of Canada and any law that is inconsistent with the provisions of the Constitution is, to the extent of that inconsistency, of no force or effect." Section 33 of the Charter itself contains the power for the legislature expressly to derogate from or to amend or repeal any of the provisions of the Bill of Rights. ("Parliament . . . may expressly declare in an Act . . . that the Act or a provision of thereof shall operate notwithstanding a provision included in section 2 or sections 7 to 15 of this Charter" (s.33(1)). For background and commentary see D. Greschner and K. Norman, "The Courts and Section 33" (1987) Queen's L.J. 155.

[70] *op. cit.* p.36, n.16.

[71] Cited in n.51 above.

classic view was based principally on the *Vauxhall Estates* and *Ellen Street* cases decided in the 1930s. He considered that the Specialist Adviser "was probably putting more weight on that particular piece of ice than legally the ice would bear".[72] The statute in question in those cases was not a constitutional statute. If the legislature passed something so basic as a Bill of Rights it did not follow that the courts would take the same line as they did to the Acquisition of Land Act 1919. The courts were taking a very different approach towards constitutional questions than they did in the mid-1930s.

This seems a powerful argument — quite apart from the fact that the judges are much readier than they were in former times to approach statutory interpretation from a purposive perspective. A Bill of Rights Act would be likely to be treated as special by the courts — legislation of fundamental significance like Magna Carta, the Act of Union, or accession to the European Community. If Parliament formally and consciously enacted a Bill of Rights with a provision requiring express amendment, it does not seem the least far-fetched to predict that the courts would give it full effect.

Lord Irvine, then Shadow Lord Chancellor, suggested as much in stating that such a clause would have the advantage that it would permit the legislature in a time of national crisis to curtail individual rights but it would have to do so openly and expressly "as in a democracy ought always to be the way".[73] It would also, he thought, make it almost impossible for either existing or subsequent law to be interpreted as being inconsistent with the E.C.H.R. "Judges would know that Parliament had to hand a means of making clear that it was derogating from the Convention, but did not use it."[74] This ingenious suggestion is based on the (seemingly unrealistic) assumption that the legislature would always be (or be deemed to be) aware of potential inconsistency between the Bill of Rights and other legislation. It seems unlikely that the courts would be prepared to adopt such a view.

It is true that, theoretically, a government could use a "notwithstanding clause" cynically as a matter of course in every statute (or at least in case of any doubt) as a way of ensuring that its legislation would always be upheld by the courts. But the reality is that governments appear to be remarkably reluctant to use the clause. Thus in over a decade of experience with the Canadian Charter there are only a handful of examples of use of the "notwithstanding clause" — and almost all concern the special case of Quebec. Professor Roland Penner wrote in 1996 that section 33

---

[72] "Minutes of Evidence", *op cit.* p.25, n.78 above at p.16, col. 2.
[73] D. Bean (ed.), *Law Reform for All* (1996), p.18.
[74] *Ibid.*

119

had so far not been used at all by the Federal Government which preferred to ask Parliament to amend legislation invalidated on Charter review by the courts so as to bring it into conformity with the court's concerns.[75]

Some supporters of the Bill of Rights concept regard the "notwithstanding clause" as an undesirable sop to the "Parliament-is-sovereign" view. I regard it rather as an acceptable compromise between no special protection for the Bill of Rights and too much. It would, I believe, be unfortunate if governments felt politically wholly unable to use the "notwithstanding clause". That would mean that there had *de facto* been a transfer of final power to British judges. I would prefer to leave final power within the country to the legislature[76] — with the possibility of appeal to the judges at Strasbourg as a final authority as to the meaning of the E.C.H.R.. As Professor Ronald Dworkin has put it:

> "No doubt that condition would, in practice, prevent a government from introducing legislation it might otherwise enact. That is the point of incorporation ... But forcing Parliament to make the choice between obeying its international obligations and admitting that it is violating them does not limit Parliament's supremacy, but only its capacity for duplicity. Candour is hardly inconsistent with sovereignty."[77]

However, Lord Bingham was perhaps correct when he said in a lecture in 1993, given as Master of the Rolls before he became Lord Chief Justice, that all this technical discussion of the issue of "entrenchment" was beside the point:

> "Suppose the statute of incorporation were to provide that subject to any express abrogation or derogation in any later statute the rights specified in the Convention were to be fully recognised and enforced in the United Kingdom according to the tenor of the Convention. That would be good enough for the judges. They would give full effect to the Convention rights unless a later statute very explicitly and specifically told them not to. But the rights protected by the Convention are not stated in absolute terms[78]: there are provisos to cover

---

[75] Penner, *op. cit.*, (1996) Publ.L. 104, at 110. Details of the sparing use made of the "notwithstanding clause" is also given by Justice Beverley McLachlin of the Supreme Court: "The Canadian Charter and the Democratic Process" in C. Gearty and A. Tomkins (eds.), *Understanding Human Rights* (1996), p.37, n.4.

[76] For a powerful plea for this under s.33 of the Canadian Charter, see W. A. Bogart, *Court and Country* (1994), pp.310–313.

[77] R. Dworkin, *A Bill of Rights for Britain* (1994), pp.31–32.

[78] Whilst that is correct for most of the provisions of the E.C.H.R. it is not true of all. Thus the prohibition in Art. 3 on torture or inhuman or degrading treatment is absolute.

120

pressing considerations of national security and the like. Save in quite extraordinary circumstances one cannot imagine any government going to Parliament with a proposal that any human rights guaranteed by the Convention be overridden. And even then (subject to any relevant derogation) the United Kingdom would in any event remain bound, in international law and also in honour, to comply with its Convention obligations. I find it hard to imagine a government going to Parliament with such a proposal. So while the argument on entrenchment has a superficial theoretical charm, it has in my opinion very little practical substance."[79]

Nevertheless, he did not envisage the courts, as under Community law, declaring statutes to be invalid.

"Judges would either comply with the express will of Parliament by construing all legislation in a manner consistent with the Convention. Or, in the scarcely imaginable case of an express abrogation or derogation by Parliament, the judges would give effect to that provision also."[80]

The writer, with respect, takes leave to doubt whether Lords Bingham and Browne-Wilkinson are correct that the courts could not declare a statute to be invalid. Certainly, if a court refused to give effect to a statutory provision because it conflicted with the Bill of Rights that would be declaring it to be *pro tanto* invalid. But since the complainant would still have a right to take the matter to Strasbourg, the difference is in reality unimportant. If an English court construed legislation to conform to the E.C.H.R., that decision could be challenged before the Strasbourg court if the complainant considered the ruling to be inconsistent with the E.C.H.R. Equally, if the court held a statutory provision to be invalid as contrary to the Bill of Rights and that ruling were in turn cancelled by subsequent and express legislation, such legislation could be the subject of a challenge to Strasbourg.

In other words, the final arbiter of the meaning of the E.C.H.R. is the Strasbourg court and special protection (or "entrenchment") therefore exists ultimately on the international plane.

A Bill of Rights would further delay the remedy

Since we already have the European Convention on Human Rights with its enforcement machinery, a domestic Bill of Rights

[79] T. Bingham, "The European Convention on Human Rights: Time to Incorporate" (1993) L.Q.R. 390, 396.
[80] *Ibid.* See also Lord Browne-Wilkinson, "The Infiltration of a Bill of Rights", (1992) Pub.L. 397. Lord Browne-Wilkinson suggested (at 398–399) that a statutory requirement of express repeal would not permit the courts to declare a statute invalid.

would add an extra series of courts to the process and would thereby lengthen the process of getting a decision from Strasbourg. The E.C.H.R. requires that all available local remedies first be exhausted, and a Bill of Rights would obviously qualify as the basis for a possible local remedy. For cases that ultimately reach Strasbourg the point is valid but it does not seem a major objection unless it could be supposed that a large proportion of cases that get started in the United Kingdom courts would end in Strasbourg. This is exceedingly unlikely. Belief in the advantages of having a domestic Bill of Rights is obviously premised on the assumption that a significant proportion of cases brought under it would succeed in the United Kingdom courts and that that process would be far speedier than seeking a remedy in Strasbourg which, as has been seen, takes many years. Since the Government has no right of appeal to the Strasbourg system, for such cases that would be an end of the matter. The litigant who loses in the United Kingdom courts would have the option of appealing to the Strasbourg system. Some would take advantage of this possibility; others would not.

But speeding up the process of getting a remedy is only part of the reason for having a domestic Bill of Rights. Another is that by providing an accessible domestic remedy more cases — probably many more cases — would be generated. It is no answer to this point to say that the cases that ultimately go to Strasbourg would take longer than if they had gone to Strasbourg direct. Previously they might not have been brought at all. To add a new string to the human rights bow seems a strength rather than a weakness of the proposal.

Bill of Rights cases would clog up an already over-loaded court system

It is impossible to predict what sort of numbers of cases might be brought under a domestic Bill of Rights but it is clear that it would be a new source of work for the courts. Moreover, whereas most civil actions settle without a trial, at least initially this would not happen to the same extent in cases brought under the Bill of Rights. In the early years there would be few decided cases from which practitioners could deduce trends so as to be able to advise clients as to their chances of success. The client would be told that the only way of discovering the attitude of the courts to the matter would be to litigate. Also, since issues under the Bill of Rights would often be matters of principle, they would not be as responsive to monetary or other offers to settle as in ordinary cases where the claim typically is one for damages. The ratio of fought cases would probably be rather high.

It is also true that there is a widespread belief that the court system is already under great stress in dealing with its existing case load. Part of the momentum behind Lord Woolf's proposals for reform of the civil justice system[81] is fuelled by this concern. But by international standards, delays in the civil justice system in the United Kingdom are at the low rather than the high end of the spectrum. Most countries would be glad to exchange our levels of delay for their own.

The danger that there would be a flood of cases swamping the system is remote. The indemnity rule of costs under which the loser pays most of the winner's costs makes lawyers cautious in advising clients with weak cases to proceed. Legal aid is only available for cases that show real promise of success — and under the plans outlined in Lord Mackay's White Paper of July 1996[82] the prospects of getting legal aid would be further reduced.

The new system of "conditional fees"[83] can be used for cases brought under the E.C.H.R. in Strasbourg and it is to be hoped that this possibility would be extended to litigation under the domestic Bill of Rights. Conditional fees may or may not bring in more clients, but lawyers are very unlikely to agree to take on weak cases on a conditional fee basis for fear of not being paid if they lose. The risk assessment in regard to prospects for success by solicitors for the purposes of conditional fee agreements will probably not be very different from risk assessment in regard to legal aid.

Precisely the same would apply to assessment by interest groups such as Liberty, MIND, JUSTICE, Interrights and similar organisations which can be expected to assist and promote Bill of Rights test case litigation. They will not wish to go ahead and thereby to risk their slender resources on cases unless they show a reasonable prospect of success.

The likelihood therefore is that a domestic Bill of Rights would generate a fair amount of new litigation, a good deal of which would end as contested cases which have to be tried. But it would be very suprising if it proved to be of unmanageable proportions

---

[81] *Access to Justice*, Interim Report, June 1995; Final Report, July 1996.

[82] *Striking the Balance: The future of legal aid in England and Wales*, July 1996, Cm. 3305.

[83] Under a conditional fee arrangement the client agrees to pay his own lawyer nothing in respect of his fees if the case is lost but an enhanced fee if the case is won. The enhanced fee is based on an agreed percentage of the lawyer's costs — up to a maximum of 100 per cent. The Law Society has recommended solicitors to agree not to take more than 25 per cent of the damages by way of the success fee. See Michael Napier and Fiona Bawden, *Conditional Fees-a Survival Guide* (1995); Michael Zander, *Cases and Materials on the English Legal System* (7th ed. 1996) pp.469–476.

and the majority of cases brought would be ones that seemed to show reasonable prospects of success.

A Bill of Rights would generate a great deal of frivolous litigation

Justice Beverley McLachlin of the Canadian Supreme Court dealt recently with the fear that a Bill of Rights would generate masses of trivial or vexatious claims.

> "One concern is that entrenchment of rights gives rise to a flood of frivolous litigation — Charter mania, as it is dubbed. In Canada there was a surge, but not a flood, of litigation after adopting the Charter. Such actions as were clearly frivolous were generally disposed of in the usual way at early stages through motions to strike. What remained tended to be serious questions. Twelve years after the adoption of the Charter, I am informed by trial justices that Charter work comprises only a small proportion of their docket. In short, the evidence simply does not support the allegation that the Charter has opened the gates to floods of frivolous litigation, although it may have increased it somewhat."[84]

A Bill of Rights would require an elaborate machinery to enforce it

This is not so. A Bill of Rights *could* be implemented without any machinery other than the existing system — including of course the availability of legal aid. If enforcement were left to the ordinary courts (see pp.143–145 below), there would be no need for additional machinery. As will be seen, it is suggested below that there would be good grounds for setting up a Human Rights Commission as an additional resource but a Bill of Rights on its own would be perfectly viable.

The time is not ripe for a Bill of Rights

Two opposing schools of thought have in the past advanced the view that the enactment of legislation to establish a Bill of Rights would be premature. (The argument has not been heard much recently but it is included here for the sake of completeness). One school suggested that before such a step be considered there

[84] "The Canadian Charter and the Democratic Process" in C. Gearty and A. Tomkins (eds.) *Understanding Human Rights* (1996), p.32.

should be a detailed review of the less drastic steps that might be taken to promote the better protection of human rights. Thus the Law Reform Committee of the Law Society, commenting on the Inter-Departmental Discussion Document published in June 1976 (p.20 above) said that what was required was a wide-ranging inquiry into all the issues in which the Law Commission and the Scottish Law Commission should be asked to play a part. Such an inquiry, it suggested, should consider, *inter alia*, the possible extension of remedies against administrative acts and omissions and the possible establishment of an administrative division of the High Court. But even more, it was necessary to inquire whether there was any case for so major a constitutional change as that proposed by the advocates of a Bill of Rights. The proposal to enact into our law "a series of directly enforceable human rights formulated in the vaguest and most general terms, and subject to almost equally vague qualifications" was "totally at variance with traditional methods of law-making in this country".[85] It only made sense in the view of the Law Society "as part of a proposal for a complete overhaul of our fundamental constitutional arrangements"[86] as proposed, for instance, by Lord Hailsham. It was "far too soon to express any firm view on whether a case [had] been made out for any such new constitutional settlement, with entrenched rights and limits on parliamentary sovereignty, subject to judicial control".[87] But, as has been seen (p.39 above), in 1993 the Council of the Law Society changed its mind and joined the chorus of those who were calling for incorporation of the E.C.H.R. into United Kingdom law.

The opposite camp which reached a somewhat similar conclusion included Professor O. Hood Phillips, a distinguished academic lawyer. Professor Hood Phillips was asked by the Chairman of the Select Committee of the House of Lords whether he thought incorporation of the E.C.H.R. was worth having without a written constitution. His answer was that the more he thought about it the more he doubted it.[88] What was needed, he thought, was to have a Bill of Rights that was entrenched against the legislature. That could only achieved "if a wholly new constitution were to be established of which a Bill of Rights would merely form one part, and that not the most important part".[89] The likelihood of wide-ranging constitutional reform seems to this writer to be remote. If

[85] "Minutes of Evidence", *op. cit.,* p.25, n.78 above at pp.64, 65, para. 7.
[86] *Ibid*.
[87] *Ibid*.
[88] *Ibid*, p.279, Q. 582.
[89] *Ibid*, p.277.

that is right, postponement to await the event is equivalent to permanent postponement. It seems an unconvincing argument. If a Bill of Rights makes sense, it makes sense regardless of whether there is drastic constitutional reform.

Having a Bill of Rights would achieve either too little or too much — the Canadian experience

In 1960, Canada enacted a Bill of Rights.[90] Fifteen years later, Professor Harry Arthurs, one time President of the Canadian Civil Liberties Association[91], told the House of Lords Select Committee that in his view it had proved a great disappointment.[92] The Canadian Bill of Rights was not enshrined in the Constitution nor was it applicable to the exercise of provincial (state) legislative power. To the extent that it neither assumed a written constitution nor a federal system it was therefore possibly an important precedent for the United Kingdom.

The Bill provided that "every law of Canada . . . shall be so construed and applied as not to abrogate, abridge, or infringe" certain enumerated rights and freedoms. There were two exceptions. One was where legislation expressly declared that it should operate notwithstanding the Bill of Rights. No such legislation had been enacted. Secondly, any act done under the War Measures Act was deemed not to infringe the Bill. Subject to this the Bill was meant to prevail over other statutes.

In *R. v. Drybones*[93] the Supreme Court of Canada held that the Bill of Rights made inoperative previously enacted legislation which contravened one of the rights and freedoms protected by the Bill. In spite of this, according to Professor Arthurs, in the Supreme Court "the cause of civil liberties [had] lost, if not the war, at least most battles and an entire campaign".[94] The Supreme Court had offered substantive comment on the Bill of Rights in 32 cases. In 25 of these cases the Bill of Rights had been violated. In six cases the Court had relied on the Bill as a factor in the decision. But even in these six cases it had played less role than might at first

---

[90] See Walter Tarnopolsky, *The Canadian Bill of Rights* (2nd ed. 1975).
[91] Professor Arthurs was also formerly Dean of the Osgoode Hall Law School and later served as President of York University.
[92] For literature on the Canadian Bill of Rights generally see J.Hucker and B.C. McDonald, "Securing Human Rights in Canada" (1969) 15 McGill L.J. 220; Elmer A. Driedger. "The Meaning and Effect of the Canadian Bill of Rights: A Draftsman's viewpoint," (1977) 9 Ottowa L.Rev. 303.
[93] [1970] S.C.R.282.
[94] "Minutes of Evidence", *op. cit.* p.25, n.78 above, at p.241, para. 9.

appear. Two cases held that the failure to provide an interpreter in court was a breach of the Bill of Rights. (In one a conviction for non-capital murder was quashed and in the other a deportation order). Two cases held there had been a breach of the Bill of Rights where an appellate court quashed an acquittal and entered a conviction without giving the appellant an opportunity to be heard. In a fifth case a conviction of a motorist was quashed because he ought to have been allowed to contact a lawyer before taking a breath test. These five cases in Professor Arthur's view added little to the protection of civil liberties. This left only the *Drybones* decision in which the court invalidated a provision of the Indian Act which penalised Indians but not others for drunkenness.

It was clear, Professor Arthurs said, that after nearly two decades "the Bill of Rights has had a negligible impact upon the Supreme Court of Canada".[95] In many more than the six cases described, the Bill "could and should sensibly have been applied, and whether applied or not, deserved more extended and sympathetic attention than it in fact received".[96] There was room for disagreement as to the reasons but there was little difference of opinion on the proposition that the Bill of Rights was not a significant factor in the decision-making processes of the Supreme Court.

Nor was there any evidence that the Government was concerned to promote or enhance the effectiveness of the Bill of Rights. The Bill, for instance, required the Minister of Justice to report to the House of Commons any inconsistency between any Bill introduced into the House and the Bill of Rights. He had made no such report. The commitment of the Government to the Bill of Rights was at the level of rhetoric. There was an almost complete absence of organised effort to secure observance of its principles.[97]

The Canadian experience with the Bill of Rights shows that mere enactment of a Bill of Rights changes nothing. As Professor Arthurs put it: "Only when the Bill begins to command the loyalty of individuals — judges, politicians, policemen, bureaucrats, ordinary citizens — will its aspirations be translated into reality. Insofar as those who are in official positions have developed fixed views and well established patterns of behaviour concerning the matters addressed by the Bill, their loyalty will not quickly be given."[98]

However, the position in Canada changed dramatically with the adoption of the Canadian Charter of Rights and Freedoms as part of Prime Minister Trudeau's repatriation of the Constitution which

[95] *Ibid*, p.242, para. 13.
[96] *Ibid*.
[97] *Ibid*, p.242. paras. 16–20.
[98] *Ibid*, p.244, para. 25.

became law in April 1982. The Charter has unquestionably made a very considerable impact.[99] A study by political scientists showed that already by the end of 1985 there were some 500–600 reported cases per year involving Charter issues — with a success rate of 31 per cent.[1] No doubt many of these were criminal cases in which the defendant took a Charter point. But many no doubt were cases initiated because of the Charter. As has been seen the Charter emerged out of a major collective experience in constitution building. Judge Forrest of the New Brunswick Court of Appeal referred to this in 1983:

> "The Canadian Bill of Rights was known to be an expression of self-restraint by Parliament. It was an instruction by Parliament to the courts regarding the manner in which they read Acts of Parliament. But the courts were quite naturally inhibited from cutting down an Act of Parliament ... the Charter is the basic law of the land to which Parliament and legislatures themselves are subject. The psychological difference also flows from a more general situation. The public is now being told in a fundamental document agreed upon by all or almost all our governments and all our federal political parties that there are individual and group rights beyond the reach of government. These will be looked at by the citizen and the public will ... expect both governments and courts to take this seriously."[2]

Opinions vary greatly as to what kind of impact the Charter has had. Are civil liberties better protected than before? There are Charter enthusiasts and Charter sceptics[3]. Professor Roland Penner, Professor of Law and former Attorney-General of Manitoba, in his recently published article in *Public Law*[4] wrote:

---

[99] There is an enormous literature on the Canadian Charter. The reader will find some of the main texts listed in the Select Bibliography on p.165 below. The journal *Public Law* has carried several articles on the subject. See especially the issue of Autumn 1988 which had three valuable articles on the subject and Roland Penner, "The Canadian Experience with the Charter of Rights: Are there Lessons for the United Kingdom?" (1996) Pub.L. 104–125.

[1] See (1987) Can.H.Rts.Yrbk. 65, cited by Judge Strayer of the Federal Court of Canada in (1988) Pub.L.355.

[2] Can.Bar Rev., March 1983, 22–23.

[3] A bibliography of the writings of the Charter critics can be found in R.Sigurdson, "The Left-Legal Critique of the Charter: A Critical Assessment" (1993) 13 Windsor Yrbk.of Access to Justice,117 at 118, nn.3 and 4. Both Professor Keith Ewing and Professor Conor Gearty are to be included among the critics of the Charter jurisprudence — see their *Democracy or a Bill of Rights* (1993), See also p.130, n.20 below

[4] (1996) Pub.L. pp.104–125.

"Without in any way denigrating popular, parliamentary and shop-floor politics of protest and persuasion, it is my view that the experience with the Charter has both generally and specifically advanced the cause of human rights in Canada.[5]
. . . It is just a little more than 13 years since the Charter was proclaimed, yet one can cite in support of the Charter and the role of the judiciary in implementing it, scores of cases dealing positively from a human rights perspective with, *e.g.* abortion rights for women, equality rights, rights for religious and language minorities, the rights of immigrants and asylum seekers, equality rights for seniors and others in benefit programs, the recognition (though not yet the full application) of the principle that equality rights apply to gays and lesbians as a disadvantaged group and a long list of cases, effecting major reforms in the criminal law . . . "[6]

According to Penner, both federal and provincial governments had had statutes amended either on their own initiative or because of judicial prodding to make them conform to the Charter.[7] A public opinion survey in 1990 found that no less than 90 per cent of English Canadian and 70 per cent of French Canadian respondents said they had heard of the Charter and "a substantial majority" of each group thought the Charter "is a good thing for Canada".[8] The fact that most respondents appeared to have little knowledge as to what is in the Charter is neither surprising nor significant.The significance of the survey is that eight years on, the Charter was apparently held in esteem by the majority of the Canadian population. It is also worthy of note that over 60 per cent of respondents thought that courts rather than legislatures should have the final say when a law was found to be unconstitutional on the grounds that it conflicted with the Charter. By contrast, when a sample of 500 elected politicians were asked the same question over 60 per cent thought that legislatures should have the final say![9]

In Penner's view, despite some serious lapses,[10] the Canadian judiciary as a whole had "taken rights seriously"[11] and creatively. The Charter was primarily a shield to protect basic political, legal,

---

[5] *Ibid*, p.112.
[6] *Ibid*, p.114.
[7] *Ibid*, pp.114–115.
[8] P. Russell,"Canada's Charter: A Political Report" (1988) Pub.L.398. The survey was carried out by Professor Russell, Professor of Political Science at the University of Toronto, with three colleagues.
[9] *Ibid*.
[10] Of which he cites examples — *op. cit.* p.128, n.99 above, at 122, n.81.
[11] To adopt Dworkin's phrase.

minority and equality rights and was not intended to to be in the vanguard of transformative politics. Taken on its own terms "the Charter has been a substantial success".[12] It had been a success not only in particular cases[13] but "perhaps more importantly in enhancing the 'culture of liberty' in Canada".[14]

One unanticipated effect of the Canadian Charter had been the way that different groups had identified with particular provisions: "women's groups identify with section 28, the multicultural community and visible minorities with sections 15(1),[15] 15(2)[16] and 27,[17] the disabled community with section 15(1) and aboriginals with section 35".[18] For such groups the Charter had introduced a new weapon that could be deployed not only in the courts but in political debate and argument. (In the context of the debate in the United Kingdom about incorporation of the E.C.H.R. it is important to appreciate, however, that some of the most controversial provisions of the Canadian Charter have no analogue in the European Convention.)

For a sceptical discussion of the impact of the Charter, see W. A. Bogart[19], *Courts and Country: The Limits of Litigation and the Social and Political Life of Canada*.[20] The theme of Bogart's book is the limits of litigation. Empirical studies of the effect of litigation in achieving social change in the United States suggested that it tended to be negligible.[21] Judicialisation of fundamental social and political questions, in his phrase, "enervates politics". Bogart warns that:

> "With some exceptions, litigation in the name of reform has achieved little real change. What it frequently has done is act

[12] *op. cit.*, p.128, n.99 above at 123.
[13] Including, "left critics to the contrary, cases on some important labour relations issues", *ibid*.
[14] *Ibid*.
[15] The right to equal protection without discrimination based on race, national or ethnic origin, colour, religion, sex, age, or mental or physical disability (s.15(1)).
[16] Permits affirmative action programmes for persons disadvantaged by such discrimination as is referred to in s.15(1) and 15(2).
[17] "This Charter shall be interpreted in a manner consistent with the preservation and enhancement of the multiracial heritage of Canadians." (s.27).
[18] s.35 recognises the "existing aboriginal and treaty rights of the aboriginal peoples of Canada". See A. Cairns, "Citizens and their Charter: Democratizing the Process of Constitutional Reform", in M. Behails, (ed.) *The Meech Lake Primer: Conflicting Views of the 1987 Constitutional Accord* (1989) 119–120.
[19] Professor of law at the University of Windsor.
[20] (1994).
[21] He cited in particular G. Rosenberg, *The Hollow Hope — Can Courts Bring About Social Change?* (1991); J. Handler, *Social Movements and the Legal System: A theory of Law Reform and Social Change* (1978).

as a lure to deflect groups and their limited resources away from the political process where more deep and longlasting change might have been secured . . . "[22]

The Canadian experience suggests that the context in which a Bill of Rights is introduced is important. There seems to be no possibility that the Conservative Party in Britain will agree with Labour and Liberal Democrats on the incorporation of the E.C.H.R. into United Kingdom law. If the next Labour government goes ahead with the project, there would not therefore, be the kind of political consensus that would provide the ideal conditions for so important an initiative. Nor is it likely that incorporation of the E.C.H.R. would generate the kind of public debate that took place in Canada in the period leading up to the adoption of the Charter. In both these respects the introduction of a Bill of Rights for the United Kingdom would get off to a less than ideal start.

The success of the enterprise would therefore be somewhat unpredictable. Much could turn on the accidents of litigation and whether the concept of litigating under the E.C.H.R. Bill of Rights caught the public imagination or whether, to the contrary, the first high profile decisions gave people a sour impression of such litigation. It is not to be expected that one would altogether avoid some early decisions that would make sensible people wonder about the wisdom of the undertaking. But a Bill of Rights cannot be judged by how people feel about it a year or two after it has been passed. The test is how people feel about it twenty, fifty, a hundred years later. One would hope that over a period of many years during which both the two main political parties would have been in government the Bill of Rights would become established as a valuable part of the system. If, however, it were seen to be a political football that would not occur. It would only be capable of playing the role for which a Bill of Rights is intended if it were generally an accepted and valued institution. Whether that could be achieved would be a severe test both for the judiciary and for the wider community of commentators, especially both the quality and the popular press and politicians. The level of such debate in recent years arising, for instance, out of European Community law decisions or decisions of judges striking down the acts of Ministers has not always been the most elevated. "Judge bashing" has come to be regarded in some circles as acceptable. Indeed one commentator has suggested that judge bashing has been consciously adopted by government as part of a strategy to cope with legal challenge. ("Rather than taking all appropriate steps to comply

[22] *op. cit.* p.64.

131

with the law, ministers are now being much more cavalier about running risks that a decision may be subject to challenge. That they feel able to do so is because there is now a climate in which it is possible to denounce any unfavorable judgment or judge aggressively".[23]) Such ill-considered or immature commentary damages the body politic. It could affect the prospects for a Bill of Rights in the United Kingdom at least in the short term. The fear would be that if the road proved too rocky the experiment might be terminated prematurely by an incoming government before it had had the time to prove itself.

Making people more rights conscious is harmful

One of the results of enacting a Bill of Rights is to increase the occasions when people go to court to assert "their rights". That is indeed the main point of the project. Yet claiming one's rights is not from all points of view a blessing. One does not relish the thought of a society where citizens reach for a lawyer and a writ like a six-shooter in the Wild West.

From the classic Marxist/socialist perspective rights are seen as inextricably linked to the ideology of individualism.

> "The paradigm instances of rights are those expressed in terms of individual interests: the liberal individual is an agent whose subjectivity is expressed in the assertion of rights, the corollary of which is the objectification of others whose interests are sacrificed in the fulfillment of the right . . . By putting the emphasis on rights as claims, and as entailing the imposition of duties which can be coercively enforced against others, the liberal discourse of rights seems to abandon any aspiration to a world in which mutual co-operation might be a central political ideal, and thus abandons the possibility of any real commitment to a socialist vision."[24]

From a non-socialist perspective this position has no persuasive power. For those who basically hold or incline to the socialist view,

---

[23] Andrew Le Sueur, "The Judicial Review Debate: From Partnership to Friction", (1996) 31 Gvt. and Opp. 8, 23. The article provides a valuable reference source for the details of recent events in terms of attacks on judges by politicians and the media, and an assessment of recent case law. See also D. Woodhouse, "Politicians and Judges" (1995) 401–418, (1996) 423–40.

[24] N. Lacey, "Are Rights Best Left Unwritten?" (1989) 60 Pol. Qtrly. 433 at 435–436. See also Jeremy Waldron, "A Right-Based Critique of Constitutional Rights" (1993) 13 Oxf.J.of Leg.St. 18–51; and James Allan, "Bills of Rights and Judicial Power" (1996) 16 Oxf.J.of Leg.St. 337–352.

it may have some power. But at least some of these may share the view put by Nicola Lacey that, despite its shortcomings, from a socialist perspective, securing a Bill of Rights would make a modest but real contribution to social justice. ("In the context of Thatcher's Britain, it is asking too much of socially-minded citizens to engage in what amounts to passive resistance by refusing to engage in rights-asserting debate"[25]).

A very different perspective on the danger of promoting too much "rights talk" was eloquently expressed in a book with that title written by Professor Mary Ann Glendon of the Harvard Law School.[26]

> "Discourse about rights has become the principal language that we use in public settings to discuss weighty questions of right and wrong, but time and again it proves inadequate, or leads to a stand-off of one right against another. The problem is not, however, as some contend, with the very notion of rights, or with our strong rights tradition. It is with a new version of rights discourse that has achieved dominance over the past thirty years. Our current American rights talk is but one dialect in a universal language that has developed during the extraordinary era of attention to civil and human rights in the wake of World War II. It is set apart from rights discourse in other liberal democracies by its starkness and simplicity, its prodigality in bestowing the rights label, its legalistic character, its exaggerated absoluteness, its hyperindividualism, its insularity, and its silence with respect to persona, civic and collective responsibilities."[27]

A rapidly expanding catalogue of rights — "extending to trees, animals, smokers, non-smokers, consumers and so on, not only multiplies the occasions for collisions, but it risks trivializing core democratic values".[28] A tendency "to frame nearly every social controversy in terms of a clash of rights (a woman's right to her own body versus a foetus' right to life) impedes compromise, mutual understanding and the discovery of common ground".[29] Glendon specifically disclaimed any intention to deny the value of rights in general or of any particular right.

> "Let us freely grant that legally enforceable rights can assist citizens in a large heterogeneous country to live together in a

[25] Lacey, *op. cit.* at p.440.
[26] *Rights Talk: The Impoverishment of Political Discourse* (1991).
[27] *Ibid*, p.x.
[28] *Ibid*, p.xi.
[29] *Ibid*.

reasonably peaceful way. They have given minorities a way to articulate claims that majorities often respect, and have assisted the weakest members of society in making their voices heard." [30]

Her complaint was about a particular narrowness and stridency of approach to the discourse of rights.

"When we assert our rights to life, liberty and property, we are expressing the reasonable hope that such things can be made more secure by law and politics. When we assert these rights in an absolute form, however, we are expressing infinite and impossible desires — to be completely free, to possess things totally, to be captains of our fate and masters of our souls. There is pathos as well as bravado in these attempts to deny the fragility and contingency of human existence." [31]

Rights asserted on behalf of groups could suffer from just the same deformation. "Rights asserted on behalf of groups tend to pit group against individual, one group against another, and group against state". [32] Her plea was for a broader, more nuanced, more balanced approach to rights discourse. [33]

But in the United Kingdom, far from the rights discourse being too strident, it could be said that it is too muted. Study by Francoise Hampson, [34] of the cases involving the United Kingdom decided by the Strasbourg Court resulted in the conclusion that most often they involved people in the custody of the State (defendants in criminal cases, prisoners, mental patients) or who have turned to it for help (parents of children in care, immigrants, asylum seekers). "By definition, they are amongst the most vulnerable people. The cases suggest a lack of respect for them as individuals . . ." [35]

"Bureaucratic convenience is allowed to prevail. It is not even a question of the balancing of competing rights; these individuals are not seen as having any. In the United

[30] *Ibid*, p.15.
[31] *Ibid*, p.45.
[32] *Ibid*, p.137.
[33] She took as her model a decision of the European Court of Human Rights on the the validity of a Northern Ireland law prohibiting homosexual acts between consenting adults (*Dudgeon v. United Kingdom*, 3 E.H.R.R. 40 (1980)), which she compared favorably for its method and approach with the decision on the same subject of the U.S. Supreme Court in *Bowers v. Hardwick*, 478 U.S. 186 (1986).
[34] Reader in Law, Essex University.
[35] Francoise J. Hampson, "The United Kingdom before the European Court of Human Rights", 9 Yrbk.Eurpn.L. 121, 173.

Kingdom, it would appear that moral virtue does not consist in respecting the rights of other individuals but in conforming. Where those who step out of line are not in the custody of the authorities and do not require any other form of assistance, they will be tolerated. A wide range of religious groups, for example, are free to practise their beliefs. Similarly, there is a wide measure of freedom in relation to sexual activities, provided they do not involve children and are conducted in the privacy of the home. The situation is very different for those in the custody of the authorities such as prisoners and mental health patients, and for those who require the help of Government, such as those whose children are taken into care. The cases reveal a lack of respect for them as individuals. Once within the control of the authorities, they appear to find their rights replaced by privileges. They may be seen as 'problems', whose treatment will be determined by the administrative convenience of the appropriate system — the prison system, the medical system, and the child care system."[36]

Ms Hampson suggested that neither the executive nor the legislature seemed to think in terms of rights for these categories of problems — and that the same is true of the public at large.

"There are innumerable voluntary agencies for the relief of various types of suffering and special interest groups in certain fields. This does not, however, address the fundamental question of whether people think in terms of the rights of others, including the right to be different, the right to challenge assumptions, but above all, the right to be respected as a human being, even whilst receiving help".[376]

Perhaps the severest test of commitment to human rights was the recognition of the rights of those who break the law or who need help. In other fields, such as the right to free speech, one could call on a certain reciprocity. ("I will recognise your right to free speech because I claim the same right.") But in regard to those who break the law there was no equivalent reciprocity. "To make 'rights' conditional upon conformity or reciprocity, however, is to make them privileges and not rights."

The problem, Ms Hampson suggested, lies not in the legal system so much as in the educational system:

"Once demands are made on the majority, their starting point is not the right of the other to be different, which would

[36] *Ibid*, 149.
[37] *Ibid*, 163.

require a justification for any interference in his rights. The starting point is the rights of the majority. There is an assumption that what the majority wants is morally better. Such attitudes are a product of education in the broadest sense. We are not brought up to respect the rights of others as a matter of moral or political obligation. Nor does an awareness of rights appear to be developed in our schools. There is little education in the fields of philosophy, civics, or human rights, all of which are seen as political . . ."[38]

But she did not think that incorporation of the E.C.H.R. would necessarily make a great difference.

"Until the climate of opinion requires each branch of Government to make the protection of human protection of human rights a priority, both in legislation and in the implementation of that legislation, the same types of breaches of the European Convention on Human Rights as have already been examined are likely to recur. They are not isolated cases of an individual exceeding the scope of his authority. They reflect the predisposition of the constitutional system and the public attitudes that maintain it."[39]

Incorporation of the Convention "simply would not address those issues" — though "it might, however, have a part to play in the education of the general public, including the Government, the legislature and the judiciary".[40]

Granted that there is something in Ms Hampson's thesis, it may be that it is a shade too pessimistic. There seems to be general agreement that in recent years there has been something of a revolution in the use of the law by pressure groups[41] and especially in the use of judicial review.[42] Michael Beloff Q.C., a leading public lawyer, in a recent wide-ranging lecture considered the conditions which led to the enormous development of this branch of law.[43] The foremost, he thought, was the growth of what he called "the

[38] *Ibid*, 164
[39] *Ibid*, 164–165.
[40] *Ibid*, 165.
[41] See especially C. Harlow and R. W. Rawlings, *Pressure through Law* (1992).
[42] The most comprehensive statement of the law is to be found in de Smith, Woolf and Jowell, *Judicial Review of Administrative Action* (5th ed., 1995). See also W. Wade, *Administrative Law* (7th ed., 1994) and P. P. Craig, *Administrative Law* (3rd ed., 1994). For an analysis of the statistics see M. Sunkin, L. Bridges and G. Meszaros, *Judicial Review in Perspective* (1995).
[43] Michael Beloff, "Judicial Review-2001: A Prophetic Odyssey", (1995) 58 M.L.R. 143–159.

regulated society", the result of "increasing intrusion, by governments of whatever political colour, into the affairs of the citizen".[44]
This tendency had waxed greatly during the years of Conservative
rule:

> "Since 1979, under a Conservative Government nominally
> dedicated to the principle of the light touch, we have been
> 'forced to be free'. But there are few areas of national life —
> education at all levels,[45] health, transport, welfare, financial
> services, the law itself — that have not been subjected to new
> and often controversial legislative schemes. Where privatisa-
> tion of industry has taken place, a tier of regulation is
> interposed between the consumer and the provider —
> OFTEL, OFGAS, OFRAIL *et al*, who themselves become
> potentially amenable to regulation by the courts. *Quis
> custodiet ipsos custodes*? was as urgent a question in Major's
> Britain as it was in Juvenal's Rome. There is simply more for
> the courts to review."[46]

Beloff referred also to the diminution in the power and effectiveness of political control over the executive:

> "the subservience of backbenchers disciplined by whips and
> ambition alike; the limitations on the powers of the opposi-
> tion, hampered by lack of access to information — except at
> the discretion of disobedient civil servants; inadequate
> powers and resources for the Select Committees compared,
> say, with their American counterparts; the decline, it may be,
> of the number of MPs with the stamina to inquire and the wit
> to criticise" . . .[47] It is for political scientists to debate the
> relative significance of these factors. But that there has been
> a vacuum cannot be doubted; and the judges have filled it."[48]

The judges were "more activist . . . — no longer hands off, but
over your shoulder". Judicial review had become a paying proposition for the legal profession — not just with the rights of the less
advantaged, such as the homeless, immigrants, students, social
security recipients "but with the affairs of the City, the construction
industry, aviation, the information superhighway and the like"[49].
Hence the rationale for publications such as *Commercial Judicial*

---

[44] *Ibid*, 144.
[45] Beloff's footnotes are omitted here.
[46] Beloff, "Judicial Review 2001: A Prophetic Odyssey", (1995) 58 M.L.R. 143 at
144–145.
[47] *Ibid*, 145.
[48] *Ibid*.
[49] *Ibid*, 145–146.

Review Bulletin and the *Environmental Judicial Review Bulletin*. A fifth factor was "the increasing awareness of the potentialities of public law among individuals" and, in particular, pressure groups. "These conditions", Michael Beloff suggested, "will surely subsist through the nineties and into the new millenium".[50]

Whether the development of greater rights consciousness could reach the level deplored by Professor Glendon obviously cannot be predicted with certainty. It would be wise to be conscious of the danger. But there are factors here that make it unlikely. One is a legal-political culture that is not hospitable to unqualified or absolute statements of right. The fact that so many of the provisions of the E.C.H.R. are drafted in a format emphasising the "on the one hand — and on the other hand" nature of most of the issues should help to reduce the risk. The courts will inevitably be involved in a process of weighing options and proportionality.[51] Nevertheless, it would be wise to expect some heightening of aggressive rights talk — the sound of which will not always be pleasing.

---

[50] *Ibid*, 146.

[51] In *Attorney-General of Hong Kong v. Lee Kwong-kut* [1993] 3 All E.R. 939 the Privy Council had to consider whether two statutory provisions affecting the burden of proof had been repealed by the Bill of Rights Ordinance s.11(1) — "Everyone charged with a criminal offence shall have the right to be presumed innocent until proved guilty according to law". It held that one did and one did not fall foul of the Bill of Rights. It said that there was a degree of flexibility in s.11(1). In a borderline case the court should determine whether the statutory objective was of sufficient importance to warrant overriding a constitutionally protected right or freedom and, if so, whether the means adopted passed the test of proportionality. "While the Hong Kong judiciary should be zealous in upholding an individual's rights under the Hong Kong Bill of Rights, it is also necessary to ensure that disputes as to the effect of the Bill of Rights are not allowed to get out of hand. The issues involving the Hong Kong Bill of Rights should be approached with realism and good sense, and kept in proportion. If this is not done the Hong Kong Bill of Rights will become a source of injustice rather than justice and it will be debased in the eyes of the public. In order to maintain the balance between the individual and the society as a whole, rigid and inflexible standards should not be imposed on the legislature's attempts to resolve the difficult and intransigent problems with which society is faced when seeking to deal with serious crime. It must be remembered that questions of policy remain primarily the responsibility of the legislature" (*per* Lord Woolf, at p.940).

4. IF A BILL OF RIGHTS, WHAT KIND AND WHAT MACHINERY?

Should the Bill of Rights be the European Convention on Human Rights?

If there is to be a United Kingdom Bill of Rights there are two main alternatives. One is to incorporate the working provisions of the E.C.H.R. into United Kingdom law, the other is to incorporate an amended version of the E.C.H.R. or to draft a new free-standing Bill of Rights. In regard to these alternatives there appears to be a substantial measure of agreement that, at least as a first step, the E.C.H.R. should be incorporated into United Kingdom law. Some, though not the writer, would go further to see some "better" Bill of Rights enacted.

The House of Lords Select Committee, which was otherwise deeply divided, was unanimous that if there were to be a Bill of Rights it should be the E.C.H.R. As was seen in Chapter 1, that view has been expressed by most of those who have supported the idea of a domestic Bill of Rights. The Labour Party's view is that the E.C.H.R. should be incorporated as a first step.

There are several obvious advantages in incorporating the E.C.H.R. as it stands:

   (a) Britain has for decades been a party to the E.C.H.R. and has, therefore, throughout that period signified its willingness to abide by its terms. Both major political parties have, as Governments, accepted the fact of the E.C.H.R. and the right of individual petition. Its adoption into United Kingdom law should therefore command the maximum amount of support in all parties that can be mustered for a Bill of Rights. It is hard to believe that any alternative version could command the same level of support across the political spectrum.
   (b) To adopt into United Kingdom law obligations that are already binding internationally should be a relatively minor step psychologically and politically by comparison with the process involved in deciding on a new text.

(c) It could be inconvenient to have two different Bills of Right — the E.C.H.R. binding on the United Kingdom externally and a different version binding internally.

(d) If we are willing to trust the judges of the Strasbourg Court with the interpretation of the Convention, we are presumably even more (or at least, no less) willing to trust English judges with the same task.

The main disadvantage of incorporating the E.C.H.R. is that everyone agrees that it could be improved upon. It lacks some valuable provisions. Its style and content are somewhat outdated. It is not in every Article as broad and open textured as might be desirable to achieve potentially the best results.

Some commentators and bodies of consequence have argued that it is important to improve on the E.C.H.R. But the task is bound to prove difficult of achievement. If it were given to a Royal Commission, or a similar body, it would be likely to take years and to involve much controversy and disagreement. No doubt the process of discussion and debate during the time of such a Commission's work would be beneficial from the point of view of educating the public, the lawyers, judges and politicians on the issues involved. But there is no certainty that the final product would be an improvement on the E.C.H.R., even if agreement were possible — and agreement is uncertain. The House of Lords Select Committee cited the experience of Austria as a reason for preferring the E.C.H.R. A Commission was set up there in 1966 to draw up a code of fundamental rights but after 12 years it had succeeded in producing a text in respect of only two rights and even then only in the form of alternative drafts. The Select Committee concluded that "to attempt to formulate *de novo* a set of fundamental rights which would command the necessary general assent would be a fruitless exercise".[1] I share that view.

Those who urge that work on a free-standing Bill of Rights in addition to or in eventual substitution for the E.C.H.R. would repay the effort and who have made detailed proposals include Liberty[2] and the Institute for Public Policy Research (IPPR).[3] The provisions they would wish to add to the British Bill of Rights which are not to be found in the E.C.H.R. include the following: no one shall be subjected without consent to medical or scientific experimentation, testing or research (Liberty, Art. 3.2[4]); arrested

[1] "Select Committee Report' *op. cit.* p.26, n.80 above, at p.21, para. 10.
[2] *A People's Charter*, 1991.
[3] *A British Bill of Rights*, 1990.
[4] The source is the International Covenant on Civil and Political Rights ("IC"), Art. 7.

140

persons should be treated with humanity and respect for the dignity of the human person;[5] arrested persons should normally be segregated from convicted persons and have separate treatment;[6] juveniles should be held separate from adults;[7] all persons are equal before the law and are entitled without discrimination to the equal protection of the law;[8] defendants are entitled to be tried by a jury in all cases involving potential loss of liberty;[9] defendants should not be compelled to testify against themselves or to confess guilt;[10] where a substantial doubt arises about a conviction there should be a right to have the case reviewed and investigated;[11] confessions should only be admissible if made in the presence of a solicitor and if corroborated by independent evidence;[12] evidence obtained in breach of the law should not be admissible in criminal proceedings;[13] everyone has the right to be secure against unreasonable search and seizure;[14] victims of miscarriages of justice should be compensated;[15] everyone has the right to know what public and private authorities hold information on them and for what purposes;[16] everyone has the right of access to information about them held by any public or private authority;[17] no one should be required to carry an identity card;[18] no marriage shall be entered into without the free and full consent of the spouses;[19] spouses shall have equality of rights as to marriage, during marriage and at its dissolution;[20] children shall be protected from all forms of neglect, cruelty and exploitation;[21] children born out of wedlock shall have equal rights with children born in wedlock;[22] children shall have the protection they need from their family, society and public

---

[5] Liberty, Art. 5 clause 6, IPPR, Art. 4(6). The source is IC, Art. 10(1).
[6] Liberty, Art. 5, clause 7, IPPR, Art. 4(7). The source is IC, Art. 10(2)(a).
[7] Liberty Art. 5, clause 8, IPPR, Art. 4(8). The source is IC, Art. 10(2)(b).
[8] Liberty, Art. 6, clause 1. The source is IC, Art. 26.
[9] Liberty, Art. 6, clause 4(g).
[10] IPPR, Art. 5(3)(f). The source is IC, Art. 14(3)(g).
[11] Liberty, Art. 6, clause 6.
[12] Liberty, Art. 6, clause 7(a).
[13] Liberty, Art. 6, clause 7(b).
[14] Liberty, Art. 8, clause 5. The sources is Art. 8 of the Canadian Charter which is based on the U.S. Bill of Rights.
[15] IPPR, Art. 5(4). A modified version of IC, Art. 14(6).
[16] Liberty, Art. 8, clause 3.
[17] Liberty, Art. 8, clause 4.
[18] Liberty, Art. 8, clause 6.
[19] IPPR, Art. 12(2). The source is IC, Art. 23(3).
[20] IPPR, Art. 12(3). The source is IC, Art. 23(4).
[21] Liberty, Art. 13, clause 2. The source is Art. 9 of the 1989 U.N. Convention on the Rights of the Child.
[22] Liberty, Art. 13, clause 3. The source is Art. 17(5) of the American Convention on Human Rights.

authorities;[23] every child born in the United Kingdom shall be entitled to United Kingdom citizenship and nationality;[24] members of ethnic, religious or national minorities shall not be denied the right to use their own language and manifest their own religion and culture;[25] everyone has the right to seek and be granted asylum if they are being pursued for political offences;[26] no refugee or asylum seeker shall be deported to a country where their life would be threatened on account of political offences;[27] workers shall enjoy protection against anti-union discrimination;[28] workers shall have the right to democratically-agreed collective action, including strike action[29].

Any of these rights could arguably strengthen a Bill of Rights. Personally I would have no problem about accepting any of them. But I would not regard it as sufficiently important to have any of them to make it right to wait until they can be agreed to be appropriate for adoption in a British Bill of Rights. Also, the act of trying to reach agreement on a different text could, if unsuccessful, damage the Bill of Rights cause out of proportion to its true importance. The fact of failure would be regarded as significant whereas in reality its importance would be slight.

Some have argued that a domestic Bill of Rights should address not just the traditional areas dealt with in Bills of Rights but socio-economic rights concerning issues such as the right to work, the right to decent housing, the right to a pollution-free environment, the right to access to medical services and the like. (As has been seen (p.49 above), the South African constitution includes such issues in its Bill of Rights.) There are two main reasons for not supporting this agenda. One is that there is no possibility of general agreement on the text of such provisions. Thus where the Left wish to see the enactment of rights designed to enhance equality, the Right will press for recognition of the opposite (protection of the right to private education, private property, private medicine, etc.) The second, and more fundamental reason is that, even if such agreement could be achieved, it would be

---

[23] IPPR, Art. 12(4). The source is IC, Art. 24(1).
[24] Liberty, Art. 13, clause 4. The source is the 14th Amendment of the U.S. Constitution.
[25] Liberty, Art. 14, clause 2. The source is IC, Art. 27 and the 1991 Hong Kong Bill of Rights.
[26] Liberty, Art. 19, clause 1, IPPR, Art. 18. The source is paras. (7) and (8) of the American Convention on Human Rights.
[27] Liberty, Art. 19, clause 3. The source is the 1951 Geneva Convention Relating to the Status of Refugees.
[28] Liberty, Art. 11, clause 2. The source is Art. 1 of the International Labour Organisation Convention on the Right to Organise and Collective Bargaining.
[29] Liberty, Art. 11, clause 3. The source is the European Social Charter.

unwise to give the judges the task of adjudicating on such issues. The adjudicative process in courts of law dealing with disputes raised by litigants is not appropriate to determining the allocation of society's resources necessarily involved in deciding such issues. Those are questions that have to be resolved by the very different political process.

If it is broadly agreed that the E.C.H.R. itself should be incorporated into United Kingdom law, at least as a first step, a question that requires attention is how much of the E.C.H.R. should be included. The view of the House of Lords Select Committee was that the material to be incorporated should include the whole E.C.H.R. and the First Protocol which has been ratified by the United Kingdom — subject to the reservation entered to the First Protocol by the Government.[30] A different view which has been adopted in many of the Bills introduced in the House of Lords is to incorporate just what may be called the provisions guaranteeing fundamental rights and freedoms (Articles 2–18 and the First Protocol.[31] the text of these provisions is printed in the Appendix at p.167 below.) The Select Committee thought that the statute should provide for a procedure whereby an Order in Council could expand or contract the terms of the domestic law in line with any changes in our international obligations under the Convention. This proposal was adopted by Lord Lester in the Human Rights Bill he introduced in the House of Lords in November 1994. It seems a wise provision.

Should there be a special human rights court?

Some have proposed that interpretation of the Bill of Rights should be the province only of a specially constituted, expert court. It is argued that this would make it somewhat more likely that the problems would be dealt with by judges reputed to be knowledgeable about, and sympathetic to human rights issues. But the history of the United States Supreme Court shows the limitations of this concept. There are not a few examples of justices apparently placed on the court by the President of the day for one purpose, whose philosophy later developed in quite different directions. Moreover there is nothing to guarantee that the specialist human rights court

---

[30] *Ibid*, p.35, para 37. The Northern Ireland Advisory Commission took basically the same view — *op. cit.*, p.23, n.75. above, at p.66.

[31] The most recent example is the Bill introduced in November 1994 by Lord Lester which included in a schedule the text of Articles 2–18, of the First Protocol subject to the Government's Reservation, and the Government's Derogation in respect of the period of detention for questioning of terrorism suspects.

would not be sabotaged by the intentional appointment of judges generally hostile to its fundamental objectives.

The advantages of a specialist court may, therefore, be somewhat speculative, whereas the disadvantages are clear. First, it would not necessarily be helpful to exclude most judges from decisions on something so fundamental as human rights. To make human rights a specialist preserve suggests that ordinary judges cannot be entrusted with such problems. It would be much healthier to involve the entire judiciary in these issues. For one thing, it would only be through such involvement that one would hope to achieve the broadening effect on judicial horizons that should be achieved by a Bill of Rights. Human rights should be a mainstream judicial activity. The chance of good (and bad) decisions is probably not significantly greater from a specialist tribunal than from the ordinary courts.

Would there nevertheless be a case for having a final court of appeal with specially selected judges? It would seem greatly preferable to use the ordinary courts even at the highest level. There is no reason to suppose that a specially selected Human Rights Appeal Court would do the job any better than the House of Lords. The House of Lords is the long-established final court of appeal with the great weight of historic authority flowing from that role. A special human rights final court of appeal could not be expected to match that authority. It would not do so even if the judges were all law lords, just because they would not be "the House of Lords". Indeed, whilst the selection of judges suitable for human rights cases might increase their stature in the eyes of some, it would diminish it in the eyes of others. (An analogy might be the attitude in the culture of the police canteen toward officers performing the role of community policing. They tend not to be held in the same esteem by colleagues.)

Lord Irvine, writing as Shadow Lord Chancellor, made clear that the Labour Party proposed that in general Bill of Rights questions should be dealt with in any court. This would avoid troublesome disputes as to which court should deal with a complaint. Also it was important that "regard for human rights pervades the work of all courts, and is recognised as an integral part of their work".[32] But he thought that at the final appellate level, "where points of funda- mental or wide-ranging importance about human rights may have

[32] D. Bean, (ed.), *Law Reform for All* (1996), pp.19–20. This was also the view of John Smith in his speech "A Citizen's Democracy" on March 1, 1993. ("It is essential that regard for human rights pervades the work of all courts, and is recognised as an integral part of their work . . ."). See equally the Labour party's policy as set out in *A new agenda for democracy: Labour's proposals for constitutional reform*, September 1993, p.30.

to be decided", there was a strong case for adding to the judges three lay persons "drawn from a panel of persons with knowledge and understanding of society and of human rights in the broad sense".[33] The lay persons would be full members of the court with an equal vote. The writer confesses that he remains to be persuaded of the wisdom of this proposal. If judges in the House of Lords do not have "knowledge and understanding of society and of human rights" they do not deserve to be Law Lords. Would the lay persons sit on ordinary appeals (many of which are highly technical tax cases) or only on cases raising points taken under the Bill of Rights? If the lay persons were felt to add something of worth to the deliberations of the House of Lords in those cases, would not the inevitable result be to diminish the authority of the decisions of the Court of Appeal which would sit without lay persons? Does not the concept of lay persons sitting with the Law Lords conflict with Lord Irvine's own stated policy that responsibility for human rights "must be put on the regular courts:and judges of those courts must be trained and be ready to respond to the challenge"[34]?

It was suggested by the Institute of Public Policy Research (IPPR) that although in general any court should be permitted to rule on points arising on the Bill of Rights this should not apply to decisions as to the validity of an Act of Parliament. It thought that the normal method of challenging the acts of public authorities would be by way of proceedings for judicial review but that it ought also to be possible for a Bill of Rights point to be taken, for instance, by a defendant at his trial in a criminal case. However, no court below the High Court, it suggested, should have the power to declare any provision of an Act of Parliament to be invalid.[35] The suggested procedure was that if there was a challenge under the Bill of Rights to the validity of a statutory provision in a court below the level of the High Court, that court would refer the matter to the High Court for decision — unless it considered that the challenge was clearly hopeless. If the High Court dismissed the challenge, the case would proceed in the lower court. Liberty makes essentially the same proposal.[36] It seems sensible.

Would there be a need for a new system of selecting judges?

There is an argument that introduction of a domestic Bill of Rights would create a need for a different system of judicial

[33] *Ibid.*
[34] *Ibid.*
[35] IPPR, *A British Bill of Rights*, 1990, p.21.
[36] See *Liberty's Bill of Rights — a People's Charter*, (1991), Art. 25, p.86.

appointment. The argument is based on the belief that because decisions under a Bill of Rights involve broader social policy issues it would be more important than now to know something about the views of the judges. The argument is mostly put by those who oppose a Bill of Rights — knowing that all right thinking people would be aghast at the idea of adopting anything like American-style investigations into the views and attitudes of judicial nominees. So, for instance, Lord Mackay, the then Lord Chancellor speaking in July 1996 said that if the E.C.H.R. were incorporated or a Bill of Rights enacted,

> "The question which would then be asked, and to which an answer could not be postponed indefinitely, is whether the introduction of such a political element into the judicial function would require a change in the criteria for appointment of judges, making the political stance of each candidate a matter of importance as much as his or her ability to decide cases on their individual facts and the law applicable to those facts."

Following on from that, he suggested, was the question whether their appointment should be subjected to political scrutiny of the sort seen recently in the United States.[37]

But the argument is not persuasive. That it is possible to have a Bill of Rights without needing to inquire into the socio-political opinions of judges is demonstrated by the Canadian system. The introduction there of the Charter did not lead to a change in the traditional methods for the appointment of judges.

A different but related argument which has been aired in recent years in England is that the system of selecting judges should be reformed in the direction of making the procedure more open and accessible to a wider range of candidates. The argument has not arisen specifically in the context of the debate over introduction of a Bill of Rights but plainly that debate could be said to raise the question. The issue was addressed by the House of Commons Home Affairs Select Committee in a report published in June 1996.[38] The Report gave a detailed account of the present system in which the Lord Chancellor made or advised on appointments on the basis of "a structured, organised, rolling programme of quite extensive consultations".[39] Recently the process had been altered

[37] "Parliament and the Judges — A Constitutional Challenge", Speech to the Citizenship Foundation, July 8, 1996.
[38] *Judicial Appointments Procedures*, Home Affairs Committee, Third Report, H.C., 52–1, 1995–96.
[39] *Ibid*, para. 36.

146

by a new system of advertising judicial posts at all levels up to Circuit Judge.[40] But this new system did not apply to senior judicial offices and the Select Committee said that it accepted the Lord Chancellor's view that advertising for positions of High Court judges and above would be neither practicable nor useful. As to practicability, the fact that such appointments were made only rarely and at short notice made advertisements inappropriate. As to utility, since candidates for such positions were known to the Lord Chancellor and his senior officials there would be little point and little scope for widening the pool of candidates.[41]

In regard to all but two of the 269 paragraphs of the report the members of the Select Committee were unanimous about the text and the recommendations. There were however two paragraphs on which they divided on party lines. The first concerned the question "Is the judiciary drawn from too narrow an educational background?" The Report[42] cited an article in the October 1994 issue of the journal *Labour Research* which contained figures to the effect that the proportion of those holding higher judicial office who were educated at an independent school had risen from 70 per cent in 1987 to 80 per cent in 1994 and that the proportion educated at Oxford or Cambridge had risen from 80 per cent to 87 per cent.[43] Commenting, the Report said

"It is certainly remarkable that such a high proportion of the senior judiciary attended either Oxford or Cambridge University, but we are not convinced that this is a sign of bias; rather we believe that it reflects the background of those entering the legal professions 30 years ago."

The Report continued (para.117):

"Whereas it might have been arguable in the past that an Oxford or Cambridge University education was largely

[40] See a Consultation Paper *Developments in Judicial Appointments Procedures*, issued by the Lord Chancellor's Department (LCD), May 19, 1994. There was a published job description and statement of criteria for selection. Selected applicants were interviewed by a panel of three consisting of a serving judge, a senior member of the LCD and a lay member. The purpose was to make the process more open and "to ensure that all those who are eligible and wish to be considered for appointment are encouraged to make known their interest and to ensure that all those available are considered" (Memorandum of evidence from the LCD to the Home Affairs Select Committee, quoted in its Report, p.xiv.). For further details see the Select Committee's Report pp.xiii–xix.

[41] *Ibid*, para. 150.

[42] *Ibid*, para. 113.

[43] A memorandum supplied to the Committee by the Lord Chancellor's Department showed that 80 per cent of the senior judiciary, 51 per cent of circuit judges and 12 per cent of district judges obtained their first degree at either Oxford or Cambridge. (*ibid*.)

reserved for those from 'privileged' backgrounds, the proportion of entrants from state schools has risen to meet that of entrants from independent schools."

This is indeed the case. In 1995, 43 per cent of incoming Oxford students were from state schools compared with 46.4 per cent from independent schools (the remaining students mainly came from abroad).[44] In Cambridge the comparable figures in 1995 were 45 per cent from state schools, 45 per cent from independent schools and 9 per cent, "Other and Overseas".[45]

The Select Committee said "We have received no evidence that candidates for judicial appointment who attended neither independent schools nor Oxford or Cambridge University are disadvantaged in their applications".[46] The conclusion reached was "we are confident that decisions on judicial appointment are not guided by information on where candidates were educated".[47] The Committee's draft report was considered by the Committee on June 5, 1996. A motion moved by Labour Members sought to replace the text of paragraph 117 by a very different paragraph standing in the name of Mr Chris Mullin:

"Inevitably, given the lengthy and expensive training necessary for entry to the legal profession, a disproportionate number of successful lawyers are likely to come from privileged backgrounds. We are concerned, however, to notice that an astonishing 80 per cent of the senior judiciary were privately educated (as compared to 7 per cent of school age children in the country as a whole). We note that far from improving, this trend appears to be increasing. We are also concerned that the senior judiciary are predominantly graduates of Oxbridge. We accept that, since Oxford and Cambridge universities attract some of the brightest law students, it is not surprising that they should be disproportionately represented in the upper levels of the profession. However we find it hard to think of a good reason why four-fifths of senior judges should come from the same two universities."[48]

The motion said it was appreciated that the present generation of senior judges graduated 30 years ago but the situation did not

---

[44] University of Oxford "Fact-Sheet 1995–96", p.2 — supplied by the Oxford University Press and Information Office.
[45] *Cambridge University Reporter*, vol.cxxvi, December 1, 1995, p.2.
[46] *op. cit.*, para. 117
[47] *Ibid*.
[48] *Ibid*, p.lxxxvi.

seem to be changing. "As the figures demonstrate, there is no downward trend". It continued:

"We believe that this situation is an indictment of the present system of appointments. Although impossible to prove, we believe there is strong circumstantial evidence that there is a glass ceiling beyond which lawyers who lack the appropriate background and contacts find it difficult, if not impossible, to progress. We acknowledge that the reforms recently introduced by the present Lord Chancellor may well improve this wholly unsatisfactory situation, but we are not convinced that they will prove adequate to overcome the very considerable forces of inertia and complacency at the highest level of the legal profession. We believe that further measures of reform will be required."[49]

The motion was however defeated by the Conservative majority who attended on the day.

The second focus of disagreement on party lines concerned paragraph 142 of the Select Committee's Report which stated the Committee's conclusion on the question whether it would be better to have judges selected by some form of Judicial Appointments Commission. This is a concept which has been advanced in recent years by various bodies as a way of broadening the process of consultation and decision in selection.[50] Views differed as to the composition and nature of such a body but its essence is to transfer responsibility for judicial appointments, either in full or in part, from the executive to an independent body whose members could include lay persons. The model proposed by JUSTICE for instance had seven lay members out of thirteen, with three barristers and three solicitors.[51] It thought that the Commission should initially only advise the Lord Chancellor by submitting lists of approved names, but that eventually it should take over the task of selection. The Law Society proposed membership divided between serving judges, legal academics and practitioners, lay persons with expertise in recruitment and training methods, and lay persons representing the community.

The Lord Chancellor, Lord Mackay, opposed the idea of the Commission. In his view, it would split the responsibility for

---

[49] *Ibid.*
[50] The Select Committee's Report (para. 131) stated that it was supported by JUSTICE, the Law Society, the National Association for the Care and Resettlement of Offenders (NACRO) and the Howard League for Penal Reform. It had also been proposed by the Labour Party — see Labour Party Consultation Paper, "Access to Justice", February 1995, section C(i).
[51] *Ibid*, para. 133.

149

appointments and blur his responsibility and accountability. It would not be possible to pass to such a body comments gathered through the consultative process. It was opposed equally by the Judges' Council which dismissed the argument made by some that such a Commission would remove the process of appointing judges from political interference, arguing that in fact a Commission would "introduce politics into the process rather than exclude them". The then Lord Chief Justice, Lord Taylor, agreeing, suggested that members of such a Commission would fight the corners they represented. He pointed to the example of Presidential nominations to the Supreme Court of the United States and to political "battling" by members of the Senate Committee formed to hold hearings in order to confirm the nominee for office. He described the prospect of such an experience in this country as "horrific". But the Committee's Report suggested that this contrast was not strictly appropriate since it was not suggested that such a Commission should be composed of politicians.

The Select Committee's Report said the key question was whether a Commission would improve the quality of appointment that exists today. It concluded it would not:

> "From the·evidence we have taken, we have not been persuaded that the quality of appointees would necessarily improve if a Judicial Appointments Commission were to be established . . . (W)e believe that the value of a consultation network might be diminished if a Judicial Appointments Commission were to play a part in selecting judges. We accept that a Commission would appear more open in the eyes of candidates, particularly those who saw themselves as disadvantaged under the present system; but we do not see that the creation of a Commission would be necessary in order to meet such concerns."[52]

Reform might be necessary but the majority on the Committee rejected the option of a Commission. The Labour minority disagreed. It thought there was room for improvement in the quality of the judiciary and referred in that connection to the role of the senior judges in "the disastrous miscarriages of justice in the 1970s and 1980s" and "the legendary stubborness of the Court of Appeal in facing up to what had gone wrong".[53]

> "Neither do we accept assurances that the heavy preponderance in the higher judiciary of upper middle class males,

[52] *Ibid*, para. 142.
[53] *Ibid*, pp.lxxxvi. The motion was again in the name of Mr Chris Mullin who himself played a significant role in these cases, especially that of the Birmingham Six.

educated at the same handful of schools and universities will necessarily melt away with the rise of a new generation of lawyers. On the contrary, we believe that evidence exists of a glass ceiling between the middle and higher judiciary beyond which those of the "wrong" background or gender find it difficult to progress. Finally we believe that the existing system of appointment is open to political manipulation by a Lord Chancellor less scrupulous than the present incumbent."[54]

The minority therefore concluded that a judicial appointments commission might well be the best means of achieving the transparency in judicial appointments necessary to retain public confidence.[55]

My own view is that, whatever the merits of making the system of selecting judges more open or of changing the procedure, there is no sufficient reason to suppose that it would improve the quality of the bench. Thus, for instance, there is, I believe, no worthwhile evidence that candidates for judicial appointment of sufficient ability are being rejected because they are women, members of ethnic minorities or persons with the "wrong" educational background. It follows that I do not regard this as an important reform whether a Bill of Rights is introduced or not. The issue, in my view, has more to do with political correctness than with the quality of the bench.

Remedies

There must be effective remedies under a Bill of Rights but the question is what are effective remedies? The remedies available should be the ordinary ones — an action for a declaration and the other forms of remedy available under judicial review (*certiorari*, *mandamus*, prohibition), damages and where appropriate, injunctions. Traditionally injunctions were not available against the Crown. This rule was rejected by the House of Lords in 1993 in *M. v. Home Office*[56] but it may nevertheless be desirable to put the matter beyond doubt by spelling it out in the Bill of Rights. A declaration in lieu of an injunction has normally sufficed in actions

---

[54] *Ibid*, p.lxxxvii.
[55] *Ibid*.
[56] [1993] 3 W.L.R.433. The House of Lords held that the Home Secretary had properly been found to be in contempt in failing to comply with a court order to secure the return to this country of a citizen of Zaire who had applied for political asylum but who had improperly been placed on a flight to Zaire.

against the Crown but the power to grant an injunction would be valuable in addition. It would also be important to provide specifically that damages can be obtained for a breach of the Bill of Rights. This would fill the gap caused by the rule that in the United Kingdom there is generally no right to damages for loss caused by administrative action unless the conduct can be classifed as being in a recognised common law category such as negligence or breach of statutory duty.

Lord Lester's Human Rights Bill provided that any violation of the Act would be actionable as breach of statutory duty. According to Lord Lester, as with any other breach of statutory duty, the circumstances in which a breach would give rise to a claim for compensation would have to be determined on a case-by-case basis by the courts.[57] But as a result of objections by Lord Taylor who suggested that the matter should be left to the courts' discretion[58] and Lord Woolf[59] the clause was withdrawn. It would be desirable to put the matter beyond doubt by including such a provision in the Act. Lord Lester wrote that a right to compensation for breach of constitutionally guaranteed human rights and freedoms has now been recognised in a number of common law countries — Canada,[60] India,[61] New Zealand,[62] the United States,[63] and Ireland.[64] The Judicial Committee of the Privy Council had held that the same was true in regard to breaches of the constitution of Trinidad and Tobago.[65] Section 50 of the E.C.H.R. permits the Strasbourg Court to award compensation as "just satisfaction" and it has often done so.

Should the Bill of Rights apply only against public authorities?

It appears to be widely agreed that actions brought under the Bill of Rights should lie in respect only of acts done by public authorities or by bodies that, though private, perform public functions. The point seems to be covered by the kind of provision in Lord Lester's Human Right's Bill of November 1994 which made actionable under the Act a violation of the provisions of the

[57] (1996) Pub.L. 198 at 200.
[58] *Hansard*, H.L. Vol. 568 col. 1144 (January 25, 1995).
[59] *Hansard*, H.L. Vol. 569, col. 781 (February 15, 1995).
[60] See *R. v. Schacter* [1992] 2 S.C.R. 679.
[61] *Nilibati Behera v. State of Oriss* (1993) 2 (SCC) 746.
[62] *Simpson v. Attorney General (Baigent's Case)* [1994] 3 N.Z.L.R. 667.
[63] e.g. *Bivens v. Six Unknown Fed. Narcotics Agents* 403 U.S. 388 (1970), *Harlow v. Fitzgerald* 457 U.S. 800 (1982).
[64] e.g. *Meskell v. CIE* [1973] I.R. 121.
[65] *Maharaj v. Attorney-General of Trinidad and Tobago (No. 2)* [1979] A.C. 385.

Bill of Rights by any person "in the performance of any public function".[66] An alternative approach which has been used in many previous Bills introduced in Parliament is to spell out those whose actions are affected more precisely.[67] For the avoidance of doubt it should be specifically stated that the Act binds the Crown.

It is fair to note that the House of Lords Select Committee thought that the possibility of actions against private individuals might be open under the E.C.H.R. and, if this was so, the United Kingdom Bill of Rights should not preclude it.[68] Admittedly this would leave an area of uncertainty to be settled by the courts. Admittedly too they might decide the question in a sense contrary to that ultimately established in Strasbourg. That however was a risk applicable to all aspects of the E.C.H.R. It seems preferable to confine the incorporating Act to acts of public authorities and those performing public functions.[69]

Should corporations be able to claim to be victims?

Most discussions about the Bill of Rights issue have proceeded on the assumption that claims could be brought by companies and other legal entities as much as by individuals. But there have been suggestions that claims should be restricted to individuals and this seems to be Labour Party policy. The matter was taken up by Liberty in its substantial paper *A People's Charter*, 1991. Article 21 of Liberty's proposed Bill of Rights would limit application of its rights to "natural persons". The commentary explained that "The term 'natural persons' in Article 21 is used to prevent an interpretation which apply the rights and freedoms guaranteed in this Bill to companies or 'legal persons'".[70] The Canadian Charter, which did not distinguish between natural persons and others, had been used by a supermarket chain to strike down legislation

---

[66] The New Zealand Bill of Rights Act 1990, s.3 states that it applies to the performance "by any person or body of any public function, power or duty".

[67] Thus in the Human Rights Bill introduced in the House of Commons in January 1994 by Mr Graham Allen on behalf of Liberty the Bill was stated to apply to "a) a Minister of the Crown or any person or body acting on behalf of, or for the purposes of, the Crown, and b) any statutory body, public body, or any person holding statutory office or exercising any public function . . ." "Public body" was defined to mean "a body of persons, whether corporate or unincorporate, carrying on a service or undertaking of a public nature and includes public authorities of all descriptions and any individual or body that exercises any public function".

[68] "Select Committee Report," *op cit* p.26, n.80 above, at p.37 para. 4.

[69] This is also the view adopted in the draft bill proposed by the Institute for Public Policy Research (IPPR) — see *A British Bill of Rights*, (1990), p.19.

[70] *op. cit.* at p.82.

outlawing Sunday trading on the ground that it breached the right to freedom of conscience and religion. Applying the same logic, Liberty opined, the right to freedom of expression could be used to uphold unrestricted advertising by tobacco companies.[71] Liberty suggested that "this could not reasonably be said to be a human right"[72].

The same point was made by Lord Irvine of Lairg Q.C. in his contribution to *Law Reform for All*,[73] a book of essays published by the Society of Labour Lawyers in 1996. Dealing with incorporation of the E.C.H.R. into United Kingdom law, Lord Irvine wrote:[74]"The rights to be protected should be those of the individual against the State. The Human Rights Act should therefore provide that its protections can only be relied on by individuals, and not by companies or by organisations". The policy expressed by Lord Irvine was also that expressed by John Smith, then Leader of the Labour Party in his speech of March 1, 1993 when he announced his conversion to the incorporation of the E.C.H.R.[75]

The writer disagrees. The point made by Liberty and by the Labour Party seems unconvincing. A legal person such as a body corporate may be the victim of a breach of human rights principles. An obvious example is a breach of the provisions of the E.C.H.R. in regard to freedom of expression which can and usually does concern companies that own newspapers and other media organisations. The view adopted by Liberty and Lord Irvine is also in obvious disregard of the decisions of the Strasbourg Court in cases such as *Spycatcher* or the case brought by the Sunday Times that arose out of the thalidomide disaster. It is also contrary to the clear and specific terms of the First Protocol to the Convention (ratified by Britain), Article 1 of which states, "Every natural *or legal* person is entitled to the peaceful enjoyment of his possessions" (emphasis supplied).[76]

[71] See now G. M. Giffman and R. Chapman, "Tobacco and Human Rights," N.L.J., August 16, 1996, pp.1232–1235.

[72] *Ibid*.

[73] D. Bean (ed.), (1996).

[74] *Ibid*, p.19.

[75] "The rights we seek to protect are those of the individual against the state. The Human Rights Act would therefore provide that its protections could only be relied on by individuals, not by companies or organisations. We do not want to repeat here the confusion and injustice that has occurred in some other countries, where companies and commercial organisations have tried to resist social legislation controlling their activities by claiming that it infringes their 'human rights'."

[76] The new South African Transitional Constitution (Constitution of the Republic of South Africa Act 200 of 1993, s.7(3)) applies the provisions of the Bill of Rights to "juristic persons . . . where, and to the extent, that the nature of the rights permits".

The view propounded by Liberty and the Labour Party therefore appears to be not only misconceived but to ignore the law of the E.C.H.R.

Is there a need for a scrutinising machinery?

Would there be value in establishing formal machinery to advise whether proposed new legislation conformed to the provisions of the Bill of Rights? A standing Parliamentary Committee might for instance be required to report to the House of Commons on any apparent divergence or the Attorney-General might be given this task. The House of Lords Select Committee said that it was sceptical of the usefulness of the idea.

> "It did not seem likely that such a Committee would succeed in detecting a breach of the Convention in proposed legislation which had escaped the notice of the various stages of preparation through which it would already have passed".[77]

The 1990 New Zealand Bill of Rights Act states that when a Bill is introduced the Attorney-General must "bring to the attention of the House of Representatives any provision in the Bill that appears to be inconsistent with any of the rights and freedoms contained in this Bill of Rights". By May 1996 the Attorney-General had advised the legislature in terms of section 7 in respect of four government Bills.[78] Four instances in six years is not very many but there is no way of knowing whether there were other instances in which the procedure could and arguably should have been used in which it was not used. Nor is it known to what extent the New Zealand Attorney-General has advised Government Departments informally behind the scenes to the effect that draft legislation offends against the Bill of Rights.

The House of Lords Select Committee was no doubt correct in its view that such an official scrutinising mechanism could only succeed in identifying a proportion of potential Bill of Rights hazards in pending legislation. Lawyers acting for individuals and interest groups after the legislation comes into force are likely to be better placed for this purpose. But it may nevertheless be a useful piece of Parliamentary machinery — if only to heighten awareness of Bill of Rights issues amongst parliamentarians,

---

[77] "Select Committee Report." *op. cit.* p.26 n.80 above, at pp.38–39, para. 46.

[78] Transport Safety Bill 1991, clause 17; Films, Videos and Publications Classification Bill, clause 31 and clause 121; Children, Young Persons, and their Families Amendment Bill; Fisheries Amendment Bill. It has also been used in regard to a handful of private members' bills.

ministers and civil servants. If the choice were between giving the task to the Attorney-General or to a standing parliamentary committee, the latter would be likely to bear much more fruit. It would be more independent and therefore less likely to be influenced by the attitudes of those in the Government machine. Also, the work would be done by larger numbers of persons than if the responsibility were confined to the Attorney-General and his staff. It is likely that as a result more problem areas would be identified — not least because it would be easier for interest groups outside parliament to lobby a parliamentary committee than the Attorney-General. Also the value of being exposed to the issues would be more widely diffused.

As has been seen,[79] Liberty made a parliamentary Human Rights Scrutiny Committee an important part of its Bill of Rights package of proposals.[80] Its draft Bill of Rights proposes the establishment of a select committee though, unlike ordinary select committees, it would be elected rather than appointed.[81] But as envisaged by Liberty, its function would not only be pre-natal scrutiny of Bills before Parliament, but also post-natal scrutiny after they have been passed and become statutes. This is a rather different concept. Its role would be to scrutinise Acts of Parliament when asked to do so either by a minister or after a resolution passed by one third or more of either House of Parliament[82] or by the Human Rights Commission.[83] Liberty's proposed special select committee would additionally have the task of considering and advising on any statutory provision held to be invalid by a court where the Government wished to reinstate the original provision.

Should there be some form of human rights commission?

It would in any event seem highly desirable to have a specialist commission outside parliament devoted to the objectives of the Bill of Rights. The function of such a body would be to act as a focal point for human rights concerns, as an expert lobby and an educative force. The idea of having such a Commission is now a familiar one. In Britain they have mainly been established for

[79] See p.31 above.
[80] Liberty, *Bill of Rights: A People's Charter*, (1991), Art. 31.
[81] So as to reduce the risk of dominance by any party, the proposal is that membership should be by reference to the number of votes cast for each party, not the number of Members in the House.
[82] It is not stated how it could be established what constitutes one third of the membership of the present House of Lords.
[83] Article 31(a).

specific topics — the Commission for Racial Equality[84] and the Equal Opportunities Commission.[85] In Northern Ireland there are equivalent agencies — the Fair Employment Commission dealing with religious and political discrimination[86], and Equal Opportunities Commission.[87] There is also the Standing Advisory Commission on Human Rights[88] whose function is purely to advise and which therefore has no power to make findings or pursue legal actions. In Canada and Australia commissions have been established with broad remits.[89] In New Zealand there has been a Human Rights Commission since 1977, established by the Human Rights Commission Act of that year.[90] The idea received the imprimatur of the UN General Assembly in December 1993[91], which emphasised that such commissions should be independent of government and sufficiently well funded to give them effective independence.

The Labour Party has made the establishment of such a Commission part of its policy. Lord Irvine said "to assist the courts, and also to assist individuals in asserting their rights, there could be established an independent Human Rights Commission along the lines of the very successful Equal Opportunities Commission and Commission for Racial Equality."[92]

The Commission should have the duty to work generally for the protection of human rights and to keep under review the working of the Bill of Rights. It should have the duty to issue an annual report and the power itself to undertake or to commission others to conduct research. It should be entitled to make proposals for changes in law or practice.

The more difficult problem is whether such an agency should have the power to compel the production of persons and papers in the course of its inquiries, and even more, whether it should have

[84] Set up under the Race Relations Act 1976.
[85] Set up under the Sex Discrimination Act 1975.
[86] Set up under the Fair Employment (Northern Ireland) Act 1989.
[87] Set up under the Sex Discrimination (Northern Ireland) Order 1976.
[88] Set up under the Northern Ireland Constitution Act 1973.
[89] In Canada a federal Human Rights Commission was established in 1977; in Australia a federal Human Rights and Equal Opportunities Commission was established in 1986.
[90] See "The Human Rights Commission — Educator or Enforcer" (1979) N.Z.L.J 467. The Commission's existence now derives from the Human Rights Act 1993, s.4.
[91] Resolution 48/134. See also *Principles relating to the status of national institutions* (the Paris Principles), adopted at the first International Workshop on National Institutions in Paris in 1991 — UN Doc.E/Cn.4/1992/43 and Add. 1.
[92] D. Bean (ed.) *Law Reform Now* (1996) p.20. See equally the Labour Party's policy — *A New Agenda for Democracy*, 1993.

the power or even the duty to take up the legal cudgels on behalf of complainants. Should it, for instance, have the power to take legal proceedings in its own name like the Equal Opportunities Commission under the Sex Discrimination Act 1975 and the Commission for Racial Equality under the Race Relations Act 1978. Both have the power to investigate discriminatory practices on their own initiative and powers to require the production of relevant information. They also have the power to issue "non-discrimination notices" to deal with unlawful discrimination. Such notices require the cessation of the identified practices and are enforceable in the courts by way of injunction. Lord Irvine proposed that the Commission should have the power in appropriate cases to institute cases.[93] This would ensure "that the protection of the public was not left to the accident of individual enthusiasm or willingness to pursue cases".[94]

One difference between the Commission for Racial Equality or the Equal Opportunities Commission, on the one hand, and the proposed civil rights or human rights commission, on the other, is that, whereas the former have a relatively precise and limited remit,[95] the latter would have a vast and open-ended area of operation. It may be more problematic to give it power to seek to stop, of its own motion, conduct which it thought contravened the Bill of Rights. The role of interpreter of the Bill of Rights should be confined to the courts.

But should it, nevertheless, have the power to investigate alleged complaints with a power to call for production of documents and papers? The existence of such a power would in practice greatly strengthen its hand. It would seem that there is a strong case for such powers to be given to the Commission.

The Commission should have power to undertake inquiries in relation to complaints brought by individuals or organisations, whether relating to grievances affecting only a particular individual or large numbers. It should also have the power to investigate matters of its own motion — but only perhaps in general terms — in order to discover whether existing law or practice required alteration. Such inquiries would not identify individual malefactors so much as identify a problem requiring attention.

This still leaves the question whether the Commission should itself be permitted to undertake legal proceedings for alleged

[93] *Ibid.*
[94] *Ibid.*
[95] For a review of the EOC's role as a litigator see Catherine Barnard, "A European Litigation Strategy: the Case of the Equal Opportunities Commission" in Jo Shaw and Gillian More (eds.) *New Legal Dynamics for European Union* (1995), pp.253–272.

158

breaches of the Bill of Rights. On balance, it would seem better to leave the bringing of proceedings to the persons actually affected. The Commissions's role should be limited to encourage, promote and assist. But it might usefully be given the capacity (similar to that of the Equal Opportunities Commission) to assist complainants before the courts. As recommended by the Northern Ireland Advisory Commission,[96] this would be a power to be exercised by the Commission in its discretion where it thought the case raised a question of principle or it was unreasonable, having regard to the complexity of the matter or the relationship of the complainant to the other party or for some other reason, for the complainant to deal with the case unaided. Assistance might consist of giving advice or procuring or attempting to procure the settlement of any matter in dispute or arranging for the giving of legal advice or assistance by a professional lawyer or arranging for legal representation for the complainant. Lord Irvine has suggested that the Commission should have the right "where necessary itself to institute cases to confirm or clarify particularly important issues".[97]

It would also be desirable that rules of court provide that in any litigation pending before the courts which raised a Bill of Rights point, the Commission would have standing to intervene as *amicus curiae*. The Bill introduced by Mr Robert Maclennan in 1983 included a provision that whenever a case raised "A Convention issue" the court would order that notice of the point be given to the Attorney-General who could then, if he chose, take part in the proceedings on that point. If the parties were caused additional costs as a result of such intervention by the Attorney-General, the court could order costs to be paid out of public funds. This too seems a worthwhile procedure which should be adopted.

One question that would have to be decided is whether the Human Rights Commission would swallow up existing agencies such as the Commission for Racial Equality or the Equal Opportunities Commission or whether, rather, they should co-exist. It would seem greatly preferable to allow the various existing agencies all to continue.[98] If rationalisation by amalgamation seemed

---

[96] *Op. cit.*, p.23, n.75 above, at p.73. para. 7.22.
[97] D. Bean (ed.) *Law Reform Now*, (1996) p.20.
[98] There was strong opposition from most of those in Northern Ireland to a suggestion in 1986 from the British Government that the various discrimination agencies and perhaps also the Standing Advisory Commission on Human Rights should be combined in a single Human Rights Commission. (See K. Boyle, C. Campbell, T. Hadden *The Protection of Human Rights in the Context of Peace and Reconciliation in Ireland,* (1996), p.56; *Equality of Opportunity in Northern Ireland: Future Strategy Options: A Consultative Paper,* Department of Economic Employment, (1986), paras. 6.31–6.35.)

desirable it could always be done at a later stage. But this would depend on how the respective organisations developed and worked together. There might be overlap problems, but the Human Rights Commission presumably would, normally, defer to the specialist bodies in regard to problems within their jurisdiction and take only problems that were not already covered by a specialist body. In theory, such overlap might cause problems; in practice it would probably be handled without difficulty. The situation would be somewhat similar to that of the Law Commission, with general responsibilities for law reform notwithstanding the existence of the Home Secretary's Criminal Law Revision Committee, the Lord Chancellor's Law Reform Committee and ad hoc Royal Commissions, departmental and inter-departmental committees. Similarly, the existence of the Bill of Rights, and the Commission should not in itself affect the jurisdiction or work of the Parliamentary Commissioner for Administration. His functions would continue in precisely the same way as now.

One of the valuable functions of the proposed Human Rights Commission would be to assist in the promotion of the broader task of education of the entire community regarding the importance of concern for human rights.

CONCLUSION

When this pamphlet was first written in 1975 it seemed that there was a real prospect that the campaign launched the previous year by Sir Leslie Scarman's Hamlyn Lectures might succeed. But although the campaign made distinct progress and won some significant supporters, it became clear in the late 1970s that neither of the two main political parties was prepared to move on this issue. It was only in March 1993 when Mr John Smith the then Leader of the Labour Party stated that Labour would incorporate the E.C.H.R. into United Kingdom law that the topic became practical politics.

At the time of writing (summer 1996) a General Election is due to take place shortly and the opinion polls indicate the likelihood of a Labour victory. It is therefore well possible that the introduction of a domestic Bill of Rights is now imminent.

For those who hope to see the European Convention on Human Rights translated into United Kingdom law one of the chief concerns must be the fact that agreement on the policy between the main political parties is unlikely. The Tories have consistently opposed incorporation of the E.C.H.R. and it would be surprising (though not inconceivable) if this opposition were to melt away. Without this, the prospects for the success of the venture would obviously be less favourable. If the Bill of Rights were seen to be a piece of "Labour legislation" in the narrow political sense there is a danger that the Tories would decide to repeal it when they came back to power. But if Labour were to bring forward the legislation early in a new Government and especially if it then went on to win a second term, there might be a sufficient period of time for the Bill of Rights to establish itself sufficiently that the next Conservative Government would feel unable to repeal the legislation (repeal of the Bill of Rights Act does not sound like much of a vote-winner). Once it had survived the first Tory period of government, the Bill of Rights would probably be there for the duration. Each time the right of individual petition to Strasbourg has come up for renewal by the British Government there has been anxiety as to whether the government would sign up again for another five years. Each time the government did so it became more difficult for its successors to consider not doing so. The same would apply to the question of repeal of the Bill of Rights. Each five year Parliament during which the Bill of Rights was not repealed would give it added authority to make future repeal less likely.

Obviously, if the Bill of Rights quickly wins popular support the question of whether it might be repealed by an incoming Government would not arise. The Tories would accept the *fait accompli*. But popular support for a Bill of Rights cannot be guaranteed. Much will depend on the accidents of litigation - the cases that happen to be brought during the early years, the particular judges who sit, the decisions they give and the reaction to those decisions from the press, the chattering classes and, more generally, the public at large.

There are almost certain to be decisions that excite great controversy and fuel the argument that a Bill of Rights is a vehicle for judges to legislate to an unacceptable extent. There does at present appear to be public support for the introduction of a Bill of Rights, but whether it could survive such early alarums remains to be seen. The rights that are sought to be protected under a Bill of Rights are not usually the rights of popular majorities. They tend typically to be the rights of unpopular minorities - defendants in criminal proceedings, prisoners, transsexuals, mental patients, demonstrators, would-be immigrants or asylum seekers. It requires some generousity of spirit and breadth of vision to see that a civilised democratic society needs to find ways of giving appropriate protection to such people and such causes.

In my own view a Bill of Rights is desirable not because human rights are grossly abused in Britain, nor to provide against the danger of future tyranny. The former is untrue: the latter unlikely. The case for a Bill of Rights rests rather on the belief that it would make a distinct and valuable contribution to the *better* protection of civil liberties. The extent of the contribution it could make must, in the end, depend on how it is regarded and interpreted by the judges. It would give them greater scope than exists in the ordinary common law and statute law. It would require of them a broader approach than has been customary. There would more argument on matters of importance in courts of law. Some of the courts' decisions would not merely be controversial but would be unacceptable to the prevailing orthodoxy whether of the Left or of the Right.

To entrust to judges more issues involving significant policy decisions is not risk free, but we have been willing to entrust such questions to the judges of the Strasbourg court for some four decades now and it is strange to suggest that English judges could not do the job at least as well.

Reflecting on the introduction of the Canadian Charter, E. R. Alexander wrote in 1989, "on balance, the [Supreme] court has risen to the formidable challenge the Charter poses, with dignity and humility, with intelligence and self-restraint, and often with a measure of grace and eloquence which few realised it possessed".[1] Another commentator, Professor Patrick Monahan, who was originally concerned about the enactment of the Charter, wrote in 1994 that in general terms "it would appear that the [Supreme] Court is off to a very good start indeed".[2] Many critics, including Monahan, had warned that the Charter would permit the judiciary to roll back the considerable achievements of the modern welfare state but he was "happy to report that this fear has not materialised in the first decade of the Charter, and there is little evidence at this point to suggest that things will change for the worse in the future".[3] The Court, he said, "has evinced a very considerable sensitivity for the trade-offs between competing social interests that most modern regulation requires".[4] Particularly in the field of social and economic regulation, "it has been willing to accord to the legislature a 'margin of appreciation' in which the legislature is not required to follow the judges' ideas as to the 'best possible means' of achieving its objectives".[5] The Court had been most activist in fields in which it had expertise such as criminal law. What was remarkable, he suggested, was "the near absence of public criticism of the Court's Charter rulings over the past decade".[6]

> "In effect, the Court has conducted itself in a politically astute fashion, intervening in discrete areas where its perceived legitimacy and authority are high, while deferring to the legislature in the broad majority of cases. This approach - which might be described as 'selective activism' - helps to explain the fact that Canadian politicians and the broader public seem to have absorbed the Charter into the Canadian political system in an almost effortless fashion."[7]

Whether this is what has actually occurred in Canada is a matter of dispute. Some commentators would paint a far less rosy picture[8]. For the time being the jury is still out.[9]

---

[1] E. R. Alexander, "The Canadian Charter of Rights and Freedoms in the Supreme Court of Canada" (1989) L.Q.R. 561, at 598.

[2] *Professor Patrick Monahan,"The Charter Then and Now" in Protecting Rights and Freedoms: Essays on the Charter's Place in Canada's Political, Legal and Intellectual Life*, Bryden, Davis, Russell (eds.) (1994) p.117.

[3] *Ibid.*

[4] *Ibid.*

[5] *Ibid.*

[6] *Ibid*, p.118.

[7] *Ibid.*

[8] W. A. Bogart lists fifteen different works by Charter sceptics - *op. cit.*, p.130 above, at n.60, pp.291–292.

But how would introduction of a domestic Bill of Rights play here? It is predictable that some of the consequences will be unpredictable. It is predictable that some of the consequences will be unwelcome. The crucial question is whether the judges would take it on sensibly and whether the politicians, the media and the public would come to regard the Bill of Rights as essentially a useful or a troublesome innovation? How will so major an innovation bed down and develop in the complex of institutions in this particular mature democracy? A satisfactory answer to these questions could only be given well into the twenty-first century. But I believe that the experiment is well worth undertaking and that by the time the E.C.H.R. has been in force in the United Kingdom for a couple of decades people will wonder why the issue was ever thought to be so problematic.

---

[9] Professor Bogart, who regards the Charter as a mistake, neverthless concedes that he could be wrong: "I must allow that my prognostications, which are decidedly gloomy at times, may not turn out to be so bad. I freely admit that I could be wrong, on one condition, that those with high hopes for litigation, in turn, will allow that they could be left with hollow ones". (*op. cit.*, p.310)

Select Bibliography

Literature on the Canadian Charter of Rights and Freedoms

Bogart, W. A., *Courts and Country: The Limits of Litigation and the Social and Political Life of Canada*, (OUP, Canada, 1994).

Bryden, P., Davis, S. and Russell, J. (eds.), *Protecting Rights and Freedoms*, (University of Toronto, 1994).

Gibson, D., *The Law of the Charter: Equality Rights*, (Carswell, 1990).

Hogg, P., *Constitutional Law of Canada*, *(3rd ed. 1992)*.

Mandel, M., The Charter of Rights and the Legalisation of Politics in Canada (Wall & Thompson, Toronto, 1992).

McLachlin, B., "The Canadian Charter and the Democratic Process" in Gearty, C. and Tomkins, A. (eds.), *Understanding Human Rights* (Mansell, 1996).

Ratushny, E. and Beaudoin, G. (eds.), *The Canadian Charter of Rights and Freedoms*, (2nd ed. 1989).

Schneiderman, D. (ed.), *Freedom of Expression and the Charter* (1991).

Tarnopolsky, W. A. and Beaudoin, G. A. (eds.), *Canadian Charter of Rights and Freedoms: Commentary* (Carswell, 1982).

Trakman, L., *Reasoning with Charter*, (Butterworths, 1991).

See also many other references footnoted in Roland Penner, "The Canadian Experience with the Charter of Rights: Are there Lessons for the United Kingdom" (1996) Publ.L. 104–25.

Literature on the European Convention on Human Rights

Clements, Luke, *European Human Rights: Taking a case under the Convention* (Sweet & Maxwell, 1994).

Dickson, B. and Connelly, A., *Human Rights and the European Convention*, (Sweet & Maxwell, September 1995).

van Dijk, P. and van Hoof, G. J. H., *Theory and Practice of the European Convention on Human Rights* (2nd ed., Kluwer, 1990).

Gearty, C. A., "The European Court of Human Rights and the Protection of Civil Liberties: An Overview", (1995) 52 Camb.L.J. 89–127.

Gomien, D., Harris, D. J. and Zwaack, L., *Law and Practice of the European Convention on Human Rights and the European Social Chapter*, (1996).

Harris, D. J., O'Boyle, M. and Warbrick, C., *Law of the European Convention on Human Rights,* (Butterworths, 1995).

Jacobs, Francis G., *The European Convention on Human Rights,* (2nd ed. OUP, 1995).

Kinley, D., *The European Convention on Human Rights: Compliance without Incorporation* (1993).

Mahoney, P., "Judicial Activism and Judicial Self-Restraint in the European Court of Human Rights: Two Sides of the Same Coin", (1990) 11 H.Rts.L.J. 57–88.

Robertson, A. H., *Human Rights in Europe: A Study of the European Convention on Human Rights* (3rd ed., Manchester University, 1993).

Appendix

THE EUROPEAN CONVENTION ON HUMAN RIGHTS

Articles 1 to 18 and First Protocol

The Governments signatory hereto, being Members of the Council of Europe,

Considering the Universal Declaration of Human Rights proclaimed by the General Assembly of the United Nations on 10th December 1948;

Considering that this Declaration aims at securing the universal and effective recognition and observance of the Rights therein declared:

Considering that the aim of the Council of Europe is the achievement of greater unity between its Members and that one of the methods by which that aim is to be pursued is the maintenance and further realisation of Human Rights and Fundamental Freedoms;

Reaffirming their profound belief in those Fundamental Freedoms which are the foundation of justice and peace in the world and are best maintained on the one hand by an effective political democracy and on the other by a common understanding and observance of the Human Rights upon which they depend;

Being resolved, as the Governments of European countries which are like minded and have a common heritage of political traditions, ideals, freedom and the rule of law, to take the first steps for the collective enforcement of certain of the Rights stated in the Universal Declaration;

Have agreed as follows:

Article 1

The High Contracting Parties shall secure to everyone within their jurisdiction the rights and freedoms defined in Section 1 of this Convention.

Section 1

Article 2

(1) Everyone's right to life shall be protected by law. No one shall be deprived of his life intentionally save in the execution of a

167

sentence of a court following his conviction of a crime for which this penalty is provided by law.

(2) Deprivation of life shall not be regarded as inflicted in contravention of this Article when it results from the use of force which is no more than absolutely necessary:

(a) in defence of any person from unlawful violence;
(b) in order to effect a lawful arrest or to prevent the escape of a person lawfully detained;
(c) in action lawfully taken for the purpose of quelling a riot or insurrection.

Article 3

No one shall be subjected to torture or to inhuman or degrading treatment or punishment.

Article 4

(1) No one shall be held in slavery or servitude.

(2) No one shall be required to perform forced or compulsory labour.

(3) For the purpose of this Article the term 'forced or compulsory labour' shall not include:

(a) any work required to be done in the ordinary course of detention imposed according to the provisions of Article 5 of this Convention or during conditional release from such detention;
(b) any service of a military character or, in case of conscientious objectors in countries where they are recognised, service exacted instead of compulsory military service;
(c) any service exacted in case of an emergency or calamity threatening the life or well-being of the community;
(d) any work or service which forms part of normal civic obligations.

Article 5

(1) Everyone has the right to liberty and security of person.

No one shall be deprived of his liberty save in the following cases and in accordance with a procedure prescribed by law:

(a) the lawful detention of a person after conviction by a competent court;
(b) the lawful arrest or detention of a person for non-compliance with the lawful order of a court in order to secure the fulfilment of any obligation prescribed by law;

(c) the lawful arrest or detention of a person effected for the purpose of bringing him before the competent legal authority on reasonable suspicion of having committed an offence or when it is reasonably considered necessary to prevent his committing an offence or fleeing after having done so;

(d) the detention of a minor by lawful order for the purpose of educational supervision or his lawful detention for the purpose of bringing him before the competent legal authority;

(e) the lawful detention of persons for the prevention of the spreading of infectious diseases, of persons of unsound mind, alcoholics or drug addicts or vagrants;

(f) the lawful arrest or detention of a person to prevent his effecting an unauthorised entry into the country or of a person against whom action is being taken with a view to deportation or extradition.

(2) Everyone who is arrested shall be informed promptly, in a language which he understands, of the reasons for his arrest and of any charge against him.

(3) Everyone arrested or detained in accordance with the provisions of paragraph 1(c) of this article shall be brought promptly before a judge or other officer authorised by law to exercise judicial power and shall be entitled to trial within a reasonable time or to release pending trial. Release may be conditioned by guarantees to appear for trial.

(4) Everyone who is deprived of his liberty by arrest or detention shall be entitled to take proceedings by which the lawfulness of his detention shall be decided speedily by a court and his release ordered if the detention is not lawful.

(5) Everyone who has been the victim of arrest or detention in contravention of the provisions of this Article shall have an enforceable right to compensation.

Article 6

(1) In the determination of his civil rights and obligations or of any criminal charge against him, everyone is entitled to a fair and public hearing within a reasonable time by an independent and impartial tribunal established by law. Judgement shall be pronounced publicly but the press and public may be excluded from all or part of the trial in the interests of morals, public order or national security in a democratic society, where the interest of juveniles or the protection of the private life of the parties so

require, or to the extent strictly necessary in the opinion of the court in special circumstances where publicity would prejudice the interests of justice.

(2) Everyone charged with a criminal offence shall be presumed innocent until proved guilty according to law.

(3) Everyone charged with a criminal offence has the following minimum rights:

- (a) to be informed promptly, in a language which he understands and in detail, of the nature and cause of the accusation against him;
- (b) to have adequate time and facilities for the preparation of his defence;
- (c) to defend himself in person or through legal assistance of his own choosing or, if he has not sufficient means to pay for legal assistance, to be given it free when the interests of justice so require;
- (d) to examine or have examined witnesses against him and to obtain the attendance and examination of witnesses on his behalf under the same conditions as witnesses against him;
- (e) to have the free assistance of an interpreter if he cannot understand or speak the language used in court.

Article 7

(1) No one shall be held guilty of any criminal offence on account of any act or omission which did not constitute a criminal offence under national or international law at the time when it was committed. Nor shall a heavier penalty be imposed than the one that was applicable at the time the criminal offence was committed.

(2) This Article shall not prejudice the trial and punishment of any person for any act or omission which, at the time when it was committed, was criminal according to the general principles of law recognised by civilised nations.

Article 8

(1) Everyone has the right to respect for his private life and family life, his home and his correspondence.

(2) There shall be no interference by a public authority with the exercise of this right except such as is in accordance with the law and is necessary in a democratic society in the interests of national security, public safety or the economic well-being of the country, for the prevention of disorder or crime, for the protection of health

or morals, or for the protection of the rights and freedoms of others.

Article 9

(1) Everyone has the right to freedom of thought, conscience and religion; this right includes freedom to change his religion or belief and freedom, either alone or in community with others and in public or private, to manifest his religion or belief, in worship, teaching, practice and observance.

(2) Freedom to manifest one's religion or beliefs shall be subject only to such limitations as are prescribed by law and are necessary in a democratic society in the interests of public safety, for the protection of public order, health or morals, or for the protection of the rights and freedoms of others.

Article 10

(1) Everyone has the right to freedom of expression. The right shall include freedom to hold opinions and to receive and impart information and ideas without interference by public authority and regardless of frontiers. This Article shall not prevent States from requiring the licensing of broadcasting, television or cinema enterprises.

(2) The exercise of these freedoms, since it carries with it duties and responsibilities, may be subject to such formalities, conditions, restrictions or penalties as are prescribed by law and are necessary in a democratic society, in the interests of national security, territorial integrity or public safety, for the prevention of disorder or crime, for the protection of health or morals, for the protection of the reputation or rights of others, for preventing the disclosure of information received in confidence, or for maintaining the authority and impartiality of the judiciary.

Article 11

(1) Everyone has the right to freedom of peaceful assembly and to freedom of association with others, including the right to form and to join trade unions for the protection of his interests.

(2) No restrictions shall be placed on the exercise of these rights other than such as are prescribed by law and are necessary in a democratic society in the interests of national security or public safety, for the prevention of disorder or crime, for the protection of

health or morals or for the protection of the rights and freedoms of others. This Article shall not prevent the imposition of lawful restrictions on the exercise of these rights by members of the armed forces, of the police or the administration of the State.

Article 12

Men and women of marriageable age have the right to marry and to found a family, according to the national laws governing the exercise of this right.

Article 13

Everyone whose rights and freedoms as set forth in this Convention are violated shall have an effective remedy before a national authority notwithstanding that the violation has been committed by persons acting in an official capacity.

Article 14

The enjoyment of the rights and freedoms set forth in this Convention shall be secured without discrimination on any ground such as sex, race, colour, language, religion, political or other opinion, national or social origin, association with a national minority, property, birth or other status.

Article 15

(1) In time of war or other public emergency threatening the life of the nation any High Contracting Party may take measures derogating from its obligations under this Convention to the extent strictly required by the exigencies of the situation, provided that such measures are not inconsistent with its other obligations under international law.

(2) No derogation from Article 2, except in respect of deaths resulting from lawful acts of war, or from Articles 3, 4 (paragraph 1) and 7 shall be made under this provision.

(3) Any High Contracting Party availing itself of this right of derogation shall keep the Secretary-General of the Council of Europe fully informed of the measures which it has taken and the reasons therefor. It shall also inform the Secretary-General of the Council of Europe when such measures have ceased to operate and the provisions of the Convention are again being fully executed.

Article 16

Nothing in Articles 10, 11 and 14 shall be regarded as preventing the High Contracting Parties from imposing restrictions on the political activity of aliens.

Article 17

Nothing in the Convention may be interpreted as implying for any State, group or person any right to engage in any activity or perform any act aimed at the destruction of any of the rights and freedoms set forth herein or at their limitation to a greater extent than is provided for in the Convention.

Article 18

The restrictions permitted under this Convention to the said rights and freedoms shall not be applied for any purpose other than those for which they have been prescribed.

First Protocol to the Convention

The Governments signatory hereto, being Members of the Council of Europe.

Being resolved to take steps to ensure the collective enforcement of certain rights and freedoms other than those already included in Section 1 of the Convention for the Protection of Human Rights and Fundamental Freedoms signed at Rome on November 4, 1950 (hereinafter referred to as 'the Convention').

Have agreed as follows:

Article 1

Every natural or legal person is entitled to the peaceful enjoyment of his possessions. No one shall be deprived of his possessions except in the public interest and subject to the conditions provided for by law and by the general principles of international law.

The preceding provisions shall not, however, in any way impair the right of a State to enforce such laws as it deems necessary to control the use of property in accordance with the general interest or to secure the payment of taxes or other contributions or penalties.

Article 2

No person shall be denied the right to education. In the exercise of any functions which it assumes in relation to education and to teaching, the State shall respect the right of parents to ensure such education and teaching in conformity with their own religious and philosophical convictions.[1]

Article 3

The High Contracting Parties undertake to hold free elections at reasonable intervals by secret ballot, under conditions which will ensure the free expression of the opinion of the people in the choice of the legislature.

Reservation to Protocol No 1

"At the time of signing the present Protocol, I declare that, in view of certain provisions of the Education Acts in force in the United Kingdom, the principle affirmed in the second sentence of Article 2 is accepted by the United Kingdom only so far as it is compatible with the provisions of efficient instruction and training, and the avoidance of unreasonable public expenditure."

INDEX